WRITE TO DEATH

WRITE TO DEATH

NEWS FRAMING OF THE RIGHT TO DIE CONFLICT,
FROM QUINLAN'S COMA TO KEVORKIAN'S CONVICTION

Elizabeth Atwood Gailey

Westport, Connecticut
London

Library of Congress Cataloging-in-Publication Data

Atwood-Gailey, Elizabeth.
    Write to death : news framing of the right to die conflict, from Quinlan's coma to Kevorkian's
conviction / Elizabeth Atwood Gailey.
      p. cm.
    Includes bibliographical references (p.) and index.
    ISBN 0–275–97713–7 (alk. paper)
    1. Euthanasia.   2. Euthanasia—Social aspects.   3. Right to die.   4. Right to die—Social
aspects.   I. Title.
R726.A89   2003
179.7—dc21   2002037057

British Library Cataloguing in Publication Data is available.

Library of Congress Catalog Card Number: 2002037057
ISBN: 0–275–97713–7

First published in 2003

Praeger Publishers, 88 Post Road West, Westport, CT 06881
An imprint of Greenwood Publishing Group, Inc.
www.praeger.com

Printed in the United States of America

The paper used in this book complies with the
Permanent Paper Standard issued by the National
Information Standards Organization (Z39.48–1984).

10 9 8 7 6 5 4 3 2 1

For Richard, Glen, Mom, Barbara, Nancy, Billy, and the rest of the clan. Without you none of it matters.

CONTENTS

PREFACE

In talking to academic colleagues, students, friends, and casual acquaintances about this book, I have been struck repeatedly by the intense interest the topic of euthanasia generates. Perhaps this stems in part from the taboo that still constrains public discourse on mortality in the United States, a nation renowned for its disavowal of death (see, e.g., Gorer 1965; Becker 1963; Aries 1974, 1981). Of course, the issue's resonance may also reflect the personal stake individuals have in finding solutions for themselves or relatives forced to confront the exigencies of medicalized death and dying. Or it may simply be that people feel compelled to examine and resolve some of the agonizing philosophical contradictions that plague this issue—including their innate reverence for life versus the universally unwelcome prospect of an expensive and protracted "technologized" death. Whatever its genesis, the public's keen interest in euthanasia appears to cut across boundaries of age, class, gender, and ethnicity, tapping into enduring religious, ethical, and cultural beliefs.

It is not only euthanasia itself that attracts unusual attention, however. The news media's role in framing the debate over the "right to die" proves almost equally compelling. Americans, it seems, have a solid grasp of the pervasive influence of the mainstream media, which function both as society's central storytellers and its major purveyors of "mimetic capital"—the set of images used to render "material existence meaningful, comprehensible, resonant" (Greenblatt 1992, 6, 36). Even casual news consumers realize that the press does far more than alert and inform us about social problems, such as the conflict over euthanasia. The news media play a vital role in the social construction of social issues by calling attention to (or marginalizing) them, by labeling them "problems," by authorizing and legitimating particular versions of their histories and causes, and by encasing them within symbolic cognitive structures—or "frames"—that advance particular interpretations and policy solutions.

Nowhere is this process more evident—nor more worthy of scrutiny—than in news stories pertaining to the end of life, that most mysterious, unsettling, and therefore symbolically weighted, of human passages. Like the abortion conflict preceding it, as well as embryo research, cloning, genetic mapping, and the string of other controversial technologies that have followed it, the struggle over a "right to die" has raised some of the most searing, contentious, and perplexing questions faced by modern societies. A small sample of these include:

- Does the nation's commitment to individual autonomy and its desire to prevent suffering at the end of life justify social and legal recognition of a right to die—including access to lethal drugs administered by a doctor?

- What rights, if any, should be granted to the state, medical professionals, and families to truncate the lives of individuals too ill to authorize this act themselves?

- Does the state's interest in preserving and allocating finite economic, social, and medical resources justify its sanctioning of physician-assisted suicide (PAS) for dying or seriously incapacitated individuals?

- If doctors and medical institutions are to be empowered by the state to assist in their patients' suicides, how might the poor, minorities, and members of other traditionally disadvantaged groups be protected from potential abuses of this power?

As these questions make clear, few social conflicts have more potential to disrupt the moral order than the battle over euthanasia and PAS, which pits American society's vigorous technological imperative and innate impulse to prolong life against its finite economic and medical resources and fundamental commitment to individual autonomy and human rights. As ground zero for these overlapping and contradictory forces, euthanasia news stories published in the national, mainstream press offer a window into a cultural realm "where negotiations over core ideologies, values, and myths surface and make themselves available for evaluation and analysis" (Fox 1977).

It is just such evaluation and analysis that is at the center of *Write to Death*, which examines national print news coverage of euthanasia within the context of the key historical, social, and economic forces giving rise to the right-to-die (RTD) debate. More than most social problems, the outcome of the struggle over euthanasia will crucially impact *all* Americans. Fallout from the policy decisions and public attitudes shaped in part by news stories about the controversy will be imprinted on the lives of elderly, severely disabled, and incompetent Americans well into the future. Unfortunately, if history is any judge, legalization of PAS, in particular, will result in certain groups in society—most likely women, minorities, the physically and mentally disabled, the poor—finding themselves confronting the darker side of the nation's sweeping new "right" to choose suicide.

ACKNOWLEDGMENTS

I am deeply indebted to a number of individuals whose generosity and assistance helped make this book possible. Next to the encouragement and patience of my husband Richard, the book benefited most from the support of Dr. Kittrell Rushing, an accomplished media historian and my department head at the University of Tennessee in Chattanooga (UTC). Since I arrived at UTC to teach media studies courses six years ago, Kit has gone out of his way to provide course releases, technical assistance, and a sympathetic ear when my efforts to juggle the book with my teaching and advising duties threatened to overwhelm. Because this book began as my doctoral dissertation at The University of Tennessee in Knoxville, I also owe Drs. Dorothy Bowles and Paul Ashdown a great deal of credit for their guidance and personal mentorship during that formative experience. Other colleagues at UTC also played important roles in the book's completion, including: Dr. Karen Adsit, whose expertise in media technologies has helped shape my research and teaching in so many ways; Dr. Betsy Alderman, whose support and people skills have guided me through rough shoals more times than I can say; my good friend Dr. Laura Lovett, whose affection and advice sustained me; and our Department secretary, Kelly Griffin, whose kindness and offers to help meant more than she realized.

I am also deeply grateful for the competence and flexibility of my Greenwood Press editors, including Michael Hermann, who shepherded the book through its early stages with grace and humor, and Bobbie Goettler, whose copyediting expertise and professionalism made working with her an authentic pleasure. Finally, I'd like to thank my students, whose interest in the media and love of ideas help fuel my scholarly work, my son Glen, whose honesty and character remain a central source of inspiration for me, and my sisters Nancy and Barbara, whose faith in me infuses my life with warmth, energy, and emotional strength.

INTRODUCTION

There is but one truly serious philosophical problem,
and that is suicide.
Judging whether life is or is not worth living amounts to answering
the fundamental question of philosophy.
— Camus 1955

Before twentieth-century advances in technology dramatically altered the capacity to extend life, the concepts of "death" and "rights" were seldom, if ever, coupled. Yet in recent decades, in industrialized countries around the globe, the notion of a "right to die" has attained widespread cultural currency. In the United States, catchphrases such as "living wills," "death with dignity," and "quality of life" have become embedded in the popular vernacular. And public approval of both passive and active euthanasia[1] has spiraled upward since the *Quinlan* case galvanized public and media attention in the mid-1970s.[2] By the dawn of the twenty-first century, polls showed close to 75 percent of United States citizens in favor of some form of euthanasia (Neergaard 2000), and by 2001 fully 65 percent of American adults approved of PAS (Taylor 2002).[3] In contrast, only 37 percent of the population in 1947 and only about half of those polled in 1977 expressed support for some form of euthanasia (Pugliese 1993; Hamil-Luker and Smith 1998).[4]

This broad public mandate for a "right to die" is striking not only for the swiftness with which traditional barriers to euthanasia appear to have crumbled, but in terms of the power and prestige of the institutions allied against it. Opponents of PAS object to it for reasons varying from its perceived corruption of the doctor-patient relationship to its violation of religious law. In addition to opposition from the American Medical Association (AMA)—arguably the nation's most visible and recognizable symbol of medical authority—PAS has been denounced by virtually all Evangelical Christian denominations, the Roman Catholic church, and Orthodox Jewish, Greek, and Islamic faiths, among others. Despite the enormous reach and authority of these institutions, their efforts to mobilize public sentiment against PAS have been notably ineffectual in the United States.

Clearly, a significant shift has taken place in public attitudes toward individual autonomy over the time and circumstances of death and, more broadly, in the fundamental meaning of what constitutes a "good death" in American society. This shift gives rise to a number of compelling questions, the most intriguing of which relates to the public's near-sweeping endorsement a "right to die": How, in less than two decades, did the central question in the euthanasia debate evolve from, "Should we allow comatose patients to be disconnected from artificial life-support systems?" to "Should we allow doctors to take proactive steps—even injecting lethal drugs—to end the lives of terminally ill and comatose patients?" As newspaper columnist Ellen Goodman (1997) notes, "Somewhere along the way the right-to-die movement went from asking about stopping treatment to asking for a doctor's help in dying" (p. A27).

Although a number of routes might be pursued to investigate the questions raised by this issue, the approach adopted in *Write to Death* involves tracking the role of the *news media*—among our culture's most potent instruments of legitimization—in conditioning public understanding of and consensus on the euthanasia conflict. All human societies erect socially approved "firewalls" against the reality of death, including standards and rituals designed to mitigate the existential trauma and uncertainty associated with mortality. In the modern era of "technologized" death, however, the task of designating the norms associated with a death has grown infinitely more complex. In post-capitalist societies like the United States, knowledge about life's end, including the meanings and interpretations attached to it, is no longer inscribed and codified primarily in religious and healing rites, the arts, or even legal rulings—but increasingly in mass media discourse.

SCOPE AND PURPOSE OF THE BOOK

Given the gravity of the euthanasia conflict, its serious long-term implications for the health and well-being of Americans, and the pitched discursive battle waged between pro- and anti-euthanasia forces during the last quarter of the twentieth century, it is surprising that news coverage of euthanasia, PAS, and the right-to-die (RTD) movement has failed to attract adequate scholarly attention and analysis. Whereas scores of euthanasia-related books have been published over the past several decades, none provide more than a cursory examination of the news media's role in constructing and conditioning popular perceptions of this ethically and technically complex issue. Meanwhile, the few researchers who have published peer-reviewed journal articles exploring some aspect of euthanasia news coverage have focused narrowly on Dr. Jack Kevorkian, ignored news coverage of euthanasia prior to 1990, and/or neglected to draw on and integrate historical, ideational, and other contextual material into their findings (see, e.g., Kalwinsky 1988; and Kenny 2000). Despite its inevitability, death and its attendant rituals are never culturally neutral; they take place and assume prominence within specific historical, economic, social, ideological, and political contexts—all of which must be examined *in tandem* with analysis of news media coverage. This is nowhere more important than in scholarly investigations of divisive, multilayered, and profoundly consequential issues such as the euthanasia controversy.

Write to Death seeks to overcome these and other deficiencies in euthanasia research by situating its analysis of euthanasia news stories published over more than two decades within the context of the key socio-cultural and historical factors serving as catalysts for mobilization of the RTD movement in the 1970s. The period selected for news analysis includes the "flash point" of the debate—the interval between Karen Ann Quinlan's coma in the mid-1970s and Dr. Jack Kevorkian's final, nationally televised "mercy killing" and subsequent conviction for murder in the late 1990s. Mass communications research suggests that the news shapes audience cognition in multifaceted ways (e.g., Katz 1980; Roberts and Maccoby 1985). News reports transmit information to the public on key issues and events; they set public and policy agendas by singling out particular social problems as salient (e.g., McCombs and Shaw; 1972); and news stories move some issues to center stage while backgrounding or warehousing others (see, e.g., Gitlin 1980; Lang and Lang 1983). These functions reflect only the outer stratum of news media influence, however. Mainstream news also serves as a chief cultural conditioner and circulator of values and beliefs (see, e.g., Carey 1975, 1988; Hall 1979). Reporters not only filter which and when, but how information is conveyed—the mix of images, metaphors, anecdotes, sources, and other discursive elements used in the construction of social problems for public consumption (see, e.g., Schudson 1978; Gitlin 1980; Gamson and Lasch 1983; Snow and Benford 1988; Entman and Rojecki 1993). In the process, news reports do more than highlight the significance of specific events and issues. They reinforce, crystallize, and alter collective knowledge about pressing social problems and their solutions. They legitimate or delegitimate specific ideologies, individuals, and interpretations. They manufacture consent (Chomsky and Herman 1988). And they cultivate general perceptions about social reality (see, e.g., Noelle-Neumann 1974; Gerbner et al. 1978; Tuchman 1978; Gans 1979).

The threshold task of this book, then, is to illuminate some of the major ways in which journalists and editors—while cloaking themselves in claims of objectivity—deployed cultural symbols in the service of ideology in their coverage of the euthanasia controversy. The book takes as its starting point the notion that deep-seated cultural values and beliefs reside in news texts and are accessible through analysis of the language, images, and other discursive symbols journalists use to encapsulate them. Moreover, it assumes these symbolic structures to embody specific ideologies (Fiske 1987). Drawing on examples from news articles on euthanasia published in four high-circulation, mainstream, national news media sources—*Newsweek, Time, U.S. News & World Report,* and *The New York Times*—over more than two decades, the book amasses an array of discursive evidence to illustrate how the national press systematically promoted pro-euthanasia views and marginalized or omitted anti-euthanasia frames.[5] Meanwhile, it demonstrates how journalists' framing selections and emphases implied the appropriateness of *particular* policy decisions on euthanasia and, in the process, advanced new definitions of and prescriptions for achieving a "good death." Another original contribution of this research involves the detection of the three major framing *stages* through which euthanasia coverage evolved during the period of analysis.

A second, related objective of *Write to Death* involves exploration of the complex dynamic between the news media, social movements, and social change. If, as Gurevitch and Levy (1985) assert, the news media serve as "a site on which various social groups, institutions, and ideologies struggle over the definition and construction of social reality" (p. 19), the battle is joined fundamentally over news media "frames"—the "codes of emphasis, interpretation and presentation" journalists use in stories about social issues (O'Sullivan et al. 1994, 281). By analyzing the repeated images, representations, and messages found in euthanasia news narratives, some of the ways in which ideological positions are packaged, presented, and made palatable to news audiences become evident. As the most efficient means of packaging and disseminating ideology, news frames represent potent weapons in the symbolic struggle social movement activists wage over competing definitions and interpretations of social problems (Gamson 1992b, 67). As with all social movements, the contest between RTD and pro-life (PL) forces is fundamentally a battle over *cultural meanings*—the version of social reality activists wish the public and policymakers to view as "fact" (Wolfsfeld 1993). This book highlights the way in which the mainstream press intervened in this process by authorizing and dispensing particular cultural "truths" about euthanasia and PAS during the peak period of public attention and consideration of the issue.

A final purpose of this book, which adopts a cultural studies approach to news research, involves exploring the wealth of data on American cultural characteristics and trends contained within euthanasia-related news narratives. Among other advantages, analysis of euthanasia news frames offers a rare glimpse into the social construction of public morality and social control. Just as abortion news stories embody the struggle over institutional versus individual control over women's bodies and reproductive rights (see, e.g., Grindstaff 1994), news narratives about euthanasia bring into focus the cultural dimensions of the contest waged between individuals, medical institutions, and governmental agencies over control of the bodies of the aged, incompetent, severely disabled, and dying. Such stories convey information on subterranean fault lines, fissures, and contradictions in social beliefs and attitudes—sites where the seeds of social change are most likely to germinate and take root. Of particular relevance to scholars interested in the social construction of death and dying in America, these stories carry within them intelligence on evolving notions of what constitutes a good death in contemporary society. Although ideas on achieving a "good" or "bad" death vary across historical eras and cultures, the desire to avoid pain and suffering at the end of life—as well as the need for myths and narratives that render death and dying meaningful—are universal values. Indeed, Lifton (1979) describes the need to imbue death with meaning and a sense of continuity as "the central quest of human history" (393).

The creation of acceptable versions of a good death not only helps neutralize this most destabilizing of human experiences, but is considered crucial to the welfare and future viability of all social systems.

Media Construction of Social Problems and Movements

The news media analysis at the heart of this book draws on two distinct yet compatible theoretical and research strands: (1) a *cultural* studies approach that views the news media as a symbolic system that both structures and is structured by society (Hall 1977, 1990); and (2) *framing theory* (Goffman 1976), which provides insights on the media's role in the social construction of reality by wedding journalists' specific language selections to larger cultural values, beliefs, and practices. Inspired by what one scholar refers to as "the phenomenon of the idea," *Write to Death* is broadly concerned with the process through which ideas on the appropriateness of euthanasia and PAS came into being and attained cultural currency in the last decades of the twentieth century (Kral 1994, 245). To investigate this puzzle, the book examines how the debate over legalized euthanasia was "framed"—or organized cognitively to support specific interpretations and perceptions—during the period when the issue loomed largest in national debate.

A Cultural Approach to News Analysis

Like all cultural experiences, death and dying are attended by a "relevant public discourse"—that is, "a particular set of ideas and symbols that are used in the process of constructing meaning" (Gamson 1988b, 165). Of all the ideational and symbolic forms used to represent reality, *language* is the most critical. Aside from facilitating human interaction and cohering individuals into communities, language "enables the manufacture and maintenance of history and culture" (DeFleur and Ball-Rokeach 1988, 21). As Hall's (1982) phrase, "The world has to be *made to mean*," suggests, language—including that circulated in news media discourse—plays a dominant role in the construction of social reality. Cherished American values and myths are vital components in the lexicon of symbols reporters use to explain and interpret social phenomena. The routine use in news stories of familiar and widely accepted "truths" or commonplace understandings both increases their credibility and interpretive power and functions ideologically. The news, in other words, not only spotlights specific problems, but situates them structurally and contextually in ways that aid particular judgments and interpretations. In this way news stories, which draw on widely recognized cultural symbols and ideas, may be seen to play a major role in establishing, reaffirming, and reproducing culture.

News Framing Theory

Framing theory is among the few perspectives available to mass media scholars that approaches news as a cultural resource journalists and news consumers use to constitute social reality (see, e.g., Tuchman 1978; Gans 1979; Fishman 1980; Edelman 1988). Functioning both as theory and analytical technique, framing is particularly useful for the study of the mass mediated symbols, images, values, and definitions journalists and editors use to promote particular views of social reality, including construction of the euthanasia debate and popular ideas related to achieving a "good death." Although framing theory has been applied in a confusing array of contexts and academic disciplines (see, e.g., Entman 1993), researchers employing the approach generally share the fundamental notion of a frame as "an interpretive schemata that simplifies and condenses the 'world out there' by selectively highlighting certain information" (Snow and Benford 1992, 137). Applied to news, framing theory suggests that the influence of frames results not so much from specific statements intended to persuade, but from the "persistent patterns of cognition, interpretation, and presentation, of selection, emphasis, and exclusion, by which symbol-handlers routinely organize discourse, whether verbal or visual" (Gitlin 1977, 7). In Foucauldian terms, news frames, like all discursive practices, establish "regimes of truth . . . the rules and standards by which individuals define what is good and bad; reasonable and unreasonable; rational, irrational, and non-rational" (Foucault 1973).

At this point it is fruitful to provide a brief explanation of how news frames are thought to operate cognitively. At the most fundamental level, news frames provide audiences with cues about the salience of events and issues, as well information on the best way to decipher and categorize social phenomena. One way in which they do so is by helping audiences process and organize new or unfamiliar social data into pre-existing cultural "scripts." By linking novel information with prior meanings, memories, and associations, news frames build bridges between the uncommon and the everyday, the known and the unknown, the prosaic and the peculiar. Frames, then, direct audiences to "imagine the new in terms of the old" (Covert 1992). This process is effective because, as Donati (1992) reminds us, "Cognition is nothing more than recognition, and people make sense of things by 're-cognizing' them as elements of a meaningfully ordered world. The consequence, in a sense, is that nothing can be perceived which is not known already" (p. 141).

The impact of a given news story frame has been found to intensify under certain circumstances, as when counterframes with opposing meanings and ideological messages are omitted or marginalized (see, e.g., Zucker 1978; Iyengar and Kinder 1987). Framing scholars have also found that news frame influence is amplified when audiences have no direct experience or are unfamiliar with news issues, such as foreign affairs or in stories about highly technical and ethically complex social issues (Zucker 1978; Iyengar and Kinder 1987). As an ethical dilemma arising from advances in medical technology, as well as dramatic population growth and a host of other historical, religious, and social forces, the euthanasia debate may be among the most complex confronted by American news audiences.

The notion that audience members find certain frames more credible than others highlights the concept of "frame resonance," a term signifying the capacity of a frame to "resonate with larger cultural themes" (Gamson and Modigliani 1989, 6) or align with prevailing cultural perceptions, experiences, and myths (Snow 1986; Snow and Benford 1988). As this suggests, the way in which readers process and accept frames is contingent on cultural preconditioning. In Schudson's (1989) words, "What is 'resonant' is not a matter of how 'culture' connects to individual 'interests' but a matter of how culture connects to interests that are themselves constituted in a cultural frame" (169). Compounding this effect, news frames are structured in a way that guides audiences toward a "dominant" or "preferred" reading that constrains alternative meanings (see, e.g., Morley 1980; Sigman and Fry 1985; Radway 1984; Carragee 1991). Hence, although frames are theoretically "polysemic"—open to multiple interpretations (Barkin and Gurevitch 1987; Newcomb and Hirsch 1984; Fiske 1987)—readers' interpretive freedom is rather rigidly circumscribed both by their cultural preconditioning and the cognitive structure of frames themselves, which promote particular meanings and discourage others (Gergen and Semin 1990).

News Framing of Social Problems and Movements

The news analysis presented in *Write to Death* benefits from the work of a number of framing scholars, including Gamson and Lasch (1983), who identified five "symbolic devices" and three "reasoning devices" that signal the presence of frames.[6] Also fundamental to news framing research and theory are Gamson and Modigliani's (1989) conceptualization of news frames as the core of "interpretive packages"—clusters of harmonious ideas about a social problem that aid in its interpretation, including the formulation of causes and solutions.

Gamson and colleagues also provide valuable insights on *framing stages*—the way in which dominant news media frames change over time to integrate the emergence of new information and/or events into an ongoing conflict. Charting longitudinal changes in dominant euthanasia news frames represents an important focus of this book, which seeks insights on the news media's role in the dramatic shift in public attitudes toward euthanasia during the past few decades. Among the many additional studies providing guidance on framing stages, the work of Silverstein (1992) and Condit (1990) are particularly useful. In Silverstein's study of news framing of the animal-rights conflict, she found that news coverage grew "increasingly respectful" and abundant as time progressed, reflecting growing acceptance of activists' terms and definitions of the debate. Condit, who investigated changes in abortion rhetoric over time, found that both pro- and anti-abortion forces involved in the early stages of the debate were hampered by a lack of symbols, terms, relevant cultural experiences, and other cognitive links used in frames to make sense of novel issues and events. These studies have obvious relevance to this book's longitudinal study of the euthanasia dispute, which not only erupted full-scale with Quinlan's coma in 1975, but presented reporters with an array of challenges, not the least of which was the unspoken taboo against the publication of graphic details of the suffering associated with advanced age and death. The issue's densely complex medical, religious, sociological, legal, and technological dimensions no doubt also proved difficult for journalists searching for a way to frame euthanasia.

For guidance on investigating news framing of the two social movements involved in the euthanasia debate—the right-to-die (RTD) and pro-life (PL) movements—*Write to Death* draws from the somewhat limited literature on the interaction between the news media and social movements. Social movement scholars have used framing analysis to explore the news media's role in mobilizing movement participants (see, e.g., Klandermans 1988; Snow et al. 1986; Snow and Benford 1988; Johnston 1995), as well as to identify trends in news coverage of social movements and the impact of news on movement goals (Gitlin 1980; Ryan 1991; Entman and Rojecki 1993; Gamson and Wolfsfeld 1993). However, rather large gaps remain in theoretical understanding of the interaction of the news media and social movements—including the role of the news media in social change and the way in which reporters frame the efficacy, credibility, and ideologies of social movements involved in ongoing conflicts (see, e.g., McQuail 1979). A study offering promising insights into this latter area of scholarship is Entman and Rojecki's (1993) work on "framing judgments"—their term for the inferences journalists make about the viability and credibility of social movements. In their research on news framing of the Reagan-era nuclear freeze movement, they identified seven such judgments made by reporters, including the protest movement's level of rationality, expertise, public support, partisanship, unity, extremism, and power (Entman and Rojecki 156–57). Aside from the impact framing judgments are likely to have on the success or failure of a social movement, they provide a relatively unobstructed view of the ideological workings of news stories on social movements.

Scholars have also found that even when social movements are able to attract media attention (something that frequently proves difficult, particularly for those clamoring for radical change), they are often depicted unsympathetically or even with outright hostility (see, e.g., Tuchman 1978; Gitlin 1980; Halloran, Elliot, and Murdock 1970; Morris 1974). Gitlin (1980), for example, found that student- and black-led protest movements in the 1960s were framed primarily as "civil disturbances"—a depiction he contends led to lack of public support for antiwar and civil-rights protestors (792). Similarly, Gamson (1995), who analyzed news framing of protestors' occupation of a nuclear reactor site in Seabrook, New Hampshire, in 1977, found that the mainstream news media trivialized the goals of the youthful antinuclear activists by framing them as "indulged children of the affluent who have everything they need" (102).[7] The obvious lesson from these studies is that the more radical and nonmainstream a social movement's goals and activities, the more likely it is to suffer at the hands of the press. This is likely to be true until and unless new events, sympathetic public authorities, and/or charismatic movement leaders (e.g., Kevorkian) intervene and override journalists' basic mistrust of and sometimes overt hostility toward emerging protest movements.

The Ideological Function of Euthanasia News Frames

If, as the above discussion of framing research strongly suggests, news frames perform ideological work, how might ideology manifest itself in news framing of the euthanasia controversy? On the surface the conflict over the appropriate role of euthanasia in American society might appear to raise few if any direct ideological concerns. Unlike, say, abortion, welfare reform, organized labor, affirmative action, or other politically charged issues, euthanasia fails to evoke immediate political associations. No social issue, however, is immune from the shaping influence of special interests, the most powerful of which are government and corporate representatives (see, e.g., Hall 1978; Carey 1989). Working from a media hegemony perspective, media scholars have found close parallels between dominant news frames and official government positions on a host of issues, ranging from air strikes on enemy aircraft and dissident social movements to labor disputes and the Persian Gulf War (see, e.g., Halloran, Elliot, and Murdock 1970; Hall 1977, 1978; Tuchman 1978; Gitlin 1980; Hallin 1986; Hufker and Cavender 1990; Carragee 1991; Entman 1991; Solomon 1992). Supporting this research are numerous studies that demonstrate journalists' heavy dependence on and promotion of the views of official sources, a phenomenon that occurs even when alternative (nonofficial) sources are available (see, e.g., Sigal 1973; Gamson and Modigliani 1987). Moreover, studies show that when journalists do include frames from nonofficial sources, they frequently "handicap" them by organizing stories in ways that position official frames as "the starting point for discussing an issue" (Gamson and Modigliani 1987, 166).

Research on the ideology of news frames also illuminates various ways in which news about social issues promotes ideologies that foster unequal distribution of economic and cultural resources through representations that uphold and reinforce racism, sexism, classism, homophobia, ageism, or other stereotypes and prejudicial positions (see., e.g., Hall 1977; Hall et al., 1978; Ericson 1987; Van Dijk 1992, 1995; Fowler et al. 1979; Hodge and Kress 1979; Binder 1993). As Nelkin (1991, 295) notes, "Selective use of language can trivialize an event or render it important; marginalize some groups, empower others; define an issue as an urgent problem or reduce it to a routine."

Based on the above discussion, an obvious initial approach to exploring the ideological implications of the euthanasia debate involves examining the social institutions with the most to gain from the routine incorporation of active and passive euthanasia in care of the incompetent and dying. Central among these are the insurance and medical industries, as well as state and federal government agencies. Conversely, the most obvious potential losers in public policy decisions about euthanasia and PAS are older Americans, who comprise less than 15 percent of the population, yet consume roughly a quarter of all medical resources. Most euthanasia cases are, of course, elderly citizens, a group distinguished by lower-than-average status, income, and educational levels. Health care in the United States is burdened by a history of discrimination, manifested not only through the patriarchal attitude of physicians traditionally, but in gender-, class-, age-, and race-based inequities in medical care. Women also comprise a significant majority of both passive and active euthanasia cases, leading some scholars to view euthanasia as inherently sexist (see, e.g., Wolf 1996; Kalwinsky 1998).[8] Because mental illness is responsible for some 90 percent of all suicides in the United States, concern also exists that mentally disabled individuals will disproportionately request and receive PAS (Gorsuch 2000). Still another anxiety relates to the risks euthanasia and PAS may pose to the poor, minorities, and other traditional victims of discrimination, including AIDS sufferers.[9] These worrisome facts, coupled with increasing pressures to cut medical and social security benefits for the aged and disabled, have fueled concerns that legalized euthanasia will be used to purge society of its elderly and other nonproductive groups. As implausible as this anxiety may initially seem, evidence of historical mistreatment of aged citizens would appear to justify concern: "It is [an] irony of modern civilization that the more highly industrialized and affluent a society becomes, the more readily and completely it tends to 'discard' its older people; or, as Cowgill has expressed it, 'modernization' tends to decrease the relative status of the aged and to undermine their security within the social system" (Heffernan and Maynard 1976, p. 74).

The controversy over euthanasia has arrived at a critical juncture in United States social and economic history. Mounting healthcare costs combined with the corporatization and concentration of ownership of healthcare institutions have revolutionized—and, many would say, compromised—the practice of medicine, "with doctors and hospitals rewarded for doing less for their patients" (Meier 1998, A23). What most troubles ethicists, gerontologists, and other advocates of the aging is that this trend coincides not only with the breakdown of traditional constraints governing euthanasia, but with the burgeoning of the elderly population—the cohort most in need of adequate pain treatment, personalized medical advice, and "reasonable attempts to prolong . . . life when death is not imminent" (Meier 1998). Worse, the pressures the elderly, disabled, and incompetent place on the nation's healthcare and economic systems promise only to intensify in the future, as baby boomers reach retirement age and medical costs continue to escalate (Longino 1994). Healthcare already consumes nearly 15 percent of the nation's gross domestic product (GDP), most of it spent on care for the elderly (Centers for Disease Control 2001). If, as one government study predicts, the number of Americans on Medicare doubles by the year 2030, the government will be forced to find new ways of shouldering the economic burden of caring for the population of older Americans (Centers for Medicare & Medicaid Services 2002). It would be unreasonable, given these fiscal realities, to ignore the many financial incentives likely to structure official frames on the subject of the appropriate use of active and passive euthanasia in care of the aged and incapacitated.

Having addressed the many troubling ideological implications of the euthanasia controversy, it is important to make a systematic inquiry into the nature of news media framing of the conflict: What, if anything, do news media frames communicate about the issue of who stands to benefit or lose from legalization of PAS? Do news frames alert the public to the potential abuses and inequities of medically and legally sanctioned euthanasia for society's marginalized groups (e.g., the poor and elderly)? Do they as a whole suggest a unified answer or solution to the question of the appropriateness of legalizing euthanasia or the social problems that originally gave rise to the debate? What *policy directions* do news frames on euthanasia imply or suggest? Who or what do they implicate or *blame* for the problems associated with the euthanasia controversy? Do frames predict *consequences* if particular actions are or are not taken?

ORGANIZATION OF THE BOOK

Serious social conflicts such as euthanasia, which emerge from dramatic technological advances and embody a wealth of ethical, religious, economic, sociological, and ideological perspectives, are inherently multidisciplinary. For this reason, readers drawn to this book are likely to come from a broad array of disciplines ranging from religion and law to medical ethics and cultural studies. General-interest audiences and students should also find the book's focus on media framing of the euthanasia issue both personally and politically relevant. In keeping with the book's multidisciplinary audience and its dual focus on news media coverage of the euthanasia conflict and the historical, sociocultural, and ideational forces giving rise to the contemporary debate, the book is organized into two main parts:

Part I presents contextual and background information, including details on the political, economic, cultural, and critical events culminating in the eruption of the late-twentieth-century conflict. To create a sense of the cultural climate and passions swirling around the issue, the first chapter opens onto one of the most dramatic developments in euthanasia history—the passage of the Oregon Death With Dignity Act (DWDA), the world's first law permitting physicians to provide death as a medical "service" to qualifying patients. This chapter also traces the evolution of news media attention to euthanasia beginning with the *Quinlan* case in the mid-1970s.

Chapter 2 anchors the dispute over euthanasia in a discussion of the evolution of social attitudes toward suicide and "mercy killing" throughout the course of Western history. Whereas the current right-to-die conflict is only a few decades old, euthanasia dates back to ancient Greece and beyond. Understanding historical and cross-cultural uses of and attitudes toward the practice—including the widespread acceptance of euthanasia in pre-Christian Western civilizations—provides a contextual framework for understanding the evolution of the current controversy, which is both informed and complicated by historical and religious traditions.

Of course, historical forces and conditions are not the only mechanisms that drive social change. As Max Weber and other social theorists have argued, sociocultural, ideational, and material factors figure heavily in major shifts in social attitudes, beliefs, and behaviors. Among the elements responsible for the dramatic changes over the past several decades in cultural attitudes toward euthanasia include revolutionary advances in medical technologies, the ascendance of scientific authority and concomitant erosion of religious dominance, major shifts in the financing and practice of healthcare, and the ballooning of the elderly population in the United States over the past 100 years. Chapter 3 offers an in-depth discussion of these factors, as well as key legal and technological milestones in euthanasia policy in the United States in the latter half of the twentieth century.

Part II of the book, organized in chapters 4 through 7, presents the results of news framing of the euthanasia debate, the research at the heart of *Write to Death*. Chapter 4 lays out and explains these results, including an in-depth description of dominant pro- and anti-euthanasia frames. Chapter 5 focuses on news framing of Kevorkian, the former pathologist who figured most prominently in the news media's notable shift in 1990 from a focus on passive euthanasia to an emphasis on PAS.

In addition to analysis of the stages through which news framing of euthanasia progressed over the more than two decades of analysis, chapter 6 considers both the ideological nature of news framing of euthanasia and what framing suggests about changing notions of a "good death" in late twentieth-century America.

Finally, chapter 7 knits together the conceptual strands introduced previously in the book, including the significance of "medicalization" of euthanasia, the dominance of "rights" frames, and the omission of alternative frames that might have been used to construct the problem of technologized death and its solutions. This chapter also discusses the implications of news media definitions of a "good death" and applies the study's results to consideration of the impact of the news media on collective understandings of significant social problems and controversies.

NOTES

1. Passive euthanasia is defined as "the withdrawal of life-sustaining care, such as artificially supplied nutrition and hydration or a respirator"; active euthanasia is "the administration of any means intended to produce death, such as the deliberate injection of a lethal dose of morphine" (Schanker 1993, 983).

2. In re Quinlan, 355 A.2d 647 (N.J.), cert. denied, 429 U.S. 922 (1976) (ruling that an "incompetent" patient's respirator may be removed to permit the patient to die).

3. The 65 percent figure is the result of a Harris poll of 1,011 adults interviewed by telephone in December 2001. Respondents were asked whether "the law should allow doctors to comply with the wishes of a dying patient in severe distress who asks to have his or her life ended." By 65 to 29 percent, respondents answered in the affirmative. When the same question was asked in 1993, 73 percent agreed and 24 percent disagreed; and in 1982, 53 percent agreed and 34 percent disagreed (Taylor 2002).

4. The question asked in the Gallop-National Opinion Research Center (NORC) poll administered to United States citizens for over five decades is: "When a person has a disease that cannot be cured, do you think doctors should be allowed to end the patient's life by some painless means if the patient and his family request it?"

5. See Appendix B for a detailed discussion of the publications and methods used in this study.

6. The five framing devices are: (1) metaphors, (2) exemplars (that is, historical examples from which lessons are drawn), (3) catchphrases, (4) depictions, and (5) visual images (e.g., icons). The three reasoning devices are (1) roots (that is, a causal analysis), (2) consequences (that is, a particular type of effect), and (3) appeals to principle (that is, a set of moral claims) (Gamson and Lasch 1983).

7. Negative framing of protest movements and activists by mainstream journalists in the United States even extends to press coverage of foreign movements. Carragee (1991), for instance, found that *The New York Times* "denigrated and depoliticized" Germany's Green movement by characterizing its members as "lost children, quasi-religious zealots, idealists, and romantics" and by portraying their political challenge "as inherently disruptive" (25).

8. A study on the practice of PAS in both the Netherlands and the United States, which included Kevorkian's assisted suicides, found that PAS recipients were significantly more likely to be female; a second study of United States oncologists found that 60 percent of their euthanasia and PAS patients were women (Emanuel 1999).

9. A New York task force assigned to investigate the impact of PAS, for example, warned that legalizing the practice might "provide an excuse for those wanting to spend less money and effort to treat severely and terminally ill patients, such as patients with Acquired Immune Deficiency Syndrome" (Gorsuch 2000).

PART I

THE QUEST FOR "A GOOD DEATH"

CHAPTER 1

"A BOMB IN THE SICKROOM": THE NEWS MEDIA AND THE FIGHT FOR "DEATH WITH DIGNITY"

Truth happens to an idea. It becomes true, is made true by events
— William James, 1907 (Strouse 2001, 10)

THE WHOLE WORLD WATCHES OREGON: HISTORICAL PASSAGE OF THE DWDA

On 8 November 1994, long after the last of the day's meager light had dissolved behind Portland's west hills, several hundred members and supporters of the Oregon Right to Die (ORTD) committee, accompanied by a large contingent of reporters from the local, national, and international media, packed into a downtown art gallery. Outside, a chill autumn rain fell like sheet metal on the city's barren streets. Inside, however, the crush of dancing and embracing bodies generated an almost tropical heat in the constricted space. Since early afternoon on this election day, Oregon's newscasters and conservative talk-radio hosts had been predicting the most sweeping Republican mandate nationwide in over a century. Yet as midnight approached, it was a decidedly liberal election return that had galvanized the crowd at First Street's Gango Gallery. Roughly an hour earlier, Oregon voters had passed the Death With Dignity Act (DWDA)—the world's first law sanctioning physician-assisted suicide (PAS).

On the heels of defeats of similar initiatives in Washington in 1991 and California in 1992, Oregon's RTD activists had realized that to succeed in their state meant seizing the moral high ground on euthanasia traditionally staked out by pro-life (PL) groups. To that end, the tiny grassroots ORTD had spent $900,000 in a bid to convince Oregonians that the most ethical course of action was to vote for a referendum, known as Measure 16, that would allow physicians to help terminally ill patients die. Opposing the ORTD's efforts was a formidable phalanx of PL groups. Bankrolled heavily by the Roman Catholic Church, this anti-euthanasia alliance—known as the Coalition for Compassionate Care—poured $1.5 million into defeating the initiative (Hubert

1994). The battle, played out largely in the news media, proved fierce. On 8 November 1994, the DWDA passed by the slimmest of margins—51 to 49 percent.

The next morning reports of Measure 16's success made headlines worldwide, rekindling interest in the euthanasia debate and seeding fresh storms of controversy across the United States. Newspapers nationwide proclaimed the historic new law "unprecedented," "a leap into the unknown," and a step onto "uncharted political and ethical ground." One local front-page story likened the vote's impact on Oregon hospitals to "a bomb in the sick room" (O'Keefe 1994). Other papers lauded the new law's "humaneness" and built-in safeguards, praising it for allowing physicians to escape the "closet" where many had practiced euthanasia in secret for years (see, e.g., Associated Press 1994).

In an attempt to explain what to many seemed inexplicable, still other news outlets attempted to shoehorn the election outcome into the category of "quirky Oregon" stories. Representing the landmark vote as an anomaly, some attributed it to Oregonians' "libertarian independence," their "preference for 'direct democracy,'" or the state's unusually low percentage of "active members of a religious congregation" (Price 1994, A17; Bates and O'Keefe 1994, 3E; O'Keefe 1994, A4). Meanwhile, on television newscasts nationwide, constituents of various interest groups were characterized alternately as "happy" or "deeply troubled" over the new law. Catholic Church officials responded to the DWDA's passage by calling for "a day of mourning for all humanity." The American Medical Association (AMA) denounced PAS as unethical. And former United States Surgeon General C. Everett Koopdeclared the referendum a threat to society's well-being.

The media shelf life of the referendum—passed narrowly by voters in a single "maverick" state—has been remarkably enduring. Oregon's unprecedented law continues to surface subtextually in national and cultural discourse on issues ranging from individual rights and rising medical costs to the decay of American moral standards and loss of social stability. Meanwhile, as if it were not newsworthy enough in its own right, a series of legal challenges,[1] including persistent efforts on the part of the federal government to overturn or seriously weaken it, have further extended its moment in the news media limelight.[2] Over eight years after its passage, the landmark law continues to make headlines in Oregon and the national press, as well as provoking sporadic debate on news-talk radio and in letters to newspapers editors.

THE CONFLICT OVER A RIGHT TO DIE

Although subsequent chapters provide a more in-depth analysis of the broad range of views activists bring to the euthanasia debate, a brief overview of the struggle between RTD and PL activists proves helpful in establishing a context for examining media coverage of the conflict. By the mid-1970s the trend toward "medicalization" of death and dying (discussed in depth in chapter 3) galvanized citizens from a broad spectrum of backgrounds to fight for a "right to die"—the freedom to die with as much dignity and control as possible, including being granted the option of choosing passive euthanasia and PAS. Considering "humane treatment" and "quality of life" preeminent moral values, RTD advocates argue that the use of "heroic" measures to extend life not only places an intolerable emotional and financial burden on families, but wastes precious economic and human resources better allocated to alleviate more pressing social problems. In place of "medicalized" death, they champion the right of severely or terminally ill individuals to exercise autonomy over a "matter of vital, exclusive importance: the timing, manner and circumstance of one's death" (Newman 1991, 171, quoting Kurtz 1991).

On the opposite side of the debate, PL activists—a loose confederation of Catholics, Christian fundamentalists, clerics, medical professionals, ethicists, philosophers, and legal scholars opposed to active and/or passive euthanasia—believe that "sanctity for life" should override "quality of life" in care of the dying and/or seriously incapacitated. Some PL activists, opposed to various forms of euthanasia on religious grounds, view both passive and active euthanasia as an affront to the authority of God and "natural law" over matters of life and death. Others, approaching the issue from a secular perspective, argue that PAS, in particular, diminishes respect for established medicine, subverts physicians' traditional roles as healers, "makes murderers of doctors," and corrupts the doctor-patient relationship. Most PL activists also raise the "slippery slope" argument against PAS—the belief that incorporation of the practice into end-of-life care will gradually undermine compassionate treatment of the elderly and terminally ill and will inevitably be used to rid society of the aged, disabled, and chronically ill, groups that they maintain already face discrimination in United States society.

MEDIA ATTENTION TO THE EUTHANASIA DEBATE

Although the euthanasia conflict may be understood as individuals fighting on one side for personal autonomy and on the other for preservation of traditional moral and social values, the controversy also embodies societal and institutional hegemonic struggles. Both the fierceness of the debate waged over the issue between the mid-1970s and mid-1990s and the struggle over PAS that persists in alternative and specialized media sources mark the issue as emblematic of enduring cultural concerns and myths (Levi-Strauss 1966). From the infinite number of potential social issues that erupt onto the public forum, it is those "that can be related to deep mythic themes or broad cultural preoccupations" that compete most successfully (Hilgartner and Bosk 1988, 71). Like the abortion debate, the euthanasia conflict points to deep-seated cultural rifts and contradictions in American society. Whereas the conflict over abortion is played out metaphorically on the bodies of women (Grindstaff 1994), however, the debate over euthanasia is enacted on the bodies of the aged, terminally ill, and severely disabled—all of whom have a high stake in its outcome. Cultural conflicts such as that waged over a "right to die" are characterized by constant flux, as special interest groups jockey to position their images and messages in ways that best support their agendas and goals (McGee 1980).

A record of the rise and fall of these cultural positions is available for analysis in media representations such as news discourse on the euthanasia controversy. Even more important, however, euthanasia news narratives provide a window into the exercise of institutional power, including that of the government, medicine, and law. The focus of investigations of institutional power, as Foucault (1971/1980) suggests, is on "how power subjugates knowledge and makes it serve its ends . . . , how it imprints its mark on knowledge, imposes on it ideological content and limits" (131). The authority wielded by institutions is inextricably bound up with knowledge—particularly that circulated in mass media images and messages. Such knowledge, as he notes, "is in itself a form of power . . . which is linked, in its existence and functioning, to the other forms of power" (Foucault 1971/1980).

Understanding the euthanasia controversy as a clash between institutions battling for power and individuals struggling for autonomy helps explain why the conflict has been joined by religious leaders and medical ethicists, along with physicians, attorneys, politicians, social justice activists, civil libertarians, and "moral entrepreneurs" who exploit social problems to garner public attention and support for their agendas (Becker 1963). It also sheds light on America's enduring preoccupation with euthanasia and why, in the national, mainstream press, coverage steadily escalated from the mid-1970s to mid-1990s. In 1975, the year the parents of coma victim Karen Ann Quinlan commenced their lengthy legal battle to remove their daughter from life support, *The Readers' Guide to Periodicals* lists only nine magazine articles published on euthanasia.[3] In contrast, a search of the Lexis-Nexis database for 1996 yielded over 6,000 hits (in the newspaper index alone).[4] Broadcast news programs and documentaries on euthanasia also proliferated in the wake of *Quinlan*.

It is not surprising that an event as explosive as the passage of Oregon's DWDA—the first law in the world allowing physicians to end the lives of patients via lethal injection—would sustain high levels of news media interest. Ironically, however, media attention to the DWDA coincides with a sharp decline in news coverage of the larger euthanasia debate since the referendum's passage. As detailed in chapters 4 and 5, news coverage of passive euthanasia—the removal or withholding of life-support systems and medical treatments from dying or seriously incapacitated individuals—had all but evaporated by the mid-1980s. Even more unexpected, however, is this study's finding that by the time of Kevorkian's arrest for murder in 1998 (a charge on which he was subsequently convicted), news about *active* euthanasia, including PAS, had also slowed to a trickle in the mainstream, national news sources included in this investigation. Based on the ebb in national, mainstream attention to euthanasia by the close of the twentieth century, it seems safe to conclude that news organizations consider the debate over euthanasia to have reached some sort of closure. If so, this conclusion not only disregards the absence of clearly defined public policy or national consensus on PAS, but ignores the intense debate over the practice that persists on the Internet, in discourse distributed by disabilities organizations and advocates of the aged, and in religious, medical, and academic publications. Certainly the decline of news media discourse on euthanasia and PAS in the United States cannot be justified by public apathy toward the topic. The notion that Americans are in denial about their mortality is something of a truism among death-and-dying authorities, including scholars who study multicultural attitudes toward death (see, e.g., Aries 1974, 1981; Becker 1973; and Kübler-Ross 1969). Contrary to Arnold Toynbee's famous nostrum that, "Death is un-American," however, United States citizens during the past half century have evinced an almost compulsive interest in end-of-life issues. As one source observed nearly two decades ago of this phenomenon, "Whether the issue is euthanasia or how to cope with grief, Americans can't seem to get enough of the subject of death" (Maloney 1983). As one indication of public interest in euthanasia, a major book wholesaler reported in 1997 that three of its top ten most-requested titles dealt with right-to-die issues.[5] Since that year, at least two dozen additional books on the topic have been published in the United States.

After the initial surge of media interest in euthanasia prompted by the *Quinlan* case, news coverage of the issue—typically triggered by legal cases or the plight of particular individuals or their families involved in conflicts with hospitals—remained consistent, albeit episodic, during the 1970s and 1980s. Media coverage of the issue spiked in 1988 with the publication of the provocative article, "It's Over, Debbie," in the *Journal of the American Medical Association* (JAMA). Startling both the public and the medical community, "It's Over, Debbie" documented a self-described "mercy killing" by an anonymous physician working as a hospital resident who injected a lethal drug into a late-stage cancer patient whom he did not know and had never previously treated.[6] Refueling the debate sparked by "It's Over, Debbie" was a second highly controversial article published four years later in *The New England Journal of Medicine*. In this essay, Dr. Timothy Quill, a respected professor at the University of Rochester, defended his decision to prescribe lethal drugs for a cancer patient named Diane who had told him that she might use pills he had previously prescribed to end her life.[7]

In 1990 two novel developments helped secure the place of euthanasia in mainstream news headlines for many more years. The first and most dramatic was the entrance of retired Michigan pathologist and RTD activist, Dr. Jack Kevorkian, into the debate. And the second was a series of ballot initiatives several states considered to legalize PAS. Although voters failed to pass any of the state ballot initiatives on PAS introduced in the 1990s (except Oregon's), Kevorkian proved irresistible to the public and journalists alike. Dubbed "Dr. Death" by the press, Kevorkian used his "suicide machine" for the first time on 4 June 1990 to assist in the suicide of Janet Adkins, a fifty-four-year-old from Portland, Oregon, diagnosed with Alzheimer's disease. For the better part of the decade that followed, he launched a direct assault on both the medical establishment and Michigan law by aiding in the suicides of over 130 individuals. By the time he was finally convicted of second-degree murder in 1999 after CBS' "60 Minutes" broadcast a videotape of him injecting a man with a lethal drug, Michigan juries had acquitted him in three highly publicized murder trials.

In addition to mainstream news media attention to euthanasia and PAS, a profusion of books on euthanasia have appeared since Karen Ann Quinlan personalized the topic for the American public in the mid-1970s.[8] RTD movement leaders contributed substantially to this trend themselves, producing several highly popular books promoting euthanasia—most notably the best-selling, *Final Exit*, written by the activist Derek Humphry in 1991.[9] A "how-to" suicide manual, *Final Exit* remained on *The New York Times* best-seller list for eighteen weeks in 1991 and sold 600,000 copies in its first two years alone.[10]

The burgeoning of mass media attention to the euthanasia controversy during the last quarter of the twentieth century is clearly indicative of the issue's enduring personal, social, and political resonance. Beyond its cultural currency, however, the media's "gaze" upon the topic serves as an example of "language use as social practice" (Fairclough 1995, 54). As a form of social practice, news media framing of the issue has much to convey about the dialectical relationship between the consciousness industry, institutional hegemony, and political action.

NOTES

1. After surviving two years of court challenges, the DWDA suffered what some predicted would be a mortal blow in June 1997, when Oregon's legislature voted to repeal the law and send it back to voters for reconsideration (Goldberg 1997). However, Oregonians resoundingly defeated Measure 51, a referendum that would have repealed the DWDA, later that same year, and the law took effect on 27 October 1997. The new law was used the first time on 25 March 1998, when doctors assisted the suicides of two terminally ill residents (Hernandez and Eure 1998). In the first year following the DWDA's implementation, fifteen individuals took advantage of it to end their lives. By the end of 2002, a total of 129 individuals had used the law to end their lives (Hedberg and Kohn 2003).

2. The most recent example began in November 2001, when U.S. Attorney General John Ashcroft authorized federal agents to take action against Oregon physicians prescribing lethal drugs under the DWDA. The directive, which was blocked by a U.S. District Court judge in April 2002, would have led to the revocation of the prescription licenses of doctors involved in PAS. Ashcroft appealed the ruling to the Ninth Circuit Court of Appeals, which will hear oral arguments in May 2003. An earlier federal attempt to abolish the DWDA came in the form of the Hyde-Nickles bill, introduced into the U.S. House of Representatives in October 1999. Had this bill been signed into law, it would have nullified the DWDA by banning the use of the lethal drugs required to carry out PAS. Although it passed by a nearly 2-to-1 margin in the House in 2000, a similar bill failed to attract sufficient votes in the Senate (Saner 2000).

3. Keywords used included "euthanasia," "mercy-killing," and "right to die."

4. Keywords used were "euthanasia," "right to die," "assisted suicide," and "mercy killing."

5. The top euthanasia titles reported by the Ingram Book Group include: *Final Exit: The Practicalities of Self-Deliverance and Assisted Suicide for the Dying*, by Derek Humphry; *Denial of the Soul: Spiritual and Medical Perspectives on Euthanasia*, by M.

Scott Peck; *and Life Support: Three Nurses on the Front Lines*, by Suzanne Gordon. Source: the Ingram Book Group's web site (http://www.ingrambook.com), 2 May 1997.

6. In severe pain the patient had reportedly said, "Let's get this over with," which the resident interpreted as a plea to expedite her death. Because the anonymous resident acted without consulting the patient's physician or family, the article alarmed the medical community and attracted national press coverage. Perhaps the most significant consequence of this event, however, was that it signaled the willingness of JAMA—among the nation's most prestigious medical journals and a "gatekeeper" for the medical profession—to inaugurate a public discussion of the surreptitious practice of PAS by medical professionals (Newman 1991, 153).

7. Along with attracting intense media coverage, Quill's article made him the focus of a New York grand-jury investigation and the New York medical ethics board. The grand jury convened but declined to indict Quill. And the state ethics board eventually rejected disciplinary measures against him on the basis that the prescription he had written was for legitimate medical use (to treat insomnia) and that it was impossible to prove he had intended the prescription be used specifically to help Diane commit suicide.

8. A small sample of recent euthanasia titles includes: Herbert Hendin's *Suicide in America* (1995); Anne Mullens' *Timely Death: Considering Our Last Rights* (1996); Gerald Larue's *Playing God: 50 Religions' Views of Your Right to Die* (1996); William Munk's *Euthanasia: Or, Medical Treatment in Aid of an Easy Death* (1977); Jennifer Scherer and Rita Simon's *Euthanasia and the Right to Die: A Comparative View* (1999); Melvin Urofsky's *Lethal Judgments: Assisted Suicide and American Law* (2000); Sue Woodman's *Last Rights: The Struggle of the Right to Die* (2001); and Ian Dowbiggan's *A Merciful End: The Euthanasia Movement in Modern America* (2003).

9. According to Humphry (personal correspondence 23 May 1997), over 1 million copies of the book have sold worldwide to date, and it continues to sell at a rate of about 1,000 copies per month in North America. A second best-selling nonfiction book on euthanasia was Betty Rollin's, *Last Wish* (1985) later made into a television movie.

10. Widespread cultural interest in euthanasia has also spawned its own film genre. Hollywood began exploring the topic of "mercy killing" as early as 1939 in the film, "Dark Victory," starring Bette Davis as a dying socialite whose doctor helps her commit suicide. More recent examples include: "Murder or Mercy?" (1974); "The End" (1978), "Promises in the Dark" (1979), "Act of Love" (1980), "Whose Life is it Anyway?" (1981), "Right of Way" (1983), "The Ultimate Solution of Grace Quigley" (1985), and "New Age" (1994). A plethora of made-for-television movies devoted to assisted suicide also appeared between 1987 and 1995, including "When the Time Comes" (ABC, 1987); "Murder or Mercy?" (NBC, 1987); "The Right to Die" (NBC, 1987); "Last Wish" (ABC, 1992); and "The Switch" (CBS, 1995).

CHAPTER 2

DEIFIED, CONDONED, VILIFIED, AND CRIMINALIZED: A BRIEF HISTORY OF EUTHANASIA IN WESTERN SOCIETIES

> The chief consolation for Nature's shortcomings in regard to man is
> that not even God can do all things. For he cannot, even if he should
> so wish, commit suicide, which is the greatest advantage he has given
> man among all the great drawbacks in life.
> —Pliny, A.D. 23–79, quoted in Larson and Amundsen (1998)

THE WHOLE WORLD WATCHES OREGON: HISTORIC PASSAGE OF THE DWDA

The right-to-die controversy is far from novel. Not only do the earliest medical records reflect dissension over the ethics and legality of "mercy killing," but these debates long pre-date the invention of advanced life-extension medical technologies (Emanuel 1994). Social attitudes toward the taking of one's own life—whether to mitigate pain and suffering or to secure the overall survival of the social system—have vacillated markedly throughout history. As one commentator observes, "In classical times suicide was a tragic option for human dignity's sake. Then for centuries it was a sin. Then it became a crime. Then a sickness" (Beschle 1988–89, 320, quoting Fletcher 1982). Clearly, "suicide, whether assisted or not, is a complex issue in any society, more so in some cultures than in others" (Larson and Amundsen 1998, 32). Depending on the culture and era, "mercy killing" and other forms of suicide have alternately been deified, condoned, tolerated, vilified, criminalized, and even (ironically) punished by death (Warrick 1991).

The purpose of this chapter is to sort through some of the contextual and historical layers informing the contemporary debate over euthanasia. Given the somewhat erratic course euthanasia has tracked throughout recorded history, it is useful to map out the major social and cultural ways in which it has been practiced, major shifts in attitudes toward "mercy killing" and suicide, and the evolution of cultural meanings attached to a "good death."

HISTORICAL BACKGROUND

Early Cultural Attitudes Toward Euthanasia

The award-winning 1983 Japanese film, "The Ballad of Narayama," provides an anthropological glimpse into one late nineteenth-century tribal culture's solution to the problem of what to do with elderly citizens who have outlived their utility and hence threaten the survival of the group. In the Northern Japanese settlement of Narayama, tradition dictated that in the autumn following their seventieth birthday, elderly villagers were loaded onto the backs of their first-born sons and hauled up the steep slopes of Mount Shinshy. Abandoned by their offspring on the summit amid the sun-bleached bones of their ancestors, the "old ones" were left to die under the watchful eye of encircling bands of vultures. The luckiest of them, according to a ballad popular in the village, were those blanketed on their first night by an early, killing snowfall.

Although few contemporary Americans would applaud Narayama's unblinking solution to the problem of providing resources and healthcare for those too old or ill to support themselves, all modern societies—including the United States—are forced to face sometimes wrenching questions about how best to allocate finite resources for care of the elderly and terminally ill. Like Narayama, cultures the world over have relied for centuries on both voluntary and involuntary euthanasia as a practical means of preserving and reallocating scarce resources, as well as a means of mitigating the pain and suffering of seriously injured and dying individuals.

Based on anthropological and historical evidence, euthanasia was remarkably common in aboriginal cultures—particularly those struggling for survival in hostile physical environments. According to an extensive survey of euthanasia use among early tribal societies, "the more severe a tribe's living environment, and the more voluntary the death by the sick or aged individual, the more noble the death was perceived in the culture" (Mullens 1996, 58). The Inuit, for example, battling among the most extreme climatic conditions on the planet, considered assisted suicide an honorable, practical, and compassionate means of dealing with terminal illness, aging, and incapacitating injury while simultaneously assuring the survival of the tribe as a whole.

Despite euthanasia's prevalence in cultures facing hostile or extreme physical conditions, it would be a mistake to assume that the practice has always been associated with threats to survival. Historical records indicate that it has been a part of cultural death-and-dying rituals in virtually every part of the globe, ranging from the North American Indians and South Pacific Islanders to the Khoikhoin of Southern Africa and the Amassalik Eskimos of Greenland (Mullens 1996; Messinger 1993; Osgood 1995). Methods early cultures used to end the lives of the seriously ill and elderly ran the gamut from hanging and stabbing to shooting and poisoning (Mullens 1996; Osgood 1995). Some tribes, such as the Aymara Indians, withheld food and water from those taking too long to die naturally (Messinger 1993, 185). Like the villagers of Narayama, Eskimos tended to abandon their hopelessly ill and elderly to the elements, assuring them both a relatively painless passing (in sub-zero temperatures) and "eternity in the highest heaven" if they met their deaths with courage (Messinger 1993, citing Humphry and Wickett 1986). Other early euthanasia methods proved more inventive, if less humane: One Ethiopian tribe tied its elderly to wild bulls; the Amboyna cannibalized their aged and weak, with loved ones "eating their failing relatives out of a sense of charity"; and members of one Congolese tribe "jumped on the tired and old until life was gone" (Messinger 1993).

Neither has euthanasia been limited to so-called "primitive" cultures. Among Western civilizations euthanasia is most famously associated with the ancient Greeks, who between 600 and 300 B.C. referred to the practice as *euthanatos*, loosely translated as "good" or "easy" death (Roberts and Gorman 1996). Poison appears to have been the method of choice for achieving the classic Greek version of a "good death." One of the earliest recorded examples involved a rite that took place on the Greek island of Ceos, where each year the elderly and infirm were gathered for a "banquet" and served poisonous drinks (Messinger 1993, 182). Later, in Athens and other population centers, aristocrats who wished to die could request poison from an official magistrate, who dispensed it from a stock of hemlock to individuals providing a "noble" reason for ending their lives (Messinger 1993). And of course, Socrates—arguably the most famous euthanasia advocate in history—quaffed hemlock both to avoid imprisonment and the discomforts of old age.

The Greeks' open tolerance, if not actual promotion, of euthanasia was grounded in three philosophical notions. The first was a fundamental trust in human *reason* (Roberts and Gorman 1996). This argument was expressed by Plato, who argued that individuals have the right to make rational decisions about the time and manner of their own deaths. Moreover, he specifically sanctioned voluntary euthanasia for adults whose lives were no longer useful to society and involuntary euthanasia for children with birth defects or serious illnesses (Roberts and Gorman 1996; Mullens 1996).[1] In the following passage from *The Republic*, which portrays Socrates praising the physician Asclepius, Plato makes the case for a "good death" through what is now called "passive euthanasia"—withholding medical treatment or therapy to the dying or incurably ill: "Where the body was diseased through and through, he would not try, by nicely calculated evaluations and doses to prolong a miserable existence . . . Treatment he thought would be wasted on a man who could not live in his ordinary round of duties and was consequently useless to himself and to society" (Mullens 1996, 60, quoting Plato's *The Republic*).

This excerpt suggests that Plato's motivation for supporting euthanasia was an interest in the welfare of the *state* rather than compassion for the suffering and dying. Plato envisioned an ideal society in which individuals sacrificed their own needs for the collective good. In such a society, he believed, only selfish individuals would insist on surviving after they could no longer contribute to the welfare of the community as a whole (Mullens 1996). Individual autonomy, the notion that "man is the master of his own body, with the right to decide his own fate" represents the second philosophical foundation from which Ancient Greek support for euthanasia grew (Messinger 1993, 182). This ideal was articulated most strongly by the Stoics, a Greek philosophical school influenced by Socratic ideals founded around 300 B.C. The Stoics considered the choice to end one's life the apotheosis of moral freedom and a dignified death the ultimate expression of character (Mullens 1996).[2] Interestingly, unlike other Greek philosophical schools, the Stoics did not privilege life over death, but considered the two "morally equal states" (Roberts and Gorman 1996, 5). At the core of the Stoics' support for euthanasia was their abiding belief in harmony with nature; they considered a life out of sync with nature not worth living.[3] Seneca (4 B.C.– A.D. 65), among the most famous Stoics, passionately defended an individual's freedom to end life: "Just as I choose a ship to sail in or a house to live in, so I choose a death for my passage from life," he wrote. Waiting passively for nature to decide the time and manner of death meant "shutting off the path to freedom. The best thing that eternal law ever ordained was that it allowed to us one entrance into life, but many exits" (Mullens 1996, 61, quoting Seneca).[4]

Finally, Greek endorsement of euthanasia was also deeply embedded in Greek cultural notions related to idealization of youth (Osgood 1995). In contrast to older citizens, whose loss of vitality was regarded as extremely unfortunate if not deeply tragic, Greeks celebrated life's earliest stages as "the only period of true happiness" (Osgood, 415). As Osgood explains in the following passage, the Greek "cult of youth" meant almost total marginalization of the infirm and aged:

During the heroic age, manhood was measured by the standard of physical prowess. Old age robbed the person of such prowess and the ability to fight like a valiant warrior and robbed males of sexual prowess. Early Greek and Roman writings were filled with images glorifying youth and beauty and denigrating old age, which was associated with the loss of youth and beauty . . . The image of the strong, young man also dominated Greek art and sculpture from the first through seventh centuries B.C . . . Except in the Hellenistic period (323–327 B.C.), Greek sculptors never portrayed older figures (Osgood 1995, 415).

In the context of the cult of youth, Greek cultural openness to euthanasia may be understood as a rational means of escaping not only the ravages of age, but of ageist attitudes and behaviors. Not only was euthanasia considered a viable means of achieving a "good death," but an appropriate option for individuals faced with debilitating or terminal illness, loss of dignity at life's end, the threat of enslavement, capture, or poverty, or a situation in which taking one's life would provide a service for others (Osgood 1995). Additionally, as Plato wrote in *The Laws*, some considered euthanasia to be justified for adults who had "disgraced themselves beyond any hope of self-forgiveness, [and chose] to atone for their actions through suicide" (Roberts and Gorman 1996, 5).

It is important to stress that while euthanasia enjoyed broad popular support in ancient Greece, it was not universally condoned. Larson and Admundsen (1998) argue, in fact, that "there is no evidence of any train of ancient pagan thought and values that endorsed suicide as always appropriate and proper for anyone desiring to die under any and all circumstances with no qualifications, restrictions or limits" (32). Among the most famous critics of euthanasia in ancient Greece was Plato's student, Aristotle, who attacked euthanasia as "an offense against the state" that robbed society of productive citizens (Roberts and Gorman, 5). In addition to the Aristotelians, the Pythagoreans objected to euthanasia on the basis that it robbed individuals of life—a sacred gift from the gods that humans had no right to take. And of course, the existence of anti-euthanasia sentiment in ancient Greece is clearly demonstrated by the Hippocratic Oath, which exhorts medical practitioners against prescribing "a deadly drug if asked, nor suggest any such counsel" (Robin and McCauley 1995).

Historians caution, however, that these and other examples of opposition to euthanasia not only represented a minority view in ancient Greece, but may actually serve as an indication of the exalted status euthanasia enjoyed in antiquity (see, e.g., Messinger 1993; Emanuel 1994).[5] The Hippocratic Oath, for example, has been characterized by some historians as evidence of the widespread *support* for euthanasia.[6] As Mullens (1996, 60) notes, "The act of helping people die was so common among physicians in Greek and Roman society that physicians in the . . . Hippocratic school wanted to set themselves apart." Moreover, according to Emanuel (1994), "it was not until some time between the twelfth and fifteenth centuries that the Hippocratic view of euthanasia became dominant."

Following the lead of the Greeks, the ancient Romans not only condoned euthanasia, but elevated it to "high fashion" at least until the second century B.C. (Alvarez 1972). To the Romans a "good death" meant ending life in the same manner as one lived: with honor and courage. According to Alverez (1972), "one's manner of going became a practical test of excellence and virtue . . . To live nobly also meant to die nobly and at the right moment." A number of notable Romans left written endorsements of euthanasia. Pliny the Elder, a naturalist who lived from A.D. 23–79, argued that the existence of poisonous plants provided evidence of the gods' approval of euthanasia for the old, suffering, and infirm (Osgood 1995). The first Roman emperor, Augustus Caesar, wrote of desiring euthanasia to end his own life and that of his family (Mullens 1996). In a similar vein, Emperor Marcus Aurelius noted the benefits of euthanasia when illness caused "intellectual decrepitude" (Messinger 1993, 184, quoting Russell 1977, 54).

Like the Greeks, ancient Romans championed euthanasia to mitigate suffering, to avoid dishonorable or undignified death, and/or to prevent enemy capture or enslavement (Messinger 1993, 184). Crucial to understanding the broad popularity of euthanasia in antiquity is the notion of *heroic* death. The focus for ancient Romans was "not on whether it was morally acceptable to kill oneself, but rather on how to do so with the 'greatest dignity, bravery and style'" (Yuen 1992, 584, citing Smith 1989). Used to this end, euthanasia was referred to by the Romans as "a *summum bonum*, or extreme good" (Messinger 1993, 184).

Judeo-Christian Attitudes Toward Euthanasia

By the third century A.D., Christianity had gained a foothold throughout Europe, emerging as the official religion of the Roman Empire (Roberts and Gorman 1996). As the influence of the Church spread, definitions of a "good death" inspired by Greek and Roman philosophers were gradually supplanted by Christian values, beliefs, and attitudes toward the taking of one's own life or that of others who were mortally ill and in anguish (Messinger 1993, 185). Early Christians differed fundamentally from the ancient Greeks and Romans in their ideas not only about the supremacy of individual reason and autonomy, but about the innate value of life itself. Perhaps the most significant distinction between Christian and Greco-Roman attitudes about death, however, is found in their conceptions of the role and meaning of suffering. Rather than viewing the physical miseries associated with death as "undignified" or something from which to be released, the Church considered pain and suffering a consequence of—and reparation for—the wages of sin. Christianity's embrace of suffering as a virtue reached a pinnacle after the eleventh century, when the Church began actively promoting martyrdom and self-sacrifice as paths to spiritual growth and salvation (Roberts and Gorman 1996).[7] This attitude toward suffering has not only survived for more than nine centuries, but remains a critical aspect of modern Catholic doctrine, a point illustrated by this statement by Cardinal Roger Mahony in 1994: "Christians, in particular, believe that loving acceptance of suffering can lead to enormous personal growth. We agree with the psychologists who have called the dying process the final stage of human growth" (quoted in Doerflinger 1995, 152).

As the Church's historical promotion of martyrdom suggests, early Christian opposition to suicide (and hence euthanasia) was not without contradictions. At the same time that early Christians opposed suicide, they also maintained "a firm acceptance of martyrdom, of testifying to the faith even if it would mean an unjust death at the hands of others" (Doerflinger 1995, 149). Meanwhile, the belief in life as a gift from God led to the Christian emphasis on the essential "inviolability" or "sanctity" of life. As Mitchell (1990, 38–39) observes, "Western civilization has been indelibly marked by Christian influences, which have imbued an assumption that, to be civilized, a society must value human life absolutely." In a reversal of the ancient Greek and Roman stress on *quality* of life, then, Christian leaders taught that *life per se* eclipsed the actual *experience* or phenomenological aspects of life.

Some historians have suggested that the fierce opposition to euthanasia that marks both Christian and Jewish religious teachings may also have roots in the persecution and subjugation of these groups at the hands of Roman conquerors.[8] As Mullens (1996, 62) writes, "Perhaps it was in opposition to the views of their Roman oppressors that followers of the Jewish and Christian religions developed an overwhelming abhorrence for suicide."[9] Other scholars have argued that a drop in the birth rate attributable to the Christian embrace of martyrdom inspired the Church's stand against suicide (see, e.g., Markson 1995). Whatever its origins, the Christian proscription against euthanasia and suicide are notably absent from the Bible. Scholars have not only been unable to identify a single example of Biblical condemnation of suicide, but have actually found limited evidence of support for the practice in both the Old and New Testaments.[10] The Bible's lack of direct prohibition of the act is striking in light of what Colt (1991) describes as, "Christianity's nearly two thousand years of intense opposition to suicide" (p. 153). He and other historians trace Christian denunciation of suicide and "mercy killing" to the highly influential Saint Augustine, who in the fifth century A.D., denounced the practice as "detestable and damnable wickedness" (Mullens 1996, 64). It was in fact Augustine who declared suicide a mortal sin and promoted the idea that those committing suicide should be condemned to hell.[11]

If the true genesis of Judeo-Christian antipathy to suicide remains somewhat mysterious, opposition to the practice was well entrenched in Church doctrine by the third century A.D. Christian teachings during this time made no distinction between suicide resulting from emotional instability and suicide as an antidote to end-of-life suffering, incapacitating injury, or incurable illness. All suicide was considered *felo de se* (self murder) (Mullens 1996). Largely as a result of Augustine's harsh condemnation of suicide, the Church began excommunicating suicides and denying them a Christian burial—the most punitive of actions given the Christian belief that such a burial is essential for salvation (Roberts and Gorman 1996).

By the eleventh century A.D., secular laws across Europe added muscle to the Church's censure of suicide. In sixteenth- and seventeenth-century England, for example, "Suicide was regarded as a heinous crime . . . a kind of murder committed at the instigation of the devil" (MacDonald 1991, 86). Legal penalties for taking one's life were severe, ranging from "confiscation of property and exposure of the corpse to scavenging animals and criminal punishment for unsuccessful suicide attempters" (Newman 1991, 154). Because a suicide's blood was considered corrupt, eligible heirs were also refused title to a suicide's property (Berk 1992). Moreover, until well into the nineteenth century in England and other Western countries, the bodies of suicides were customarily impaled on stakes and displayed prominently near roadsides (MacDonald 1991, 86).[12]

Renaissance and Enlightenment Influences

Christian stigmatization of suicide spread rapidly throughout Western Europe until the nineteenth and twentieth centuries. By the Middle Ages, however, fissures of support for euthanasia had begun to appear in discourse referring to the practice—many from unexpected sources. For example, St. Thomas More, a thirteenth-century Catholic officially canonized by the Church, wrote in *Utopia* that euthanasia for the hopelessly ill and suffering represented "an honourable death" (Mullens 1996, 67). As a general rule, the taking of one's life during this era was judged moral or immoral based on the perceived motivation for the act. Powerful elites in Medieval society—mainly military and church officials—drew clear distinctions between "egotistic suicide," which resulted in severe sanctions for the suicide's survivors as well as ill treatment of the corpse, and "indirect, altruistic" suicide, which "was set up as a model and an example of unyielding faith unto martyrdom" (p. 12).

Although motivations for suicide or euthanasia varied along class and gender lines, the act was apparently sufficiently widespread in Medieval Europe to inspire authorities to attempt to deter it. Minois (2001), who studied an array of Medieval documents ranging from journals and the memoirs of ordinary people to clerical and judiciary sources, concludes that despite severe sanctions visited on the corpse and survivors of those taking their own lives, "suicide was practiced in all social categories and by both men and women" during the Middle Ages at a rate consistent with other historical eras (p. 9). As he writes, "the many laws that were passed, both canon and civil, the number of philosophical and theological pronouncements made on the subject, the absence of expressions of surprise in the chronicles, and the dockets of court cases regarding voluntary homicide all show that suicides occurred with some regularity" (p. 10).

Moreover, "effective substitutes for direct suicide" were also fairly common in European cultures during this period, including tournaments (which Minois refers to as "gaming suicides"), duels, chivalric martyrdom and a variety of other "indirect warrior suicides" which were at times characterized as enactments of the will of God (Minois 2001).

The Renaissance saw the emergence of more overt public support for euthanasia, as poets, humanists, historians, and playwrights rediscovered Greek philosophy and began to celebrate the heroism of famous suicides from antiquity, including Cato, Brutus, and Lucretia (MacDonald 1991, 87). The progression of medical knowledge at this time also prompted a redefinition of euthanasia as a *medical option*—a development that corresponded with the emergence of medicine as a realm of knowledge and authority distinct from Church teachings (Cartwright 1977). Physicians had already begun to form professional organizations by the Middle Ages, and by the seventeenth century, medicine's image had benefited from improved physician education, training and initial efforts to standardize medical procedures. Most significant in advancing the fortunes of institutionalized medicine, however, was the advent of "natural" or scientific explanations for disease. It was during the Renaissance that physicians began dissecting cadavers and creating a classification system for understanding human anatomy. As medical science gradually adopted a view of the body "as a single system of finite materials and forces accessible to human comprehension" (Rubenstein 1995, 35), human anatomy "came to be seen more as a machine than as a divine mystery" (Roberts and Gorman 1996, 8). In the clear light of scientific observation and measurement, the body was demystified and the legitimacy of both Church teachings and folk superstitions about the causes and treatments of disease began a slow decline. Further weakening the Church's authority on health and disease issues was the rise of post-Reformation religious skepticism and "horror of religious fanaticism" (MacDonald 1991, 98; see also Rubenstein 1995).

Along with scientific explanations for disease and new conceptions of the physical body, Renaissance ardor for scientific investigation based on observation, rationality, and philosophical analysis proved highly significant in the shift toward greater tolerance of euthanasia. From their reawakened interest in the classics, Renaissance scholars acquired new respect for the role of human reason and began arguing for the existence of innate civil liberties. This led to new discourses of *human rights* and *individual autonomy*. From this foundation emerged the notion of personal freedom over one's *body*: If individuals indeed possessed "natural" rights and reasoning abilities, it followed that they should be allowed to apply these innate liberties and intellectual powers to decisions about the time, place, and manner of their own deaths.

The turn toward acceptance of the scientific method as a basis of knowledge intensified during the Enlightenment, a period in Western Europe marked by euthanasia discourse that "was more vigorous—and on the whole, more sympathetic—than it had been since the Roman Empire" (Colt 1991, 171). As medical knowledge advanced in technological sophistication, concern also arose over medicine's *unintended consequences*—including its potential to increase suffering by prolonging death (Roberts and Gorman 1996). Philosophers, poets, and statesmen, including Francis Bacon, John Donne, and David Hume, began to address this issue in their writings (Emanuel 1994; Mullens 1996). Additionally, use of "mercy killing" to mitigate suffering was championed by Voltaire, Montesquieu, Diderot, and other individual-rights advocates, whose views ultimately led to the decriminalization of suicide in France (Mullens 1996).

It is not a coincidence that it was in the eighteenth century that the term "self murder" was replaced by the word "suicide"—a development that attests to the growing clout of medicine in the social construction and control not only of the physical body and its processes, but of broader political and social values and ideologies (Minois 2001). As physicians gained increasing authority, concepts such as "patient rights" and "physician responsibility" began to achieve sufficient cultural currency in both Europe and the American colonies to pose a challenge to Christianity's unequivocal proscription against euthanasia (Roberts and Gorman 1996). Stethoscopes and other technological innovations developed during the Enlightenment established medical science as the preeminent authority on the human body. This shift away from trust in Church interpretations of human anatomy, disease, and death continued to dilute the Christian taboo against euthanasia. By the end of the eighteenth century, half of the American colonies had removed anti-suicide laws from their books. As the medical model of disease gradually picked up momentum, discourse on euthanasia moved from the theoretical and academic to the practical and legal. Increasingly, from this period on, patient-rights advocates, physicians, and legislators would search for tangible ways to ensure hopelessly ill patients "autonomous choices about their own lives" (Roberts and Gorman 1996, 9).

SOCIAL CONSTRUCTION OF A "GOOD DEATH"

Just as the triumph of science and reason over religion led to a reshaping of attitudes about euthanasia, so too have ideas about what constitutes a "good death" responded to evolving epistemologies. In fact, among the most intriguing aspects of the study of mortality—including cross-cultural and historical definitions of a "good death"—involves the dramatic way seemingly immutable notions shift over time. The French cultural historian Phillippe Aries (1974, 1981), for example, who charted shifting cultural definitions of a "good death" in Western history, contends that during the first millennium A.D., people experienced "tame death"—a calm, accepted, anticipated death experienced more or less collectively. During this era, death for everyone was essentially the same, and people were informed when death was imminent so they could prepare for it (Moller 1996; Gavin 1995). Preparation consisted of "lying down, folding one's arms across the chest, facing the wall, and other such gestures" (Gavin 1995, 22–23). The dying typically engaged in forgiveness rituals to make peace with their enemies, and death was largely a public affair attended by relations and friends.

By the Middle Ages, however, "tame death" had given way to what Aries terms "my death"—an era characterized by personalization of death. As new scientific knowledge, medical discoveries, and philosophical notions of individual rights and autonomy entered the social consciousness, a discernible shift occurred in the images, beliefs, and practices surrounding death.[13] The chief characteristic of this shift was that "the idea of a universal, collective destiny disappeared" (Moller 1996, 7), and death began to be socially represented and experienced as a "meditative, introspective experience" (Illich 1976, 177). The devotional movements that emerged in the seventeenth century after the fragmentation of Medieval religions further "privatized the attempt to achieve salvation" (Luhmann 1986, 316). The upshot of these converging forces was that death—rather than being attributed to external forces such as "the curse of an enemy, spell of a magician . . . or God dispatching his angel of death"—began to be viewed as "an inevitable, intrinsic part of human life" (pp. 199, 179). In line with the "individualization" of death was a new understanding of the *moment* of death "as the occasion for self-awareness or self realization" (Gavin 1995, 23).

Rather than an impersonal act originating from an outside agent or force, then, death became a personal experience. And rather than the responsibility of the broader community, it fell to each individual to shoulder the burden of his or her own demise (Illich 1976, 183). Beginning in the Middle Ages, "Man, faced by death, was . . . asked to be aware that he was finally, frighteningly, totally alone" (Illich 1975, 40–41). The strikingly "macabre" images and rituals used in this era were a reflection of the growing sense of alienation and anxiety spawned by what Aries (1974) calls the "unacceptability" of death (see also, Illich 1976).[14]

Possibly as a result of increased social anxiety in the era of "my death," this period was characterized by highly specific notions about achieving a "good death." Social conventions and rituals surrounding death were tied to folk practices and superstitions "designed to help people meet their death with dignity as individuals" (Aries 1974, 185). In Medieval France, for example, a widely reproduced series of engravings called the *ars moriendi* (literally, the "art of dying") provided unambiguous instructions on end-of-life conventions and expectations, including elaborate deathbed repentance rituals. Published in the sixteenth century, this "how to" manual on achieving a good death was used by "carnal and secular" people rather than the clergy (Illich 1976, 183). Popular for two centuries, its instructions ranged from the proper arrangement of loved ones around the deathbed to the most appropriate facial expressions to affect at the moment of death. It is important to note that it was the dying themselves who were expected to orchestrate their deaths, directing bystanders, for example, "to keep the doors open to make it easy for death to come, to avoid noise so as not to frighten death away, and finally to turn their eyes respectfully away from the dying . . . to leave him alone during this most personal event" (Illich 1976, 183).

By the eighteenth century, European cultures experienced a third major upheaval in social attitudes toward death and dying, as well as the specific rituals attending a "good death." Aries (1974), who labels this era "thy death," documents how unacceptability of one's own death gradually progressed to a broader resistance to the death of others. In Victorian England, for example, concern over the loss of loved ones manifested itself in rituals swathed in sentimentality, including romanticized deathbed rituals, extended periods of mourning, and lavishly decorated sympathy cards. It was during this era, significantly, that the first modern glimmerings of concern over "death with dignity" emerged: A good death in Victorian-era England and the United States was one marked by "discretion" or control over emotions, and the fact of imminent death was hidden from the dying. In the context of urbanization and industrialization, these rituals may be understood as attempts to counteract the "sense of isolation and alienation" of a death experience increasingly untethered to its traditional religious and communitarian moorings (Moller 1996, 12).

In light of the sense of isolation and alienation associated with death and dying, it should come as no surprise that by the end of the eighteenth century death came to be seen as an "enemy" or "something to be overcome" (Gavin 1995, 24). Increased dread of death, in turn, led to overt human efforts to *combat* it directly.[15] Whereas traditional responses to death and dying had been largely passive—characterized by family and friends acting mainly as spectators or bystanders—death was now a "problem" for which a solution might conceivably be found. Attempts to delay or otherwise overcome death were encouraged by the newly emergent medical profession, which (not coincidentally) had begun to use the "disease" model as a way of understanding death and dying. As secularism, individualism, and commercialization converged, death became "forbidden" in Aries' terms—hidden away in hospitals and tethered to technology. The result was that death was "redefined as a technical problem to be solved" (Gavin 1995, 29, citing Aries 1974).

Dominated by technology, death in post-industrial Western cultures has not only been characterized by the myth "that fate, or death can be defeated" (Gavin 1995), but by a progressive loss of "moral content," mystery, and meaning (Cassell 1975). This is evident in news and entertainment media discourse, where death and dying—defined increasingly in terms of the observable and quantifiable rather than the immaterial and intangible—tends overwhelmingly to focus on the "facts and artifacts" of the body, including its physiological functions, anatomical parts, and diseased organs (Cassell 1975, 45).

The various movements arising in the twentieth century to combat medicalization of death and dying testify to public dissatisfaction with these developments. The most significant example, of course, has been the rise of the RTD movement, which mobilized in direct response to medicalized death procedures, including the practice of keeping comatose and terminally ill patients alive through respiration, artificial nourishment and hydration, surgeries, and other invasive medical procedures. The work of other movements dedicated to redefining a "good death" and reclaiming the rituals surrounding death from established medicine have paralleled the efforts of the RTD movement. Some of these include the hospice movement, founded in England by Dame Cicely Saunders as a challenge to established medicine's "ineffectiveness in pain control for the dying" (Battin 1994, 7), as well as the work of Elisabeth Kübler-Ross (1969) and her followers.[16] As a result of the combined efforts of these movements, a "good death" in contemporary Western cultures has increasingly come to be defined as openly acknowledged, relatively painless, and custom-tailored to individual needs and desires (Walter 1994) or one that is "anticipated, welcomed, nonstigmatizing, and follow[s] the completion of one's central social obligations and personal desires and goals" (Kearl 1989, 497).[17] Subsequent chapters, and particularly chapter 6, address the question of the extent to which this, as well as alternative versions of a "good death," appear in narratives about euthanasia in the national press.

NOTES

1. Mullens (1996, 61), for example, notes that in order to keep disabled and ill new-borns from burdening the state, Plato, Socrates, and Aristotle favored exposing them to the elements.

2. One scholar makes an intriguing historical parallel between the Stoics and modern RTD activists, arguing that the Stoics' determination to control their deaths was a reaction to the disintegration of Greek society. Comparing the Stoics to modern RTD activists, he sees the actions of both groups as a response to times of "tremendous social change and upheaval" (Reinhold 1974, 35, quoting Harvard professor Arthur J. Dyck).

3. Zeno, the Stoics' founder and a staunch advocate of euthanasia for the terminally ill and elderly, put his personal convictions into practice by hanging himself at the age of 98 after impairing his toe (Osgood 1995).

4. Seneca's own suicide—carried out to avoid execution for treason—"was considered tremendously noble by the Romans" (Mullens 1996).

5. As Messinger (1993) writes, "Perhaps the best evidence of euthanasia in Greece is the condemnation of the practice by others, such as the Pythagoreans, Aristotelians, and Epicurians" (pp. 183–184).

6. Moreover, significant questions remain as to who actually wrote the Oath (although it is typically attributed to the Greek physician, Hippocrates), as well as to the date it was introduced and the extent of its influence in antiquity. Based on their analysis, Roberts and Gorman (1996, 6) conclude that the Hippocratic Oath offers insufficient "proof of an ancient sanction against the practice of euthanasia."

7. For example, Rubenstein (1995) notes that it was only after the eleventh century that depictions of Christ began to reflect Catholic promotion of martyrdom and suffering. Before this time, in Coptic and Byzantine churches, she writes, "Christ was uniformly portrayed as . . . a triumphant sovereign," often dressed in splendid attire and depicted as fully alive even when nailed to the cross. This image contrasts with later images of Christ, who "is portrayed as dead on the cross with his head slumped on his right shoulder, his eyes closed, and his face twisted. Often he wears a crown . . . of thorns. Tears and blood are often visible. Except for a loose-fitting loincloth that looks like it can be easily unraveled, he is naked" (p. 63).

8. For example, Mullens (1996, 64) traces Jewish condemnation of suicide to the first century A.D., "when Jewish historian Josephus dissuaded his army from mass suicide against the Roman army at Jotapata[,] arguing that suicide is cowardly, repugnant to nature, and violates the will of God."

9. Interestingly, the first record of Jewish opposition to euthanasia coincides with the introduction of the Talmud in A.D. 1—a period when Roman acceptance of euthanasia was at its peak (Mullens 1996). After the twelfth century, Jewish death rituals were governed by Maimonides, "The Misneh Torah: The Book of Judges," which equated euthanasia with murder (Roberts and Gorman 1996).

10. As Mullens (1996, 63) notes, "of the eight cases of suicide in the Old Testament and one in the New Testament, none are condemned . . . Suicide in the Bible is often depicted as appropriate behaviour [sic], such as when Sampson pulls down the temple killing himself and his Philistine captors, or when Ahithophel, the wise counselor of Absalom, kills himself after his advice is ignored leading to Absalom's defeat, or Judas, after betraying Jesus to the Romans, hangs himself from a tree."

11. Augustine gave four reasons to support his argument that suicide   was a mortal sin: It violated the fourth commandment, "Thou Shalt not Kill"; it deprived suicides the salvation of penitence and absolution before death; it insulted God by removing the power of life and death from God; and it was a cowardly act (Mullens 1996, 64).

12. The practice of impaling the bodies of suicide   s on polls and exhibiting them publicly continued in England until as late as 1823 (Mullens 1996, 66). Laws mandating forfeiture of a suicide's property remained on the books in England until the 1870s (Berk 1992).

13. Aries (1974) outlines four ways in which individualistic notions of death   began to appear in the fifteenth and sixteenth centuries: (1) in an increased emphasis on individual salvation rather than the collective salvation associated with the Second Coming of Christ; (2) in the belief that "judgment day" occurs on the day of one's death rather than at the Apocalypse; (3) in a move from unthreatening, abstract depictions of death (e.g., a reclining knight) to macabre portrayals (e.g., the worm-eaten corpse); and (4) in ever more personalized tombs, which functioned to underscore individual achievements and immortality (Gavin 1995, 23–24, citing Aries 1974).

14. "In the new iconography of the sixteenth century, death raped the living" (Aries 1974, 56). Similarly, Illich (1976) argues that the proliferation of macabre images of death, particularly after the Reformation, "underscores the growing anxiety of a culture faced with the call of death rather than the judgment of God" (p. 184). Another intriguing indicator of both the social anxiety and extent to which medical science had begun to infiltrate beliefs and attitudes about death in Europe during this era was public fascination with medical rituals (see, e.g., Illich 1976; Moller 1996). Public dissection of the human body not only became a favored subject of paintings in fifteenth- and sixteenth-century Europe, but a common sideshow at carnivals. By the seventeenth century, dissection and anatomy lectures proved so popular that social gatherings were organized around them. Described by one historian as an "ancient version of the modern cocktail-theme party,"

public dissections were accompanied by "good-natured joking, refreshments, and people wearing gay, masquerade-like apparel" (Moller 1996, 11). These and similar rituals carried out during the era of "my death," according to Illich (1976), functioned socially "to orient, repress, or allay the fear and anguish generated by a death that had become macabre" (p. 189).

15. Callahan (1993) traces the idea of death as a controllable "problem" to Francis Bacon, "who first called for medicine to seek the cure of disease" (p. 32).

16. Kübler-Ross, in crafting what might be considered a contemporary version of the *ars moriendi*, not only labored to articulate death's stages and norms and specify the requirements for achieving a dignified death, but encouraged open discussion of mortality. For example, Weisman and Kübler-Ross (1972) focused on helping patients achieve "significant survival," the ability to retain control over their daily lives and conduct rather than merely surviving. Others have emphasized the interaction between the dying individual and others as a key factor in the quality of the dying experience.

17. Other "good death " strategies developed by thanatologists range from arranging therapy groups and teaching terminally ill people Eastern meditation techniques to administering the psychoactive drug LSD to the dying, "which supposedly enhances morale, reduces depression and pain, and collapses one's orientations toward the past and future into the now, theoretically enhancing interactions with family and environment" (Kearl 1989, 491).

CHAPTER 3

CRISIS OF AUTHORITY AND THE SEEDS OF CHANGE

> The death of the patient in the hospital, covered with tubes, is
> becoming a popular image, more terrifying than the skeleton of
> macabre rhetoric.
> —Aries 1981, 614

> There is no law that is not inscribed on bodies....From birth to
> mourning after death, law 'takes hold of' bodies in order to make
> them its text. Through all sorts of initiations (in rituals, at school,
> etc.), it transforms them into tables of the law, into living tableaus of
> rules and customs, into actors of the drama organized by social order.
> —de Certeau 1984, 139

As the last chapter's review of euthanasia history demonstrates, notions of a
"good death" not only shift over time, but correlate with changes in social,
economic, and ideational models. This is also the case, of course, with social
movements, including the emergency and mobilization of the 1970s RTD (right-
to-die) movement, the culmination of a number of psychosocial, ideational, and
economic forces. It is these contextual elements that provide the impetus for this
chapter, which investigates the central factors fueling the contemporary
euthanasia debate.

IDEATIONAL AND MATERIAL FACTORS

Medical innovations and notions of human rights that originated in the
Renaissance and flowered during the Enlightenment remain central to
understanding the contours of the modern political struggle over euthanasia.
Max Weber's discussion of the characteristics of political conflict proves useful
in identifying some of the forces responsible for the explosive growth of the pro-
euthanasia movement in the twentieth century. Weber (1968) saw political
conflict as the confluence of three essential elements: (1) social movements

struggling for power, (2) institutions through which social control and dominance is exercised and pursued, and (3) ideational factors. Whereas all three elements are easily identified in the conflict over a right to die, it is the third—ideational factors—that has perhaps exercised the greatest shaping influence on the contemporary controversy over a "right to die." After all, it is ideas—particularly those centering on liberty and human rights—that inform the central catchphrases used by RTD movement activists, including "right to die," "death with dignity," and "choice in dying." Of course, as Weber (1968) notes, in order to trigger substantive change, ideas must be wedded to material and cultural conditions. It is only when a constellation of forces—including the activities of dominant institutions (including the mass media, which Weber recognized as a primary force of social control)—come into alignment with philosophical beliefs such as individual rights that social transformation is possible (Neuzil and Kovarik 1996).

Using the Weberian model as a point of departure, then, the dramatic rise in social acceptance of euthanasia in late-twentieth century Western societies may be understood as the congruence of a number of specific, underlying social, economic, and ideational factors, including: (1) the success of medical institutions in "medicalizing" death and dying; (2) social upheavals of the 1960s and 1970s characterized by an explosion of human rights movements; (3) a decline in the authority of religion as a force of moral restraint; (4) changing demographics (e.g., the dramatic rise in the population of elderly in the United States) combined with escalating medical costs; and finally, (5) the mass media, to which the fortunes of all social movements in late modern cultures are inextricably bound (see, e.g., Olien et al. 1989; Snow and Benford 1988, 1992; Gamson 1990). Because these developments have proved critical to the rise and fortunes of the contemporary RTD movement, this chapter reviews their contribution to and overall impact on the conflict over a "right to die."

MEDICALIZATION OF DEATH AND DYING

Few areas of life have been more dramatically altered by technological advances than the experience of dying in America. Although today it is difficult to imagine mortality outside the province of physicians and hospitals, prior to the Industrial Revolution, death was a "natural" and domestic occurrence, albeit one of significant social, moral, and religious import. Before the eighteenth century physicians may have been sought to attend the critically ill and dying, but they lacked an arsenal of weapons powerful enough to delay or combat death.

Given the sweeping authority the medical establishment enjoys in contemporary society, it is difficult to imagine the profession's lack of prestige and influence in its early history (see, e.g., Conrad and Schneider 1992). In fact, as Rubenstein (1995) reminds us, the notion of health as a cultural ideal did not even emerge in the United States until the mid-nineteenth century, when "research-oriented hospital medicine" led to development of the germ theory of disease, cellular pathology, improved anesthesia, and antiseptic surgical techniques which made surgery vastly safer and more effective (p. 177). Moreover, Enlightenment notions of progress were not widely applied to healthcare until the end of he nineteenth century (Callahan 1993, 61). As noted in the previous chapter, it was during this time, not coincidentally, that death came to be viewed as a problem that medicine had a "moral obligation to defeat" (Gavin 1995, 62). Once this new paradigm gained a foothold, authority over death and dying increasingly was given over to physicians and hospitals.

By the early decades of the twentieth century, hospitals—which began as squalid, unsanitary "shelters" for the poor and homeless—began taking advantage of advances in pain control to market care of the dying to middle- and upper-class individuals. By the early 1920s the number of hospitals exploded from a mere 178 in 1872 to 6,000 (Hoefler and Kamoie 1994, 68). As advances in medical technology continued to be made, established medicine not only entered the death-and-dying "business," but metamorphosed into a full-scale bureaucracy modeled on the factory: "Slowly but surely, as the Industrial Revolution progressed, the hospital began to lose its character as a family-oriented, long-term almshouse for the indigent. The modern institution took on the characteristics (and, inevitably, some of the impersonality) of the factory assembly line, with its system of raw material inputs (admissions), production (medical interventions), and product outputs (discharged patients)" (Hoefler and Kamoie 1994, 69). These changes were attended by a parallel elevation in the status and image of institutionalized medicine, which claimed responsibility for the marked drop in the incidence and mortality of diseases. Although medical advances undoubtedly contributed to this trend, sharp declines in the incidence of smallpox, cholera, and malaria also stemmed from dramatic improvements in economic and social conditions, including: "better nutrition and housing, and public health innovations like sanitation. With the lone exception of vaccination for smallpox, the decline of these diseases had nearly nothing to do with clinical medicine . . . But despite lack of effective treatments, medicine was the beneficiary of much popular credit for improving health (Conrad and Schneider 1992, 13).

The medical profession's new health-enhancing image, which Conrad and Schneider attribute in no small part to savvy public relations, gradually paved the way for a "medical monopoly" over death and dying along with virtually all matters related to care of the physical body. This monopoly was actively promoted by the government, which passed legislation favorable to the growth of institutionalized medicine. "Once scientific medicine offered sufficient guarantees of its superior effectiveness in dealing with disease, the state willingly contributed to the creation of a monopoly by means of registration and licensing" (Conrad and Schneider 1992, 14, quoting Larson 1977).

Established medicine's monopoly over the death-and-dying process during the twentieth century not only came about as a result of technological advances, but through its expanding power to define "what is normal, proper, or desirable" for the terminally ill and incapacitated. By mid-century, what "normal, proper, or desirable" in the care of the dying increasingly meant was the application of "heroic" medical interventions designed to prolong lives virtually indefinitely.

Paradoxically, As each new medical advance further expanded medicine's influence over "the American way of death" (Mitford 1963), it also reinforced the notion of death as the ultimate failure of medicine (Bugen 1979). Rather than the natural end of the human life cycle, death under the medical model gradually came to be viewed as "the end point of untreatable or inadequately treated disease or injury or [as] medicine's enemy—a reminder of [the] limitations of medical diagnosis and management" (McCue 1995, 1039). In its assault on death and association of death with the failure of technology, established medicine, in Durkheimian terms, enlarged the sphere of the profane (death), thereby secularizing formerly sacred aspects of the experience of dying (Tiryakin 1988). At the same time, in its god-like success in delaying or outwitting death for months, years, and even decades, "scientific medicine almost seem[ed] to have produced the illusion that mankind is on the threshold of immortality, so that death, when it occurs, becomes the ultimate defeat" (Seravalli and Fashing 1992, 37).

If the myth of medical omniscience and triumph over death remains an exercise in wishful thinking, it is a conceit that reflects and aligns with a number of deeply held American values, including the culture's "fascination with high-technology care and [the] . . . deep-seated need for the engineering of miracles" (Illich 1976, 106). Belief in the magical powers of medicine evolved quite naturally from the breathtaking array of medical breakthroughs made since the mid-nineteenth century. "Miracle" drugs, including antibiotics and vaccines, liberated modern nations from viral and bacterial contagions responsible for wiping out entire populations in the past. Following Louis Pasteur's 1881 discovery of an effective anthrax vaccine, vaccinations became formidable weapons against killer epidemics, helping to eradicate by the 1940s and 1950s such diseases as polio, smallpox, and measles (Rubenstein 1995). In 1950 alone measles, diphtheria, poliomyelitis, and tuberculosis killed nearly 3,000 children in the United States. In 1973, in contrast, only 43 children died from these diseases (Kearl 1989, 408). These advances, combined with the development of penicillin, tetracycline, and erythromycin, dramatically altered population patterns in the United States Whereas less than 100 years ago most Americans died from pneumonia or other infectious diseases that killed swiftly, most late-twentieth-century Americans die of cancers and other lingering, degenerative conditions (see Table 3.1).

In addition to medicine's powerful new arsenal of disease-fighting drugs were a proliferation of aggressive life-extension therapies that hospitals began to use routinely by the second half of the twentieth century. Prior to these developments, which enabled the medical profession to claim authority over death to an extent unthinkable in previous centuries, people with diseased organs and/or those unable to breathe or swallow food simply died. With the advent of cardiopulmonary resuscitation, intravenous feeding and hydration, artificial respiration, organ transplants, open-heart surgery, and other advanced surgical procedures, however, individuals could be kept alive for decades "with most of their brains destroyed, with bodily systems near total breakdown, in states of irreversible unconsciousness" (Newman 1991, 166). As the twentieth century drew to a close, a million Americans in various states of unconsciousness were being kept alive by high-tech medical machinery (Glick 1992). CAT scans, MRIs, (magnetic resonance imaging machines), kidney dialysis, EKGs (electrocardiographs), and ever more radical organ transplants were by now a routine part of healthcare practice.

Table 3.1
Comparison of Major Causes of Death in the United States, 1900 and 1990

Causes of Death 1900	%	Causes of Death 1990	%
Influenza-pneumonia	11.8	Heart disease	33.5
Tuberculosis	11.3	Cancer	23.4
Gastroenteritis	8.3	Stroke	6.7
Heart disease	8.0	Accidents	4.3
Stroke	6.2	Pulmonary diseases	4.1
Kidney disease	4.7	Pneumonia-influenza	3.6
Accidents	4.2	Diabetes mellitus	2.3
Cancer	3.7	Suicide	1.4
Infancy diseases	3.6	All others	20.7
All others	38.2		

Source: National Center for Health Statistics, United States Department of Health and Human Services, Washington, D.C., 1991.

The medical profession's tendency to attack terminal diseases with unalloyed aggression "however small the potential benefit, however high the real emotional and financial costs" resulted in profound alterations in the trajectory and experience of death in American society (Hoefler and Kamoie 1994, 81). Although the advantages of life-extension technologies are obvious for patients and their families, as well as insurance companies and taxpayers forced to foot the bill for these expensive services, their negative consequences often seem to overshadow their benefits. Dworkin (1993) argues that those most victimized by medical technology, ironically, are the dying themselves, who are "horribly crippled, intubated, disfigured by experimental operations, in pain or sedated into near oblivion, connected to dozens of machines that do most of their living for them, explored by dozens of doctors none of whom they recognize, and for whom they are not so much patients as battlegrounds" (p. 180).

The widespread use of aggressive and expensive medical life-extension therapies reflects a broader trend in United States society referred to by those who study it as the "medicalization" of society (see, e.g., Freidson 1970; Conrad and Schneider 1992; McCue 1995). Medicalization, a modern-day manifestation of Foucault's theories on the coercive workings and spread of institutional power, has been defined as the "continuously expanding conception of 'sickness' in the society" (Fox 1977). Sociologists and bioethicists who have investigated this trend express concern that death and dying—like other "natural" human behaviors including childbirth, aging, menopause, female sexuality,[1] overeating, hyperactivity,[2] shyness,[3] drug and alcohol use, criminality, homosexuality, infertility,[4] and domestic violence—have been appropriated and redefined to conform to the "disease model" (Conrad and Schneider 1992). No longer confined to biology, institutionalized medicine has pushed the boundaries of its domain to include the power to define (and hence establish policy regarding) "health and illness, normality and abnormality, sanity and insanity" (Fox 1977). It is the potential of such labels to marginalize, control, and dehumanize individuals that most concerns sociologists and other experts on the medicalization phenomenon (Fox 1977). Because medical categories attached to individual or social behaviors are by definition mutable, subjective, and nonuniversal, as well as frequently reflections of racial, gender, and class biases, they are "as much as artifacts of the preconceptions of socially biased observers as they are valid summaries of the characteristics of the observed. In this view, illness (especially mental illness) is largely a mythical construct, created and enforced by the society" (Fox 1977, 61).

The gradual migration of medicine into morality, as well as established medicine's inroads into social and behavioral science, has, as Kearl (1989) puts it, "made alcoholics out of drunkards; poorly performing students who used to be called stupid are now seen as victims of learning disorders; and the disoriented senior, who used to be understood as a victim of dramatic social change, is now viewed as senile" (p. 406). Nelkin (1994) identified a similar pattern in news discourse linking human behavior to biology. News stories, she found, attributed a broad array of human traits to genetics, including selfishness, pleasure-seeking, depression, and thriftiness, as well as "obesity, criminality, shyness, directional ability, intelligence, political leanings, and even preferred styles of dressing" (p. 28).

Although medicalization has clearly shaped both public perceptions of the causes and proper responses to an assortment of social behaviors and profoundly impacted the experience of death and dying in the United States, what does it have to do with suicide or euthanasia? Here, it is useful to point out, as Kalwinsky (1998) notes, that "suicide does not require the assistance of a physician. If the proper drugs were made widely available to the dying, for example, those wishing to end their lives could do so in the privacy of their homes and without the ministrations of a physician. The medicalization of euthanasia, then, not only aligns generally with Foucault's (1954/1976, 1975/1977) ideas on the institutional procurement of power (particularly through control over the bodies of individuals), but represents a specific example of established medicine's colonization and domination over all aspects of death and dying.

The roots of medicalization are firmly planted in the soil of United States society's biological-deterministic bias, as well as its "heroic positivist" philosophy—the quintessential American "can do" attitude that privileges action over non-action even if action proves futile. The medicalization of death in particular is also undoubtedly symptomatic of the search for certainty in increasingly chaotic times, as well as an aspect of the human drive to explain highly complex and mutable social phenomena in ever more "literal and concrete ways" (Kearl (1989). In terms of institutional empowerment, medicalization became the route through which established medicine began to seize control over the very "tempo and form of dying," determining "with precision the time and place of death" (McCue 1995, 1939). Physicians suddenly wielded vast powers, including the authority "to continue or discontinue life-sustaining technology for ideal timing of organ transplantation, to allow family to be present for a loved one's death, or to delay death for the convenience of court deliberations" (McCue 1995).

Among the most far-reaching consequences of the medicalization of death and dying has been its disruption of traditional understandings of death's place and meaning in Western cultures. By rendering death "a starkly unnatural event," medicalization spawned confusing new categories of death, including death from disease, death from removal of life-support systems, and death resulting from the purposeful administration of "palliative" (pain-killing) narcotics (McCue 1995). Even more unsettling, the atomization of death into discrete steps and technical procedures has thrown the definition of death itself in a philosophical quagmire. As Aries (1974) notes, reducing death to a series of technical steps obscures just when it is that death occurs: Is it when the patient becomes unconscious? Is it when a patient ceases to breathe on his or her own? "All these little silent acts of death have replaced and erased the great dramatic act of death," he writes, "and no one any longer has the strength or patience to wait over a period of weeks for a moment which has lost a part of its meaning" (Aries 1974, 88–89).

Perhaps the most dramatic outcome of medicalization has been the blurring of the boundaries separating life and death—the two most fundamental conditions ordering human experience. By the mid-1950s, new medical technologies had already begun to complicate definitions of death. The introduction of the concept of "brain death" into the medical literature in 1959, however, threw long-held distinctions into disarray (Roberts and Gorman 1996). Historically, death was a rather straightforward matter determined by cessation of heart and respiratory functions (Lazar et al. 1996). Once organ transplants became routine, however, "Doctors needed concrete criteria under which they could declare the patient dead, then restart the heart and keep the organs viable until they could be transplanted" (Roberts and Gorman 1996, 13). Despite the fact that brain-death criteria were developed within a decade after the concept was introduced,[5] the issue of determining death continues to be shrouded in ethical, legal, religious and scientific uncertainties. Is death, for example, the irreversible cessation of *whole* brain function (e.g., "profound coma, apnea and absence of all brain-stem reflexes") (Lazar et al. 2001, 833)? Or is death the irreversible cessation of so-called *higher* brain functions "responsible for consciousness and interaction with the world"(p. 834)? The development of artificial organs and other medical technologies in the future will only add to the complexities of defining death.

Reducing death and dying to a series of medical procedures has also, of course, inevitably led to disintegration of traditional cultural meanings attached to the experience. The technologies of death have depleted ancient death rituals, including the ways in which people have traditionally experienced the passing of relatives and friends. It is difficult for modern Americans to grasp how intricately death was once woven into the fabric of everyday life. Prior to the widespread use of antibiotics following World War II, death was a near-prosaic feature of American households, where it claimed a disproportionate number of children, in particular. One hundred years ago it was commonplace for even the youngest of family members to witness the death of a sibling, parent, or other relative. Virtually everyone, young and old, was exposed to the sight of the bodies of the dead, which, until after the Civil War, were prepared for burial at home. In contrast, most Americans today reach young adulthood without first-hand experience of either the dying process or the death of someone they know. Describing contemporary Americans as a "'death-free' generation," Hoefler and Kamoie (1994) note that on average, individuals in the United States will not experience the death of a family member until they reach 20 years of age.

Statistics testify to the striking impact of increased life expectancy combined with medicalization of death and dying on socio-cultural practices: In 1900, 80 percent of all Americans died at home. By 1950 this number had shrunk to about half, and roughly 80 percent of individuals die in medical institutions in the United States today (Field and Cassell 1997; McCue 1995; Hoefler and Kamoie 1994).[6] Medicalization has also meant that elderly Americans live longer and die more slowly today than at any time in history.

Another important consequence of medicalization of death and dying relates to the growing influence and pervasiveness of mass mediated images and messages about mortality. Unlike their forebears, whose exposure to death was personal and almost routine, the vast majority of American citizens in the twenty-first century encounter death primarily through the mass media. What has become known as the "American way of death" gradually developed between 1830 and 1920. It was in this period that the symbolic "dying of death" took place—what historian James Ferrell (1980) describes as "the practical disappearance of the thought of death as an influence bearing upon practical life." As care of the dying became relegated to hospitals, and the bodies of the dead were turned over to the "death-care industry"—which in the mid-1990s numbered some 30,000 funeral homes, crematoria, and other enterprises dedicated to the disposal of the dead—Americans accepted the commodification of death and dying. In the process, funeral directors and cemetery owners gained ever-greater control over death-related "symbolic services" (Wernick 1995).[7]

The confinement of the dying and critically ill to medical facilities designed with practicality, efficiency, and sterility in mind, rather than with interaction and meaning, inhibits even the most rudimentary of traditional deathbed customs, including the bedside vigil. "The classic deathbed scene, with family gathered around to say good-bye, is now largely an anachronism," as Hoefler and Kamoie (1994, 11) note. Patients who die in modern medical institutions typically do so in a drug-induced stupor, tangles of tubes trailing from their bodies, and their passage to death accompanied not by hushed, familiar voices, but by the high-tech drone of respirators and other life-sustaining machines. Such an environment does little to foster substantive human interaction, but rather lends an aura of detachment and surrealism to the experience of death. As Aries (1974) observes, the "tamed death" of the past, characterized by a rapid, if not totally pain-free passage to death, has given way in the contemporary era to a "forbidden" and "unnamable" death spawned by technology. The inevitable result of technologized death is increasing isolation, alienation, and loss of dignity for the dying and the broader cultural suppression of death.

In allowing the medical profession to appropriate death and dying, then, citizens of Western societies clearly struck a Faustian bargain. On the positive side, the arrangement has lifted many of the burdens of death once shouldered painfully by families and communities. The economic and socio-cultural costs attached to medicalization of death and dying, however, have also proved staggering. As discussed above, among the most serious cultural costs of this arrangement include loss of meaning and a sense of individual autonomy over the dying process. Ironically, an important original impetus for the surrender of care of the dying to medical institutions was the enhancement of individuals' sense of control over death. By enlisting doctors in technological warfare against aging and disease, Americans sought emancipation not only from care of the dying, but from death itself. Unfortunately, the more expansive the jurisdiction granted the medical community to define and control end-of-life affairs, the less autonomy individuals and families exercise over the circumstances in which they and their loved ones die.

The growing profit orientation of the medical establishment has only exacerbated the sense of isolation and alienation many terminally ill patients and their families experience. The fact that medicine has developed into a multi-billion dollar industry dominated by HMOs and hospital chains has created a deep schism not only between patients and their doctors, but between medical professionals and their own intrinsic missions as healthcare providers. Among the major consequences of the ascendancy of the "business model of medicine" is its focus on the principles of "cost-effectiveness, conservation of health resources, and connections" rather than the "caring, commitment and courage" physicians pledge to uphold in the Hippocratic Oath (Schuller 1996, 28). Charting the dramatic ways in which profits transformed the practice of medicine following World War II, Lown (1998) writes that,

Lucrative rewards hastened the shift from a health care system focused on patients to one based on disease. A doctor could earn far more from an invasive procedure requiring a single hour than from an entire day spent with patients . . . Contemporary medical practice trivialized discourse and listening. While enthralled by heroic cures, physicians remained largely indifferent to preventing disease and promoting health . . . Further distorting medical practice was fee-for-service reimbursement, which encouraged a glut of unnecessary procedures . . . And increasingly centralized hospitals, unaccountable and wildly inefficient in the way they dispensed sickness care, encouraged cost inflation (p. 25).

It is precisely such negative perceptions of the medical establishment, including its association with burgeoning costs and loss of patient autonomy, that set the stage for rapid mobilization of the RTD movement in the final quarter of the twentieth century. By the 1970s, a growing number of Americans had come to view the medicalization of death "a pernicious trend" not only responsible for wasting resources, but for depriving individuals of substantive control over their own deaths. McCue (1995, 1039) articulates this perspective in the following passage:

Viewing dying and death as merely a failure of medical diagnosis and therapy is antiholistic and trivializes the final event of our lives, stripping it of important non-medical meaning for patients, family, and society. This narrow view of dying may be a particular concern for the very elderly, for whom death is an expected and sometimes desired event. Respect for the wholeness of life requires that we not debase its final stage; art, literature, and the social sciences teach us that a good death can be a natural, courageous, and thoughtful end to life.

Public rejection of the medicalization of death and dying—part of a larger trend that Kurtz (1994) refers to as "the growth of anti-science"—manifested itself in growing antipathy toward orthodox medicine and the recasting of doctors as "demons rather than saviors." Not restricted to medical care for the dying, the nation's growing frustration with the medical profession has clearly been at the root of the "patient rights" consumer movement, as well as the astonishing growth of alternative therapies and "holistic" treatments ranging from acupuncture and massage to herbal treatments and vitamin-based therapies. At the most fundamental level, advocates of both alternative medicine and of a "right to die" are motivated by a desire to circumvent the power and limitations of organized medicine.

DEMOGRAPHIC, PSYCHOSOCIAL, AND ECONOMIC FACTORS FUELING THE DEBATE

Democraphic Shifts and New Meanings Attached to "Old Age"

The widespread sense of loss of autonomy over death, growing disillusionment with the medical profession, and the disintegration of traditional cultural rites of passage that once imbued death with meaning are critical factors explaining the rapid mobilization of the campaign for legal and social acceptance of euthanasia that emerged in late twentieth-century United States society. No discussion of the factors responsible for the growth of social acceptance of euthanasia would be complete, however, without consideration of two twentieth-century developments: (1) the emergence of new meanings attached to old age and aging and (2) the explosive growth in the population of aged citizens.

Although the elderly have, of course, been a part of every society, contemporary cultural understandings of the meaning of "old age" did not emerge until the late-nineteenth century. As Industrial Revolution interest in worker efficiency and productivity intensified, new "life stage" categories, including the notion of "'old age' as a social, cultural and biological phenomenon," gained widespread cultural currency (Hareven 1995, 121). "American society passed from an acceptance of aging as a natural process to a view of it as a distinct period of life characterized by decline, weakness, and obsolescence" (Hareven 1995, 120). Concurrent with this shift in perception, geriatrics emerged as a new medical specialty. Within a remarkably brief span of time, old age was not only given its own category, but constructed as a problematic condition marked by psychological and physiological "symptoms" requiring medical treatments (Hareven 1995). An important by-product of the medicalization of aging has been increased segregation and isolation of the elderly, as well as changes in popular representations of aging. Featherstone and Wernick (1995) argue that two opposing images of the elderly have come to dominate popular culture: Either they are represented as "heroes of aging" who have managed to stave off the decline of their bodies and maintained productive work habits, or as "abominations of human nature" whose "severe bodily decline" renders them virtually subhuman.

These changes in popular beliefs about the elderly, considered in tandem with the graying of the United States population (which is, in itself, a direct by-product of advances in medical technology), explain much about the transformation of social attitudes toward euthanasia. Life expectancy has shot up during the past century, resulting in the rapid growth of the over-sixty-five age group, which climbed from 3.1 million in 1900 to 35 million in 2000 and is projected to grow 74 percent between 1990 and 2020 (United States Census Bureau, 2000). Describing these changes as "a remarkable development, unique in all history," Omicinski (1999) notes that "before the Industrial Revolution in the late nineteenth century, people over 65 never amounted to more than 2–3 percent of the population. In today's developed world . . . they are 14 percent, an incredible change in a very short period." Even more remarkable has been the rise in the number of the "very old" elderly—citizens over age eighty-five. As the nation's fastest-growing population segment, this cohort increased by 37.6 percent between 1990 and 2000 alone (United States Census Bureau, 2000).

Such striking demographic shifts clearly have profound psychosocial, as well as economic, ramifications. Among the most troubling potential effects, of course, is an increasingly overt backlash against the elderly, who may perceive themselves as having "outlived their previous roles and sources of value and meaning" (Osgood 1995). As discussed earlier in this chapter, attitudes toward the elderly in United States society devolved with the advent of Industrial Revolution, which privileged youth and vigor as prized commodities in an increasingly commercialized culture. In fact, the elderly do exact a heavy toll on the medical and economic resources of the nation: Some 75 percent of all medical expenditures in the United States are devoted to caring for the aged (Callahan 1990, 101), with about $30 billion annually spent on individuals in their last year of life (Hoefler and Kamoie 1994, 58). Although only about 5 percent of elderly citizens in the United States live in homes for the aged, nursing-home expenditures more than doubled between 1980 and 1990—from $11 billion to $25 billion (Hoefler and Kamoie 1994, 59). Of course, the high costs of caring for the elderly are rarely if ever overtly articulated in the discourse of those promoting euthanasia. The economic implications of using "heroic" measures to keep the nation's least productive and most expensive citizens alive, however, are certainly implied in RTD collective action frames, and they almost certainly provide an important underlying explanation for the nation's increasing acceptance of passive and active euthanasia.

Erosion of Religious and Moral Barriers to Euthanasia

As mentioned earlier, the "rights" discourses that came into prominence during the civil rights movements of the 1960s and 1970s proved critical to mobilization of RTD activists, whose key discursive framework rests on the concept of the right of individual autonomy. Without the gradual decline of religious authority in American society, however, the rights frame alone is unlikely to have had sufficient resonance to mobilize public support for a "right to die." As the result of a constellation of factors, belief in religious teachings has suffered a precipitous decline in all Western societies. By the mid-twentieth century, religious and moral barriers to "mercy killing" were seriously eroded, creating a psychosocial climate conducive to the growth of the RTD.

Among other functions, organized religion serves as an institution of restraint and moral order, as "a means of gathering together, in one overpowering vessel, the sense of the sacred—that which is set apart as the collective conscience of the people" (Bell 1976, 154). For centuries organized religion not only imbued everyday life with meaning, but served as a primary political and structuring force in Western societies. As capitalism marched its way into dominance in the nineteenth and twentieth centuries, however, it ushered in what Nietsche describes as the "advent of nihilism" (Berman 1982). With the decline of religious influence, theological authority gave way to secular ways of knowing—among the most important of which is scientific knowledge. This erosion of religious authority continued unabated throughout the twentieth century, as commercialism and media representations of the "good life" heightened society's denial of—and hence decreased the vitality of religiosity as an antidote to—death.[8] By the 1970s in the United States, psychologists had documented a dramatic shift in public attitudes away from an emphasis on personal immortality and the rewards to be reaped in the afterlife to a stress on economic success and individualism—two dominant American cultural values that in many ways have supplanted the quest for traditional religious salvation and emphasis on a "higher power" (see, e.g., Feifel 1972). Despite the fact that some 98 percent of Americans profess belief in God, church attendance has fallen off significantly over the past century (Hoefler and Kamoie 1994). To a degree unknown in the past, Americans inhabit a world of secular rather than religious values, a psychosocial climate in which, "man has been thrown back on his own resources, [and] there is no higher authority to turn to for support" (Reinhold 1974, 35).

Among the myriad results of this change has been a radical transformation in the meanings attached to suicide. In the Middle Ages "voluntary death was seen as the result of diabolic temptation induced by despair or as mad behavior," and as, such, was regarded as immoral and cowardly (Minois 2001, 9). By 1700 the term "self-murder" was replaced by "suicide," a change reflecting growing interest in scientific (rather than religious) sources of knowledge (Minois 2001, 9). By 1800, as secularization and medicalization of society took root in Western cultures, the notion of suicide as a moral failing was replaced by an understanding of suicide as a "sickness" or "an insane act," a perception that led to a gradual "openness to non-Christian attitudes toward self-killing" (MacDonald 1991, 89, 93). Paralleling this shift was the more general "collapse of morality" that, according to sociologist Daniel Bell (1976), was directly tied to the elevation of the "aesthetic experience"—the belief that "experience, in and of itself, is of supreme value" (p. 157). Along with the idea that "everything is to be explored [and] anything is to be permitted," the logic of the aesthetic privileged individualism—the authority "of the 'I,' of the 'imperial self'" (p. 158).

The replacement of religious faith with belief in the individual moved "the center of authority from the sacred to the profane," (Bell 1976). In the process, attitudes about death generally and about suicide, in particular, were radically repositioned (Moller 1996). Although virtually all established religions oppose "active" euthanasia,[9] as Newman (1991) points out, even Americans who do attend church "do not always follow their religious leaders" when it comes to issues—such as euthanasia and PAS—that involve questions of individual autonomy (p. 179). In fact, roughly three-quarters of United States citizens (even those describing themselves as religious) support the practice. In a 1991 Roper poll, both Protestants and Catholics expressed strong support for PAS (including prescribing lethal drugs to terminally ill individuals who request them), as well as laws allowing family and friends to request death for a terminally ill patient by lethal injection if the patient is too ill to do so (Newman 1991, citing Roper Poll 1991). In 1987, pollster Louis Harris (p. 160) concluded that, "There is no major segment of the public that does not support euthanasia by wide margins. This includes Catholics and members of the Moral Majority whose evangelical preacher leaders vigorously oppose legalizing euthanasia."

Like medicalization, secularization also dismantled long-held definitions of what it means to experience a "good death." A significant yet rarely acknowledged outcome of the decline in the authority of religion has been the dismantling of structuring narratives once used to make the death palatable (see, e.g., Aries 1974, 1981). As Seale (1995) writes,

Religious narratives once sustained the hopes of individuals as they approached their deaths or contemplated the deaths of others. Human lives could then be cast in narratives, as at funeral orations, in which the individual was judged according to whether s/he had met the demands of higher purpose. By contrast, . . . in late modern society, with a relative absence of grand narrative structures such as religion, dying is hidden away and "denied" as it poses insuperable problems of meaning (e.g., Aries 1974; Elias 1985, 598).

As Seale suggests, religious narratives about death functioned historically as a means through which individuals, "by engaging in moral behavior, sacrifice, bravery and spiritual adventure in the service of a higher purpose" might experience vicarious versions of "heroic" death (Featherstone 1992). These narratives not only helped prepare individuals for their own mortality, but framed death in terms of honor and courage. Given death's innate potential for political and psychosocial disruption, the decline of such narratives is far from trivial. As anthropologist Bronislaw Malinowski (1972) reminds us, death, "which of all human events is the most upsetting and disorganizing to man's calculations, is perhaps the main source of religious belief" (71). Taking this idea in a slightly different direction, Giddens (1991) theorizes that humans construct religion to deal with death's inherent mysteries and contradictions—including most notably death's violation of notions of "selfhood" that make it ontologically possible for individuals and cultures to adopt an optimistic view of life (Giddens 1991). In the absence of socially viable and culturally resonant narratives that explain death and restore the sense of self and personal identity, the specter of mortality becomes a potentially disrupting force and a source of existential anxiety.

Interestingly, Kearl (1989) proposes that it is precisely such anxiety that may account for RTD activists' preoccupation with the dying process—the physical and phenomenological conditions surrounding death—rather than focusing on religious narratives that privilege the afterlife. In the move toward secularization of society, cultural fears may have shifted from damnation in hell or concern with how honorably one lived one's life to a fixation on control over one's "dignity" at death, as well as with the timing, physical environment, and other material circumstances attending death. In this context the RTD movement may be seen as essentially restorative—an attempt to repair and reinstate what Giddens (1991) refers to as the "narrative of the self" imperiled not only by the threat of mortality, but by the combination of medicalization and secularization of death.

By 1975, when Karen Ann Quinlan slipped into a coma after consuming an overdose of drugs and alcohol, the ideational and material factors required for collective mobilization of the RTD movement were already well established. In addition to the erosion of religious and moral barriers to suicide, the aging of the United States population, and the medical profession's approach to death as a problem in need of a technological solution, the availability of "rights" discourses borrowed from 1960s and 1970s civil rights activists proved crucial to mobilization of the RTD movement. Urbanization, changes in family structure, geographic mobility and, perhaps most important, mass mediated images and messages promoting materialism and commercial culture as the highest of cultural values have also been instrumental in the fortunes of the RTD cause. Along with making it easier for Americans to ignore their own mortality, these forces helped "precipitate . . . the abdication of responsibility of caring for both the dying (to hospitals) and the dead (to funeral directors)" (Hoefler and Kamoie 1994, 19). In the process, they helped foster an environment amenable to increasing social and legal acceptance of both passive and active euthanasia.

THE RISE OF THE CONTEMPORARY RTD MOVEMENT

Quinlan's ordeal not only thrust the debate over euthanasia into the public consciousness and media spotlight, but made her an instant, international symbol of the "great cultural unease" about medicalized death, which, by the mid-1970s had become pervasive in United States society (Moller 1996, 187). Following a New Jersey Supreme Court's ruling allowing her to be disconnected from life support, Quinlan remained alive for a decade in a "persistent vegetative state" (PVS)—a condition "characterized by massive and irreversible brain damage that leaves the individual unable to sense or respond to his or her surroundings" (Hoefler and Kamoie 1994, 50).[10] Like all key cultural symbols, Quinlan gave form to the invisible and intangible, challenging enduring social myths and belief in the process. In many ways she thrust the topic of death itself onto a reluctant public. As one commentator notes, "She served as the pretext for Americans to work out their beliefs, anxieties, and ambivalence about dying and death" (Filene 1999, 11). Along with throwing already beleaguered understandings of death into further disarray, the Quinlan controversy raised a host of thorny new questions, including those related to "the relative power of physicians versus family members to decide when to end heroic measures, the individual's very right to die, the role of government in ensuring the citizenship rights of life and death to its citizens, and legal decisions concerning active euthanasia" (Kearl 1989, 432).

Galvanized by the *Quinlan* case, Americans polled in 1977 expressed a 50 percent approval rating for some form of legalized euthanasia, a figure approaching 75 percent by the late 1990s.[11] In the wake of *Quinlan*, thousands of Americans have joined RTD organizations such as the Hemlock Society, the Euthanasia Society of America, Americans Against Human Suffering, Choice in Dying, and the Euthanasia Research & Guidance Organization (ERGO). The aftermath of *Quinlan* also saw new RTD organizations spring up in Canada, Western Europe, Australia, and Asia. The largest of these—the Japan Society for Dying with Dignity—boasts roughly 75,000 members. In 1997, thirty-eight pro-euthanasia societies spanned the globe, with an estimated following of 750,000.[12]

Historical Roots of the Modern RTD Movement

Although the *Quinlan* case is widely considered a watershed in the RTD movement's growth in the United States (Burnell 1993, 250), it was far from the first eruption of controversy over euthanasia in American society. The earliest organized effort to legalize euthanasia occurred some four decades earlier with the establishment in 1938 of the Society for the Right to Die and the Euthanasia Society of America (Burnell 1993; Marker 1992).[13] Of course, the roots of public debate and sympathy for "mercy killing" extend considerably deeper in American history. The first documented legal case involving assisted suicide, for example, took place in 1816 in Massachusetts. This case, which set precedent for future prosecutions of "mercy killers," involved a prisoner tried for "murder" for persuading a condemned man in an adjacent cell to hang himself to avoid a public execution. Although the law at the time equated encouraging suicide with murder, the jury acquitted the prisoner (Siebold 1992, 46).

Debate over the proper role of euthanasia in medical care has also long been a focus of physicians and the organizations representing them. The first published medical reference to euthanasia in the United States appeared in an 1884 issue of the *Boston Medical and Surgical Journal*, the predecessor to the *New England Journal of Medicine*. In this article, a physician argued that doctors should be permitted "to stand aside passively and give over any further attempt to prolong a life which had become a torment to its owner" (Emanuel 1994). Around the turn of the century, public speeches debating the merits and dangers of euthanasia were fairly common in both England and the United States, and editorials on the topic appeared in American medical journals with some frequency. "Patients' rights" movements developed on both sides of the Atlantic. In America, the fledgling pro-euthanasia movement succeeded in introducing a bill in the Ohio legislature in 1906 to legalize passive euthanasia. Although the measure was defeated, it generated widespread publicity, including letters and editorials in *The New York Times* (Emanuel 1994). In 1913, a similar bill was introduced (and later defeated) in New York, prompting the AMA to make its first of many public stands against PAS (Roberts and Gorman 1996).

Interest in euthanasia was sparked again in the early 1930s, when prominent English physician C. Killick Millard made a widely circulated speech advocating legalized euthanasia (Messinger 1993). The period between 1920 and 1940 saw a dramatic rise in "mercy killing" legal trials, which further intensified public debate on the issue. Controversy was also ignited by the publication of a provocative story in the *London Daily Mail* in 1935 that was picked up by a variety of United States newspapers. The story, in which an anonymous physician confessed to "mercy killing" five of his patients, unleashed an outpouring of requests by patients for doctors who would help them die, confessions from other doctors who had practiced euthanasia, and letters from American physicians and medical organizations condemning the practice. The passions fueled by these events led to the founding of the Voluntary Euthanasia Legislation Society in England in 1935, the first RTD organization in the world (Emanuel 1994). This organization became the model for the Society for the Right to Die, founded in the United States in 1938.

Prior to World War II, continued failure to pass bills legalizing euthanasia demoralized activists and weakened the campaign to obtain legal and social sanctioning of the practice. Most damaging to the pro-euthanasia movement, however, was the discovery after World War II of Germany's "Euthanasia Programme," used to rid German society of an estimated 200,000 physically and mentally disabled citizens (Roberts and Gorman 1996, 11). Although most historians regard Hitler's extermination of physically and mentally disabled citizens as mass murder rather than "euthanasia" (see, e.g., Lifton 1986; Newman 1991), Nazi use of the term continues to haunt RTD activists and provide ammunition for euthanasia opponents (Roberts and Gorman 1996). In the decades following the war, euthanasia's image had suffered a blow in the United States—but not a mortal one, according to one historian. In 1945 the

Euthanasia Society of America launched a new campaign in New York to make euthanasia legal, a move that attracted the public support of "a committee of 1,776 physicians and 54 Protestant ministers [who] announced that, in their view, voluntary euthanasia was not contrary to the principles of Christianity" (Messinger 1993, 195). Despite the movement's support from additional clergy, however, a proposed bill to legalize voluntary euthanasia was never introduced into the state legislature. As a result, although the 1940s and 1950s witnessed a surge in patient requests for assisted suicide, it was not until the late 1970s and early 1980s that several high-profile legal cases—most notably *Quinlan*—reactivated the pro-euthanasia movement.

Key Legal Developments

As one observer notes, "It is easy to forget how the past 50 years have changed the law governing the process of dying in America" (Cerminara and Meisel 2001, 672). Among the most dramatic examples of these changes involves shifts in jurisprudence related to the practice of passive and active euthanasia. The series of legal cases that thrust the question of a "right to die" into the public forum commenced with the United States Supreme Court's landmark 7–0 ruling in the 1976 *Quinlan* case. Since then the RTD movement has enjoyed a remarkable string of legal and social successes. Today it is difficult to believe that advance directives such as living wills—legal directives spelling out medical preferences in advance of a life-threatening illness or accident—were once highly controversial. In 1975 no state in the United States legally recognized such documents. A mere decade later, forty states had passed laws acknowledging them, and by the mid-1990s all fifty states in the United States recognized the validity of advance directives, a phenomenon due in large part to the RTD movement's promotional efforts.[14]

The impact of the *Quinlan* ruling, which allowed Quinlan's parents to remove her from life-support systems over the objections of her doctors and the institution where she was hospitalized, had an immediate impact not only on medical practices, but on the laws governing death and dying: In the three years following the case, ten states passed some form of passive euthanasia legislation to allow withdrawal of medical treatment (Daar 1995). Moreover, Quinlan served as a catalyst for a host of other legal actions challenging laws banning euthanasia. By 1994 roughly 100 right-to-die cases had entered the state courts, and 80 percent of all superior state court rulings have cited *Quinlan* as a legal precedent (Hoefler and Kamoie 1994, 172, 183).

Although many of the RTD movement's efforts to legalize PAS have been stymied at both the state legislative and judicial levels, a number of court rulings have carved out important legal victories for champions of a "right to die." In 1986, a California state court became the first in the nation to recognize the right to refuse medical care as "basic and fundamental."[15] Laying the groundwork for this ruling, a New Jersey high court one year earlier had eliminated the distinction between the removal of a respirator and withdrawal of a feeding tube, a decision effectively mandating hospitals to "starve" patients at their own or their legal surrogates' request.

Surpassing these legal triumphs was the landmark *Cruzan* decision in 1990.[16] In this case, the United States Supreme Court—weighing in for the first time on the question of an individual's inherent "right" to control the circumstances of death in the *Cruzan* decision—recognized a limited Constitutional "right to die." The high Court ruled that mentally competent patients had a constitutional right under the fourteenth Amendment to refuse medical therapies, including basic life-support systems such as those providing food and water.

The impact of these RTD milestones on medical practices has been nothing short of revolutionary. Within two decades of *Quinlan*, United States hospitals almost universally considered "passive" euthanasia a routine aspect of medical care. A 1989 survey, for example, found that nearly 90 percent of all critical-care doctors withhold or withdraw medical therapies from their patients, and research conducted in the 1990s found that half of all hospital deaths result from the withholding or withdrawal of medical care (Hall 1994). Yet another study conducted by the American Hospital Association concluded that 70 percent of all deaths each year in the United States are "somehow timed or negotiated" and result from the "withdrawal of some death-delaying technology" (In re L.W. 1992). As a capstone to these achievements, by 1995, nearly forty states had passed some form of the Uniform Rights of the Terminally Ill Act, codifying into law a patient's right to reject medical treatment even if such action hastens death (Bushong and Balmer 1995).

Although these gains have been dramatic, the RTD's legal feats have not been restricted to overcoming barriers to passive euthanasia. During the 1990s the movement made significant headway in its push to legalize PAS. Passage of Oregon's Death with Dignity Act (DWDA) in 1994—the world's first law legalizing PAS—remains the most dramatic legal example of such progress to date. In the wake of Oregon's success, twenty-five states have considered (and subsequently rejected) bills to legalize assisted suicide, including Arizona, California, Colorado, Connecticut, Michigan, New York, Wisconsin, Hawaii, and Vermont. Meanwhile, four states have offered voters the opportunity to approve PAS through ballot initiatives, including Washington and California.[17] Filene (1999), noting the narrow margins by which these two states' PAS initiatives were defeated, underscores the speed at which public acceptance of PAS progressed by the early 1990s. "Fifteen years earlier—no more than a minute or two of cultural-historical time—Americans had been hesitant to legalize living wills," he writes. "Now 46 percent voted to legalize not simply passive euthanasia, but active euthanasia by doctors." Although all state initiatives except Oregon's have so far been defeated, many lost by only a few percentage points.[18] This fact, combined with poll results demonstrating enduring public support for PAS, attests to the broad, grassroots appeal of a "right to die."

In yet another extraordinary legal development favoring the RTD movement, the highest courts in California and New York, in back-to-back rulings in late 1995 and early 1996, not only struck down laws prohibiting PAS, but recognized the "right to die" as a Constitutional guarantee.[19] Pronouncing these two decisions "a fundamental break with thousands of years of moral and medical tradition," a *New York Times* reporter predicted that the controversy surrounding euthanasia would eventually "wield a moral force and have a societal impact that rivals or surpasses that of *Roe v. Wade*" (Wilkes 1996, 24).

The RTD movement has also suffered its share of legal setbacks, among the most important of which occurred on 27 June 1997, when the United States Supreme Court unanimously ruled in a pair of decisions that states may constitutionally pass statutes banning PAS.[20] The Court's ruling in *Washington v. Glucksberg* overturned a Ninth Circuit Court of Appeals' finding that laws prohibiting PAS were unconstitutional. There is much in the ruling to cheer champions of a "right to die," however. First, the high court stopped short of denying the existence of a constitutional "right to die." Instead, Chief Justice Rehnquist, in the principal opinion signed by four other Justices, left the door open both for states to pass laws allowing PAS and for recognition of future claims to a constitutional right to doctor-assisted dying. Referring to the question of individuals' constitutional claim to PAS, he wrote, "Our opinion does not absolutely foreclose such a claim" (Greenhouse 1997, A1). Justices Souter, O'Connor, and Stevens, in concurring opinions, also gave RTD proponents considerable grounds for optimism. By creating "regulation with teeth," Souter wrote, states could overcome the Court's basic reservations about PAS, including concerns about involuntary euthanasia.[21] Similarly, Justice O'Connor stated that the Court had no objections to physicians administering pain medications to dying patients, "even to the point of causing unconsciousness and hastening death."[22] In perhaps the most openly encouraging opinion of all, Justice Stevens wrote that "a State . . . must acknowledge that there are situations in which an interest in hastening death is legitimate. Indeed, not only is that interest sometimes legitimate, I am also convinced that there are times when it is entitled to constitutional protection."[23]

Since the late 1990s PAS has remained a target of legal maneuverings on the part of both RTD and PL forces. RTD activists have continued their efforts to persuade state legislators to introduce bills legalizing PAS, while also working to get state ballot initiatives modeled on Oregon's DWDA before voters in as many states as possible. Ironically, among the most active opponents of PAS in recent years has been the federal government. In the late 1990s, members of the United States Congress made two failed attempts to pass legislation intended to nullify Oregon's DWDA.[24] These efforts were followed in 2001 by a directive issued by United States Attorney General John Ashcroft warning physicians in Oregon that prescribing lethal drugs to patients requesting PAS would result in loss of their medical licenses. In April 2002 a federal judge in Oregon ruled against Ashcroft and the Bush administration, denying the government authority to prosecute Oregon physicians who legally practice assisted suicide under Oregon's law.[25] The Bush administration has subsequently appealed this ruling.

NOTES

1. In her book, *Nymphomania: A History* , Carol Groneman (2000) contends that as medicine became professionalized in the mid-nineteenth century, women's "uncontrolled" sexuality or "nymphomania" was labeled a "disease" by the male-dominated medical profession and treated with a variety of "cures," including ovariotomies and clitorodectomies (Smith 2000, citing Groneman).

2. According to Conrad and Schneider (1992), the term "hyperactivity" was popularized in the 1950s and treated with the drug Ritalin (which they point out was conveniently developed around the same time).

3. In his book, *Better than Well: American Medicine Meets the American Dream*, Elliott (2003) cites the pervasive use of Paxil, Nardil, and similar drugs to treat shyness (now labeled "social anxiety") as an example of "medical involvement in the whole self-improvement business" (cited in Berger 2003, D7).

4. Since the late 1970s the disease metaphor has increasingly been applied to infertility. For example, a 1999 story in *The New York Times* quotes an infertility specialist who insists that a doctor who treats infertility "is no different than the doctor who treats diabetes with insulin" (Stolberg 1999, 3).

5. In 1968, the Harvard Medical School released a report redefining clinical death and specifying the criteria for determining brain death (Roberts and Gorman 1996, 13).

6. Institutional deaths include those occurring in both hospitals and nursing homes.

7. The death care industry, as Wernick (1995) notes, "has subordinated the churches that once presided over all the rituals of the life course, and has itself come to exercise a virtual monopoly over the organized symbology of death" (p. 280).

8. Several nineteenth-century theological trends further accelerated the secularization of American culture. These included exclusion of the concept of hell from after-life doctrine and Americans' embrace of and emphasis on personal and material progress rather than heavenly rewards (Wernick 1995).

9. For example, Jews oppose all forms of active euthanasia, including so-called "mercy killing" to mitigate end-of-life suffering. Unlike the Roman Catholic church—which opposes *all* forms of euthanasia—*passive* euthanasia such as withholding or withdrawing medical treatments are allowed in both Jewish and Greek Orthodox doctrine (Berk 1992).

10. She died on 11 June 1985.

11. For example, a November 1993 Harris poll found a 73 percent approval rating for PAS if safeguards were explained (Hall 1994), and an April 1995 Gallup poll found 75 percent approval for PAS for the "helplessly ill" (Wilkes 1996).

12. Between 1969 and 1975 membership in the Euthanasia Educational Council swelled from a handful of devotees to 300,000 (Siebold 1992). The Society for the Right to Die and Concern for Dying merged in 1990 to form Choice in Dying. In 1993, Americans Against Human Suffering became Americans for Death and Dying. ERGO was founded in 1976; membership figures are from Derek Humphry's listserve, ERGO's Right To Die Mailing List, 18 April 1997.

13. The Society for the Right to Die was modeled on the Voluntary Euthanasia Society the world's first group founded to promote legalization of euthanasia, founded in England in 1935 by Dr. Killick Millard, George Bernard Shaw, H. G. Wells, among others (Burnell 1993, 249).

14. In perhaps the ultimate endorsement of living wills, in 1991 Congress passed the Patient Self-Determination Act, a federal law requiring hospitals to provide information on living wills and other advance directives to all Medicare and Medicaid patients. The Patient Self-Determination Act (PSDA), Pub. L. No. 101–508, 4206, 4751, 104 Stat. 1388–115, 1388–204 (1990).

15. *Bouvia v. Superior Court*, 179 Cal. App. 3d 1227, 1137, 225 Cal. Rptr. 297 (1986). ("A patient has the right to refuse *any* medical treatment, even that which may save or prolong her life.")

16. *Cruzan v. Director, Missouri Department of Health*, 497 United States 261 (1990). Despite its acknowledgment of a constitutional right to die, the Court's decision was not considered a complete RTD victory: The court upheld a Missouri lower court ruling that states could—under certain circumstances—overrule patients' and their families' refusal of life-sustaining medical care.

17. These include California (1988, 1992), Michigan (1998), Washington (1991), and Maine (2000).

18. In November 2000, for example, the "Maine Death with Dignity Act" lost by a margin of 51 to 49 percent; in 1992 California voters defeated a similar referendum by a margin of 54 to 46 percent; and in 1991 Washington state voted down legalized PAS by 54 to 46 percent. In the wake of Maine's failed Death with Dignity initiative, lawmakers acknowledged its broad public support by passing laws expanding hospice care and reforming other aspects of care of the dying.

19. Stressing the significance of these rulings, University of Michigan law professor Yale Kamisar declared that, "In the past 30 days there have been more developments in this field than there have been in the previous 20 years" (Lemonick 1996).

20. *Washington v. Glucksberg*, 521 U.S. 702 (1997); *Vacco, Attorney General of New York v. Quill*, 521 U.S. 793 (1997). In *Vacco v. Quill*, the companion case to *Glucksberg*, the High Court ruled that a New York state law prohibiting PAS did not violate the Constitution's Equal Protection clause. In justifying its reversal of a lower court ruling, the Court relied on the AMA's distinction between "refusing life-sustaining treatment and demanding a life-ending treatment" (Bumgardner 2000, 416, quoting American Medical Association)

21. *Glucksberg*, 521 U.S. at 785 (Souter, concurring).

22. *Ibid.*, at 737 (O'Connor, concurring).

23. *Ibid.*, at 741–42 (Stevens, concurring).

24. In 1998 United States Rep. Henry Hyde of Illinois introduced a bill in the House known as the Lethal Drug Abuse and Prevention Act. An overt attempt to override the DWDA, the bill was designed to prevent Oregon doctors from using controlled substances to hasten patients' deaths. Opposed by the AMA and some 40 medical groups, the bill died in the House and never made it to the Senate (Buzzee 2001, 221). The second Congressional attempt to nullify the DWDA was the Pain Relief Promotion Act of 1999 (PRPA), which would have prohibited the use of lethal drugs by doctors performing PAS. Appended to the Controlled Substances Act (CSA) the PRPA would have empowered the Federal Drug Enforcement Administration to investigate and bring charges against any physician suspected of using a controlled substance in assisted suicides. The bill passed the House, but failed to come to a vote in the Senate (Wiley 2002).

25. United States District Judge Robert Jones, scolding Ashcroft for interfering in states rights, wrote that "the citizens of Oregon, through their democratic initiative process, have chosen to resolve the moral, legal and ethical debate on physician-assisted suicide for themselves by voting—not once, but twice—in favor of the Oregon act."

PART II

THE SHAPING POWER OF NEWS: FRAMING OF THE EUTHANASIA DEBATE

CHAPTER 4

News Frames and Framing Stages in Euthanasia Coverage

In significant ways, medicine . . . has replaced religion as the most
power extralegal institution of social control.
—Conrad and Schneider (1992, 241)

RESULTS: NEWS FRAMING OF EUTHANASIA

Among the most significant findings of this book's analysis of euthanasia coverage in the national, mainstream press is its overall support for frames that promote social and legal acceptance of euthanasia.[1] Dominant frames reflected pro-RTD interpretations in all but a handful of the stories analyzed in *The New York Times, Time, Newsweek,* and *U.S. News & World Report (USNWR),* a phenomenon that held true throughout over two decades of coverage. Although news stories typically contained at least one pro-life (anti-euthanasia) argument (e.g., that the "right to die will become the duty to die"), these tended to function as marginalized "counterframes" designed more to meet news media balancing and conflict conventions than to present a diversity of perspectives on an issue with deep repercussions in society.

As significant as which frames were selected to represent the euthanasia issue is where these frames were situated within public discourse on the issue. Although euthanasia encompasses a broad range of discursive topics—ranging from the medical, legal, and sociological to the theological and philosophical—this study's results show that journalists represented the controversy through a remarkably constricted lens. As Figs. 4.1 and 4.2 show, with rare exceptions, the articles represent euthanasia through two basic frames. Medical frames, dominant in nearly half of the stories investigated, and legal frames, dominant in roughly 40 percent of stories were overwhelmingly used to construct public understanding of the euthanasia conflict and its implications.

This chapter, which expands on these and other frame-related findings, provides an overview of the two dominant frames identified in this research (medical and legal) followed by an in-depth analysis of news framing of the euthanasia debate during the first two of the three major framing stages through which euthanasia coverage evolved over the two-decade period of analysis. These include: (1) stage one, characterized by concern over *passive* euthanasia, specifically, refusal or withdrawal of medical treatments and life-support systems ("pulling the plug" in common vernacular); and (2) stage two, also characterized by concern over passive euthanasia, but focused on the withdrawal of nutrition and hydration (the "feeding-tube controversy") rather than removal of respirators and similar life-support systems. (Results on the third framing stage, characterized by preoccupation with PAS or active euthanasia, is the subject of Chapter 5, which reports on news framing of Dr. Jack Kevorkian.)

DOMINANT NEWS FRAMES IN EUTHANASIA COVERAGE

Medical Frames

As mentioned previously, this study's findings show that print journalists covering euthanasia constructed the issue predominantly as a medical problem. Medical frames were considered dominant in any story that filtered euthanasia primarily through the viewpoints and values of the medical establishment. Specific characteristics of this frame include heavy reliance on medical sources, medical terms, and/or medical ideological positions. Medical sources—another important indicator of medicalization of the conflict—appear ten times more often than religious and five times more frequently than ethics experts (including medical ethicists). Meanwhile, sources able to provide a sociological or historical perspective on this complex and consequential issue were given scant attention (see Table 4.3).

It is significant that medical frames dominated news stories on euthanasia regardless of their overall ideological thrust—that is, whether dominant frames carried pro-RTD or pro-life positions. In addition to the pervasive pro-RTD *Humane Treatment* subframe—which argues that dying patients should be allowed to die in the time and manner of their choosing—journalists used four additional pro-RTD medical frames in the news articles analyzed. These include: *Medicine Out of Control*, *Medical Autonomy* (No Legal Interference), *Criminalizes Doctors*, *MD's are Already Practicing Euthanasia*, *Proceed with Caution*, and *Standards Needed*.[2] As Tables 4.1 and 4.2 show, these frames were dominant in roughly half of the stories.

Like all pro-life frames, those advancing medical positions and perspectives were marginalized in the news stories in this analysis (see Table 4.2). Even when they were dominant (in less than 5 percent of stories), however, pro-life frames, like pro-RTD frames, overwhelmingly advanced medical rather than religious frames such as *Sanctity of Life* (life is a gift from God and hence to be preserved at all cost) and *Divine Authority* (only God has the authority to determine the time of death). Perhaps even more surprising was this study's finding that medical pro-life frames were more dominant than the pro-life Social

Table 4.1
Comparison of Medical and Legal Frames in *The New York Times, U.S News &*
World Report, Newsweek **, and** *Time,* **1975–98**

FRAME	New York Times	USNWR	Newsweek	Time	TOTAL	Percent of Total (n =121)
Pro-RTD Medical	11	13	13	16	53	43.8
AE Medical	0	3	1	1	5	4.1
Pro-RTD Legal	16	8	11	10	45	37.0
AE Legal	0	0	0	1	1	0.8
Totals	27	24	25	27	103	85.7

subframe, *Slippery Slope*, which argues euthanasia will gradually be used to eliminate the poor, elderly, and other unwanted groups.

The four pro-life medical subframes appearing in news coverage in this study include: (1) *Contaminates Medicine* (allowing physicians to practice euthanasia violates the Hippocratic Oath and undermines the doctor-patient relationship); (2) *Medical Alternatives Exist* (hospice care or better pain treatment would render euthanasia unnecessary); (3) *Causes Worse Suffering* (certain euthanasia practices—such as withholding food and water from dying or comatose patients—actually exacerbate suffering); and (4) *Allows Doctors to Play God* (a medical frame linked to the *Divine Authority* religious frame that argues God—and not doctors—should decide the time of death).

Although all of these frames were marginalized in euthanasia coverage in this study, *Medical Alternatives Exist* and *Contaminates Medicine* appear and were dominant most often. Two frames—*Causes Worse Suffering* and *Allows Doctors to Play God*—were never dominant and appear in fewer than a dozen of the 121 articles included in the research.

Two pro-RTD medical frames, *Humane Treatment* and *Medicine Out of Control*, were pervasive aspects of euthanasia news coverage. Because *Humane Treatment*, in particular, is so central to RTD ideology and rhetoric, it is useful to examine how and within what context this collective action frame was employed in the news stories in this study. Critical to understanding *Humane Treatment* are the concepts of suffering and no hope. The following passage from *Issues in Law & Medicine*, written by an ethics scholar, helps articulate the *Humane Treatment* justification for euthanasia:

Table 4.2
Dominant Pro-RTD vs. AE Frames in *The New York Times*, *U.S News & World Report*, *Newsweek*, and *Time*, 1975–98

FRAME	New York Times	USNWR	Newsweek	Time	TOTAL	Percent of Total (n =121)
Pro-RTD Medical	11	13	13	16	53	43.8
Pro-RTD Legal	16	8	11	10	45	37.2
Pro-RTD Economic/ Pragmatic	0	0	0	1	1	0.8
Pro-RTD Religious/ Ethical	0	0	0	0	0	0
Pro-RTD Social (Public Support)	2	2	0	0	4	3.3
AE Medical	0	3	1	1	5	4.1
AE Legal	0	0	0	1	1	0.8
AE Religious/Ethical	0	0	1	0	1	0.8
AE Economic	0	0	0	0	0	0
AE Social (Slippery Slope)	0	0	1	0	1	0.8
Neutral or Ambivalent	6	1	3	0	10	8.2
TOTALS[3]	35	27	30	29	121	100

Table 4.3
Sources used in Euthanasia Stories in *The New York Times, U.S News & World Report, Newsweek* **, and** *Time,* **1975-98**

SOURCES	Percent
Politicians	3
Religious (clergy, theologians not specifically associated with pro-RTD or pro-life groups)	3
Legal and Judicial (e.g., judges, lawyers, police, prosecutors. law professors)	26
Medical (e.g., doctors, nurses, administrators, medical school professors, etc.)	30
RTD activists	10
Pro-life activists (representatives from disabilities and pro-life organizations, representatives from organized religion specifically involved in the anti-euthanasia movement, etc.)	5
Ethics & philosophy (e.g., medical ethicists, philosophy professors, other academics, etc.)	6
Lay public (patients and their families, etc.)	13
Other (e.g., polling and study results, government or organization reports, etc.)	4
Total (n = 849)	100

The highest value for suffering, terminally ill patients is to maintain control and dignity in dying by preserving the right to self-determination; when there is no longer any reasonable possibility of otherwise maintaining control or dignity, there is no significant moral distinction between allowing such a patient to die and actually causing death; when cure is no longer possible, the most important aspect of the physician's care of the patient is the relief of suffering (Reitman 1995, 299).

As this passage suggests, *Humane Treatment* is grounded in the notion that when no hope of a cure exists, it is not only cruel, but a violation of the physicians' oath to "do no harm" to prolong the lives of mortally ill, suffering individuals. In this sense, "harm" is caused not by passive or active euthanasia, but by denying suffering, mortally ill individuals the option of dying.[4] This passage also illustrates two other important components of this medical subframe: "death with dignity" and "quality of life." In addition to the harm caused by prolonging the physical suffering of the dying, "death with dignity" emphasizes the harm in forcing them to endure "indignities" such as the disintegration of their physical and mental faculties. Euthanasia advocates argue that if medicine cannot cure, it should at least do everything possible to alleviate suffering—including hastening the dying process. This also relates to so-called "quality of life" issues: If individuals are hooked to machines, totally dependent on others, and unable to enjoy or experience "normal" life, the argument here is that they are no longer "human" or "alive" in any authentic sense.[5]

A corollary to the compassion/mercy argument is the "right" of individuals to extend compassion to the suffering—an argument that allows RTD activists to attach the *Humane Treatment* frame to culturally resonant "rights" discourse. Emphasizing the role of outside parties in administering to the suffering, this argument stresses physician activism in the death process not only as a moral right, but a duty. The rhetorical question, "Why is it that animals can legally be put out of their misery—but not humans?" perhaps best expresses this element of *Humane Treatment.*[6]

As Gamson (1988a) points out, dominant frames (such as *Humane Treatment*) exist in a dialectic relationship to counterframes. Countering the *Humane Treatment* frame—which is grounded in the assumption that suffering is always negative—is the pro-life religious frame, *Suffering is Positive*, which argues that suffering has legitimate benefits for those desiring spiritual growth and "redemption" (Bernardi 1995, 14).[7]

In addition to *Humane Treatment*, journalists writing about euthanasia in this research also privileged the pro-RTD medical frame, *Medicine Out of Control*, which argues that medical technologies developed to prolong life have not only taken on a life of their own, but have turned over control of the dying process to "machines rather than nature" (Wallis 1986, 60). Other pro-RTD medical subframes appearing most frequently in the articles in this study include *MDs Already Practicing Euthanasia*, *No Government Intrusion*, and *Criminalizes Doctors*. A more detailed discussion of these frames is offered later in this chapter.

Legal Frames

As with medical framing, this study's findings show that journalists overwhelmingly privileged pro-RTD over pro-life legal frames. The most dominant pro-RTD legal frames in the articles investigated included the ubiquitous *Right to Die*, as well as *Undermines the Law* (which argues that the widespread practice of PAS, illegal in all but one state in the United States, dilutes the authority of the law) and *Criminalizes Families* (which argues that family members involved in "mercy killing" are being unfairly punished by legal authorities). Marginalized in euthanasia news coverage were legal frames supporting pro-life viewpoints and positions, including: *Euthanasia is a Crime* (Murder) and *Legal Safeguards Are Impossible.*

Of the pro-RTD legal frames used by journalists to construct the euthanasia issue in national print coverage, the *Right to Die* frame is paramount. Considered a cornerstone of American democracy, individual autonomy is based on the notion that humans—created in God's own image—possess special attributes that give rise to innate freedoms and rights.[8] As the mobilizing force behind the campaign to legalize euthanasia, the *Right to Die* frame argues specifically that individuals have the right to make decisions concerning the circumstances of their own deaths. In American society, where individualism trumps virtually all other social values, rights frames are believed to possess particular resonance. The reasoning behind the *Right to Die* frame—that if individuals have the right to control the circumstances of their lives, they should also have the right to control the circumstances of their deaths—applies not only to terminally ill patients in pain, but to anyone whose suffering makes life intolerable. Ultimately, euthanasia supporters believe that autonomy eclipses the state's interest in protecting life.[9]

Pro-life activists counter the *Right to Die* frame with the catchphrase: "The right to die will become the duty to die" (see, e.g., Appleby 1996). This catchphrase—which is particularly pervasive in literature distributed by disabilities groups opposed to legalized euthanasia, but also appears as a counterargument or balancing convention in a sizable minority of news stories investigated here—is a component of the *Slippery Slope* frame, which "warns against the potentially disastrous consequences of stepping over the boundary that separates 'allowing to die' from active killing" (Bernardi 1995, 14).[10]

FRAMING STAGES IN EUTHANASIA NEWS COVERAGE[11]

The Early Years: 1935–75: Euthanasia Discourse Before *Quinlan*

In order to grasp the significance of the three major framing stages found in this examination of news coverage of euthanasia, it is useful to understand the extent to which euthanasia—and particularly the concept of a "right to die"—had seeped into public awareness in the decades prior to *Quinlan*. As a close examination of the Euthanasia Timeline reveals (Appendix C), the RTD movement had gained a foothold in American culture well before *Quinlan*. By the end of the 1930s, for example, the United States had no fewer than three RTD organizations. Another surprising early example of the salience of the issue was a petition signed in 1947 by 1,000 New York state physicians "urging that voluntary euthanasia, or 'mercy death' for an incurable sufferer, be permitted by law" (1,000 Doctors Urge 'Mercy Death' Law 1947, 30). In 1950 Pope Pius XII made an official pronouncement of the Church's position on the use of life-support systems to prolong the lives of terminally ill and comatose patients. And by 1959 the first headline using the phrase "right to die" appeared in *The New York Times* (Beavan 1959, SM14).[12] One year later an elite group of medical authorities met to create an "official" definition of death that would better align with sweeping advances in medical technology that by this time could keep dying patients' hearts beating almost indefinitely. Perhaps the best evidence of the topic's pre-Quinlan infiltration into popular culture was television's first portrayal of passive euthanasia in a 1963 episode of "Dr. Kildare."[13] Finally, it is significant that in 1972—three years before Quinlan became a household name in America—the United States Senate was busy holding hearings on "death with dignity," a pro-RTD catchphrase that, along with "right to die," journalists adopted to construct public understanding of the issue.

Once in play, "master frames" such as "right to die" tend to remain consistent in news media reporting.[14] Congruent with this is the present study's finding that many of the catchphrases, modifiers, descriptors, and other framing elements used to cover euthanasia in the first stage of the debate continue through late-stage coverage. The catchphrase "right to die," for example, is reproduced in some form in virtually all euthanasia news stories in this study and appears repeatedly in headlines and sub-heads throughout the full period of analysis.[15]

Whatever the genesis of the Right to Die "master frame," rights rhetoric was certainly embedded in pro-RTD discourse well before Quinlan's accidental drug overdose made her a national symbol of the RTD movement. Although coverage of euthanasia did not begin in *Time, USNWR,* and *Newsweek* until the Quinlan controversy, an analysis of news reports on euthanasia appearing in *The New York Times* in the early 1970s shows that the rights frame was also well-entrenched by this time in the public consciousness. For example, half a dozen references to "rights" appear in the first seven paragraphs of a 1971 news story on euthanasia (Klemesrud 1971, 35). An editorial published in the *Times* in 1973 openly advocates "the right to die" (The Right to Die 1973), and an op-ed piece appearing the previous year not only makes a passionate case for "the right to choose death," but charges the legal system with denying "this right" to the public (Russell 1972, 29). The fact that no quotation marks were used to set off the phrase "right to die" in these pre-Quinlan articles indicates reader familiarity with a slogan widely associated with the RTD movement.

The durability of the rights frame in pre-Quinlan coverage of euthanasia is also demonstrated in the following passage from an article on living wills published in *The New York Times* in 1974—a year prior to Quinlan's accident. Although, once again, readers were assumed to be well-versed on the concept of a "right to die," note how carefully the author explicates the rights frame, comparing euthanasia with similar rights struggles over "Women's Lib" and abortion and equating the "right" to control one's body, hair, clothes, and sex life with the "right to die": "The right to die hardly competes with Women's Lib for public attention, nor is it as controversial as abortion; to many people, however, it represents one of the last unresolved issues in the battle for human rights. Many civil libertarians, for example, contending that everyone is entitled to control over his own body, assert that one's mode of dying should be as privileged a part of one's life-style as long hair, clothes and sex. Under the Constitution, they argue, the right to die is as inalienable as the right to live" (Dempsey 1974, 12).

However broad their dissemination, these early seeds of public interest and signs of social unrest did not germinate until Karen Ann Quinlan's coma—a flashpoint in the evolution of the twentieth-century RTD movement and the catalyst that would thrust the euthanasia controversy onto the media and public agendas in the mid-1970s. Social scientists have proposed a number of models to describe the stages through which social problems like euthanasia tend to progress. Although critics of such models rightly note that "the patterns of progression from one stage to the next vary sufficiently to question" the idea of issue cycles or stages (Hiltgartner and Bosk 1988, 54), the *Quinlan* case appears to offer a clear-cut example of the transition from "incipiency," a period in which latent signs of growing interest in a social problem exist but have yet to be fully defined and framed, to "coalescence," the stage in which a social issue such as euthanasia earns public acknowledgement and widespread attention (Hiltgartner and Bosk 1988). Because of Quinlan's pivotal role in mobilizing collective action around and focusing mass media and public attention on a "right to die," the mid-1970s was chosen as the starting point for this study's analysis of national print news framing of the euthanasia issue.

Stage One: Debate over Passive Euthanasia (Withholding of Life-Support Equipment and Medical Therapies), 1975–84

The brief discussion above of signs of social acceptance of a "right to die" in the decades prior to *Quinlan* helps explain how by 1975—when euthanasia entered public discourse as a legitimate social conflict—journalists had already identified the major frames that would characterize coverage of the controversy for the next two decades. Even so, journalists' seeming comfort with the terms of the debate is given its disturbing nature of the topic and the news media's traditional reluctance to offend readers with detailed discussions of mortality or agony associated with the dying process. Death, as one researcher points out, is foreign to the news media's "own abiding structure, the illusion it must maintain to remain culturally and economically viable" (Kalwinsky 1998, 93).

In addition to pro-RTD frames such as the *Right to Die* or *Humane Treatment* (and its corollary, "death with dignity") already in circulation by the time euthanasia gained sufficient momentum to attract media attention, a host of factors influenced the framing choices reporters made in the first framing stage. Like all frames used to construct social problems and issues, those used to represent euthanasia were restricted by the available inventory of cultural symbols, myths, collective memories, and common-sense understandings in circulation at the time (Swidler 1986). Equally important in constraining euthanasia frames were various events and developments playing a crucial role in propelling the issue from the fringes of social activism to the glare of media attention. Two such developments worked in tandem to catapult euthanasia into the media spotlight in the mid-1970s: The first was hospitals' routine use by this decade of life-sustaining technologies to prolong the lives of terminally ill and comatose patients. And the second, of course, was Karen Ann Quinlan's coma and the subsequent legal battle waged by her parents to force removal of her respirator. It took both developments to mobilize the disparate factions of the RTD movement, provide the media with the medical and legal frames needed to make sense of and interpret this troublesome new controversy, and launch the issue of euthanasia fully into public and mass media awareness.

At issue in the *Quinlan* case—as in the first stage of coverage generally—was passive euthanasia: Is it appropriate to hasten death by removing a respirator or withholding medical treatment from comatose or gravely ill patients at their (or their guardians') request? Analysis of the first framing stage shows the news media and the nation still clearly grappling with what one *Newsweek* reporter called, "that hard question—to pull the plug or continue living as a vegetable" (Ansen 1979, 99).

Promotion of Pro-RTD Frames

As mentioned earlier, news reports in this study overwhelmingly privileged pro-RTD frames during the full period of coverage analyzed in this research. This pattern is clearly in evidence from the first news stories on euthanasia appearing in *Newsweek, Time, USNWR*, and *The New York Times*. Along with heavy use of medical and RTD sources advocating acceptance of euthanasia, pro-RTD ideologies manifested through a broad spectrum of framing devices ranging from syntactical structures (headlines and leads), visual images, and anecdotes to catchphrases, exemplars, and depictions. Anecdotes advancing pro-RTD themes, for example, were highly favored over pro-life cautionary tales warning of the unintended consequences or drawbacks of legalization of passive euthanasia.

Although a more in-depth discussion of the ideology of news frames appears later in chapter 7, it is useful at this point in the discussion to show how journalists' use of a particular framing strategy contributed to the overall promotion of passive euthanasia in this framing stage. This framing strategy concerns the use of loaded modifiers such as "extraordinary means" and "heroic measures" to describe medical efforts to keep comatose or terminally ill patients alive. These terms, which appear sporadically throughout the two decades of coverage, were a fixture of coverage in the first framing stage.[16] In an early article on Quinlan, for instance, the terms, "extraordinary effort," "extraordinary means," "extraordinary treatment," "artificial means," and "heroic treatment" were all used to refer to patients' on life-support systems (Clark and Agrest 1975, 58). Although this article's use of these modifiers is unusually heavy, most stories in the first framing stage contain at least one reference to "extraordinary" or "heroic" efforts or resort to alternatives such as "excessive treatment," "relentless drive to extend the life of the aged," "artificial intrusions," and even "massive and heroic intervention."

Of course, it might be argued that journalists' heavy reliance on "extraordinary efforts," "heroic measures," and similar terms is justified on the basis that these are medical terms borrowed from medical professionals—the primary sources journalists draw upon in this study's news stories.[17] Their repetitious and ritualistic use outside their original medical contexts, however, not only contributes to medicalization of euthanasia coverage, but results in a distinctly different set of meanings in news stories than in a clinical context. The cumulative effect of their pervasive use is that of underscoring the pointlessness, excessiveness, and irrationality of artificially prolonging the lives of patients who are not "alive" in any qualitative sense. Moreover, the implicit message loaded modifiers such as "extraordinary measures" communicate is frequently made explicit through use of the authorial voice or that of medical authorities.

For example, a 1975 article about Karen Ann Quinlan in *The New York Times Magazine* declares that "at a certain point heroic measures to preserve life become obscene" (Halberstam 1975, 221). And a doctor in Newsweek is quoted as saying that "practically speaking, Karen Ann [Quinlan] is dead already" (Sheils and Agrest 1975, 76).

Medicalization of the Euthanasia Debate

Given the focus of this study on medicalization of the euthanasia issue, it is useful to demonstrate some of the characteristics of medical framing found in the first framing stage. For this purpose, a single news report has been selected for in-depth analysis. Titled "A Right to Die?," this early first-stage *Newsweek* article focuses on the events surrounding the *Quinlan* case (Clark and Agrest 1975). Although any number of similar articles might have been chosen, this article has a number of features that recommend it: First, it is the earliest in-depth article on euthanasia to appear in the news magazines in this study. As such, it may be presumed to have played a key role in both defining the terms and setting up the discursive boundaries of subsequent coverage. Additionally, its length (over 4,000 words) is sufficient to allow extensive evaluation of framing strategies used to promote euthanasia. Finally, it reflects the way in which journalists in this study generally marshaled sources, terms, and arguments, as well as exemplars, anecdotes, descriptive details, visual images, and other "condensing symbols" to construct the euthanasia controversy primarily as a medical (rather than a metaphysical, philosophical, ethical, political, or economic) issue.

Among the first steps in framing analysis is to examine the syntactical structure—the headline and lead paragraphs—of news texts (see, e.g., Pan and Kosicki 1993). It is significant, first of all, to note that the headline, "A Right to Die?" is a highly favored RTD movement catchphrase. Although this particular headline presents the "right to die" catchphrase in the form of a question rather than a statement, it nevertheless evokes the highly resonant individual rights (legal) frame. The implicit pro-RTD thrust of this headline becomes more apparent if one imagines an alternative headline based on a pro-life catchphrase or subframe such as "Sanctity of Life?" or "A Duty to Die?," either of which suggests a distinctly different response to the question of euthanasia's appropriateness. Whereas the headline, "A Right to Die?"—with its reference to individual "rights"—refers to the legal battle mounted by Quinlan's father to disconnect her from the respirator, the text of the article suggests the medical *Humane Treatment* subframe, which argues that Quinlan should have the right to "die in peace" or "die with grace and dignity."

Along with headlines and leads, sources represent a crucial signifier of a story's overall frame. In this article, sources were employed overwhelmingly in the service of medical viewpoints and values: Of a total of thirty-two sources used in this news story, twenty-two (or nearly 70 percent) were physicians. In contrast, the article draws from only two sources voicing theological, philosophical, or ethical perspectives.

Yet another step in framing analysis and an important cue to the directionality of news story frames involves identifying the terms or language used to interpret a social problem or issue. The *Newsweek* article serves as a case study of the medicalization of the euthanasia controversy. For example, in addition to the pervasive use of medical terms such as "heroic" and "extraordinary measures" discussed earlier, the machine that keeps Quinlan breathing is described as a "Bennett MA-1 respirator." Moreover, medical terms and jargon were used to describe an exhaustive list of phenomena, including: (1) the "definition" of death (e.g., "brain death," "the absence of brain waves on an electroencephalogram," "heart death"); (2) Quinlan's specific circumstances (e.g., "light on her respirator," "persistent vegetative state," "spontaneous respiration," "fixed and dilated pupils and no response to external stimulation," damage to nerve cells," "damage in . . . the reticular formation of the midbrain, . . . both halves of the cerebral cortex, . . . the basal ganglia, . . . the thalamus," "intravenous feedings," "metabolic in origin"); (3) cases in which euthanasia is characterized as an appropriate option (e.g., "incurable malignancy of the bone marrow," "cerebral hemorrhage," "intestinal obstruction," "encephalic," "gastrointestinal or cardiac defects," "incurable anemia"); and (4) procedures and equipment used on patients for which euthanasia may be appropriate (e.g., "injection of adrenalin," "heart-lung machine," "lethal dose of potassium chloride").

Once again, although it may seem natural or logical that Quinlan's story be told by medical sources in the language of medical technology (after all, her narrative does take place in a hospital), the impact and meaning of medical language in a news narrative differs substantially from the same language used in a patient's hospital chart. Even more crucial than the pervasive use of medical terminology outside its clinical context is the underlying message that this usage signals to readers about the appropriate domain in which euthanasia-related problems should be addressed. Telling the story in the technical language of medicine rather than the language, say, of sociology, philosophy, history, or even metaphysics unconsciously emphasizes not whether euthanasia should be practiced, but in which particular circumstances (read: medical cases diagnosed and controlled by doctors). In this way medical language itself can be seen to constrict and bias public discourse on euthanasia.

Framing of Conflict in Stage One

As with other news stories in which medical framing dominates, the news story highlighted here not only uses medical terms and vocabularies to medicalize suicide (which in reality does not actually require medical intervention), but does so by overtly championing medical views on the appropriateness of euthanasia as a "solution" to the problems facing individuals at the end of life. A prime way in which euthanasia is medicalized is through an emphasis on various conflicts, some of which reappear throughout the two decades of news coverage and others of which, interestingly, diminish in intensity over time. Like other framing elements in the first framing stage, conflicts were used to promote both pro-RTD and medical framing of the debate over euthanasia.

Of course, the primary conflict during the first framing stage is the debate—symbolized by Quinlan—over whether it is appropriate to remove respirators and other life-support systems from comatose or gravely ill individuals to bring about death. Two additional conflicts also emerge in the first framing stage: conflict between dying patients (or their surrogates) and medical professionals and conflict between the medical and legal systems over authority to make decisions involving passive euthanasia.

Given the focus of most articles in this period on the *Quinlan* case, it is not surprising that the first of these latter two conflicts—antagonism between doctors and their patients or surrogates—is most common in the first stage of coverage. An early article in *The New York Times Magazine*, for example, blames the "agonizing" Quinlan situation on her doctors' refusal to turn off her respirator despite "explicit written permission" to do so from Quinlan's father (Halberstam 1975, 221). Playing up the conflict between Quinlan's parents and her doctors more overtly, the *Newsweek* story selected for in-depth analysis describes relations between the two parties as characterized by "a great deal of bitterness" and as having "steadily deteriorated ever since the Quinlans brought their lawsuit . . . to force removal of Karen's extraordinary life-support systems." Journalists generally draw upon four specific frames to articulate this conflict: (1) *Humane Treatment; (2) Medicine Out of Control; (3) No Legal Interference;* and *(4) Right to Die.* These four pro-RTD medical frames were highly related and frequently appear together in the news stories in this investigation (Clark and Agrest 1975). As these examples show, by representing the issue as a conflict between doctors and patients (including surrogates), the issue is further medicalized.

A second major conflict played out in the first framing stage concerns the battle between orthodox medicine and the legal system over which should wield authority over decisions involving euthanasia. There is little ambiguity as to the party most articles in this framing stage support in this power struggle: In both overt and subtle ways, news frames in this stage suggest that physicians should be able to make euthanasia-related decisions (in cooperation with dying individuals or their guardians) without the encumbrance of legal oversight or regulations. The *Newsweek* article selected for in-depth analysis, for example, argues explicitly against legal "interference" in what is depicted as a medical problem. It favors the medical establishment in its turf war with legal authorities by portraying physicians who support euthanasia as both caring and ethical (e.g., "Many doctors are reluctant to use any means to hasten a patient's death") and as victims burdened with the Promethean task of attempting to treat dying patients and their families with care and compassion while being harassed by the legal system for doing so.

Other passages that portray doctors as hapless victims hounded by the legal system emphasize the potentially dire consequences of judicial interference. In an unattributed statement the article makes the point that "most physicians oppose attempts to settle cases like those of Karen Quinlan in the courts. If [the judge] should rule that Karen's treatment must be continued, . . . it will have a tremendous impact on the practice of medicine." Similarly, several passages depict medical professionals as hassled unfairly by the legal profession, which in turn is characterized as ill equipped to deal with medical questions: "No matter how well intended, . . . such decisions should not be left to the courts alone"; "Perhaps . . . the single most fundamental question posed by the *Quinlan* case is whether it or any similar moral dilemma can or should be taken to court of law for resolution"; and "The law . . . forces doctors to kill secretly [from a quote]." Finally, a quote by an AMA representative supports medical hegemony over euthanasia by arguing that because "the criteria for death will vary" and "are constantly evolving," it makes no sense to make laws that "lock" doctors "into a statutory definition of death . . . After all, it used to be that death occurred when you held a mirror to a patient's mouth and it did not fog up." In other words, this quote suggests, medical professionals need to be allowed autonomy not only to define death, but to change their definitions as they see fit. This perspective is promoted in this unattributed statement from the same article: "The decisions involved, according to this view, are too personal and depend too much on individual circumstances to be left up to the cold impersonality of the law" (Clark and Agrest 1975).

Still other passages in the article promote the notion that legal restrictions force physicians to hide their activities from the prying eyes and invasive reach of the law. As a result of legal restrictions, the story argues, doctors have no option but to "work out devious conscience-sparing ploys to accomplish their purposes." One such "ploy" involves saying to their patients, "'I have something for your pain. If you take too much, it will be harmful.' And then, in effect, the patient decides." Another tactic doctors are depicted as using to circumvent legal restrictions is the substitution of legal for illegal substances to end their patients' lives: "Instead of switching off the respirator, . . . they simply don't replace the oxygen tank when it's empty. 'They're not likely to get caught not maintaining the oxygen supply, . . . while they might get caught unplugging the machine."

The inappropriateness—and even ludicrousness—of legal rules governing the medical practice of euthanasia is stressed once again in the following passage, which describes the lengths to which doctors must go to avoid "getting caught":

Doctors seldom forget a patient whose life they bring to an end. Dr. Joel Posner . . . remembers a desperately ill man on a respirator . . . Unable to speak, the man handed Posner a note that read, "Please Don't Kill Me." Eventually, the patient became so sick that the respirator tube would slip out of his throat several times a day, causing him to turn blue from near suffocation. Finally, because of the man's suffering, Posner decided that further care on the machine was useless, and that the patient should be allowed to die. Turning off the respirator would be cruel, Posner decided, because it might take the patient twelve hours of choking to die. Morphine to put him to sleep could potentially constitute active euthanasia. So Posner turned off the respirator and administered pure oxygen through the tube. The effect was to suppress the man's respiration and put him to sleep. He died shortly afterward. "It was really no different from morphine," says Posner, "but somehow more legal."

This passage offers an unabashed example of the basic promedical thrust of news articles in this study generally. Note, first, the journalist's careful depiction of the doctor as a compassionate, cautious man who does not take euthanasia lightly ("Doctors seldom forget a patient whose life they bring to an end" and "Finally, because of the man's suffering, Posner decided . . . that the patient should be allowed to die"). Even more striking, however, is the passage's characterization of the doctor's active steps to end a patient's life as allowing the patient to die. In actuality, of course, the doctor administered a lethal dose of oxygen expressly to end the man's life—an unambiguous instance of PAS. Also significant is the journalist's inclusion of the physician's complaint about not being (legally) free to administer morphine instead of the "pure oxygen" he must resort to when ending a patient's life. This, along with the article's (euphemistic) characterization of the doctor's actions as "suppress[ing] the man's respiration" and "put[ting] him to sleep," has the effect of normalizing and legitimizing PAS. The passage also portrays legal restrictions governing physicians' care of patients as irrational: "If oxygen has the exact effect as morphine," the reporter opines, "why make oxygen legal and morphine illegal—and why punish the doctor for using one, but not the other?" (Clark and Agrest 1975).

Finally—and perhaps most significantly—this passage is notable for its conflation of passive and active euthanasia—a framing strategy that clearly promotes support for PAS. No ethical, medical, or even legal distinction is made between the act of turning off a respirator and injecting a patient with a lethal substance to end his life. Based on this and similar articles in the study, it is clear that reporters use the *Quinlan* case—ostensibly concerned with the debate over passive euthanasia—to help create a favorable climate for active euthanasia, including PAS.

References to the Quinlans' ordeal as "tragically public," a "personal plight," and "a personal tragedy" reinforce the medical view that questions pertaining to euthanasia are best addressed not in the legal arena, but by medical professionals and their patients. The frame used to express this idea is *No Legal Interference*, a medical frame that argues that issues involving euthanasia decisions are much to "delicate" for the legal system's ham-fisted procedures and solutions. Doctors, in contrast, have handled such cases "countless times, usually on the mutual agreement of patient, family and physician." However, now that "the Quinlans' private and personal plight [has come] before the public bar in a case that is probably unique in American jurisprudence," physician autonomy has been breached and the doctor-patient relationship violated (Clark and Agrest 1975).

This last sentence's characterization of the *Quinlan* case as "unique in American jurisprudence"—which underscores the unprecedented and unjustified reach of the law into medical terrain—offers an excellent example of an exemplar, a framing device that calls on past or recent cases to instruct or impart "lessons" applicable to current problems. Of the dozen or so exemplars used in this article, only two challenge the appropriateness of euthanasia. These include a reference to the Nazi euthanasia program ("the calculated euthanasia policy [of] Nazi Germany against cripples, mental incompetents . . . ") and a quote from a doctor who practices PAS that articulates the pro-life medical frame, *Causes Worse Suffering* ("I've seldom seen anybody die [via PAS] with 'peace and dignity. They have tubes and pain, and they're scared. It's not like 'Love Story'") (Clark and Agrest 1975).

Exemplars supporting pro-RTD ideologies, on the other hand, were both common and were used openly to advocate passive euthanasia in Quinlan's case. For instance, a patient similar to Quinlan who has been in a coma for thirty-four years is used as a morality tale or warning of what will befall the relatives of all comatose individuals if the legal system refuses to allow Quinlan to be disconnected from her respirator. This unfortunate coma patient, the article instructs, "is still cared for around the clock by her mother." Significantly, *Newsweek* editors selected a photograph of this particular, long-term coma patient to accompany the article on Quinlan—a choice that visually invites and reinforces parallels with Quinlan. Use of a photograph of a patient in a coma for more than three decades, of course, underscores the "rationality" or practicality of using passive euthanasia in such cases much more directly and viscerally than the verbal arguments presented in the text itself. Again, it is useful to imagine possible alternatives to this choice of photographs: What message would have been conveyed, for example, if the news magazine's editors had used a photograph of a third coma patient briefly referred to in the same article who recovered from a long coma and went on to lead a normal life?

Two additional exemplars were used to promote the idea that Quinlan should be allowed to die by linking her case with analogous cases in the past. The first introduces a couple who disconnected their daughter from life support after a doctor warned them that they would eventually resent and "may even start hating her." The second describes a deceased woman as intensely grateful to her son for agreeing to help her obtain passive euthanasia, concluding that "this was the greatest gift she had ever received from him."

As mentioned earlier, Quinlan herself figures strongly in this and other articles' promotion of pro-medical and pro-RTD ideologies. Used as a sympathetic symbol for all dying and comatose patients who languish in a metaphysical and medical limbo as a result of life-extension medical technologies, her case invites audience identification with the pro-RTD *Humane Treatment* and *Right to Die* frames. As indicated previously, one of the most important ways in which this ideological position is advanced is through promotion of the idea that Quinlan (as well as others with similar prognoses) is "dead already." This idea is expressed through the notion that "death is inevitable"—an argument that both expresses the *Humane Treatment* frame and indirectly evokes the *Economic/Pragmatic* frame (a pro-RTD frame that argues that when "no hope" of recovery exists for comatose and terminally ill patients connected to life support, keeping them alive via medical technology wastes valuable economic and human resources). This inevitability argument is expressed in such statements as, "Most of the doctors who have examined Karen Quinlan believe she has lost her consciousness of life" or "She is in a persistent vegetative state." Likewise, a physician commenting on Quinlan's condition is quoted as saying, "I don't believe she can think in any of the sense we talk of.

She can't calculate, can't reason. Lets's not confuse mental deficiency and Miss Quinlan. In my opinion, she has no awareness, no consciousness. That's a totally different world."

Vivid visual images of Quinlan's emaciated body curled into a fetal position, as well as the contrast between her present and past appearance were also used to build the case that she is already "dead" in any meaningful sense: "Once . . . Quinlan was a vivacious girl with frosted brown hair and a ready smile. Now she weighs only 70 pounds. Her hair falls on the pillow in dull, matted strands. Her skin, sallow and waxen, is stretched taut over her skull. Her mouth is in a rigid grimace, her eyes are tightly shut. Thin yellow tubes . . . trail from her nose and arm." Blame for Quinlan's plight—described in this article as "without hope"—is attributed to the "extraordinary means" used to prolong her life. Having established first, that she is essentially dead and, second, that she is being kept alive unnaturally through life-extension technologies, the article's solution is obvious: Quinlan should be "allowed to die 'with grace and dignity'" (Clark and Agrest 1975).

The argument that established medicine has gone too far in its "heroic" attempts to preserve lives is a chief component of another common first-stage frame: *Medicine Out of Control*. A look at this medical frame provides insights into the way in which even antimedical arguments were used to medicalize the euthanasia controversy. Although frequently used intensifiers such as "heroic measures," "heroic treatments," "extraordinary effort," "alive by extraordinary means," and "extraordinary treatment" generally have a negative connotation insofar as they impugn medical technology, they manage to preserve an overall positive image of doctors as healers. The word "heroic" itself casts physicians in the role of protagonists, however misguided or overzealous their efforts to prolong the lives of "hopeless" patients. What "heroic" suggests here is that doctors are too concerned about keeping death at bay; in this sense they are not so much culpable as overly duty-bound—compassionate and committed to a fault, as it were.

The fine line journalists negotiate between condemning medical technology while preserving an overall positive image of the medical system is illustrated in the delicate wording of this passage from a 1978 article by columnist George Will (1978): "Support for euthanasia legislation derives, in part, from the mistaken fear that doctors are obligated to prolong life with all available technologies, however severe the ordeal and cost" (p. 72). Although anti-medical on its face, note the passage's use of the words "mistaken fear" and "obligated," which have the effect not of discrediting the medical establishment, but merely of raising questions about particular medical practices. Elsewhere he comments that, "Perhaps not until this century did the average visit of a patient to a doctor do more good than harm. But now medical proficiency, while making living better, is making dying more problematic. Medicine should prolong life, not the process of dying" (Will 1978, 72). Here again, the phrase, "medical proficiency," manages simultaneously to praise the medical profession while indicting its life-extension medical technologies. As such, it exemplifies the way in which euthanasia narratives in the first framing stage cast doctors and the medical establishment not as antagonists, but as flawed heroes. By drawing subtle yet clear distinctions between medical professionals and their life-prolonging technologies, journalists stake out a careful middle ground between attacking medicine for having gone "too far" (a framing characterization that in itself implicitly promotes social acceptance of euthanasia), while simultaneously upholding and reinforcing medicine's institutional authority and power.

Given the fact that the *Quinlan* ruling and legislation passed to increase individuals' autonomy over death and dying eventually meant the end of medical hegemony over euthanasia-related decisions, it is significant that the news articles in stage one framed the debate so unambiguously from the perspective of medicine rather than law. A final example from a different news article further illustrates this phenomenon. Interpreting the power struggle between medicine and the legal system primarily through the medical subframe *No Legal Interference* described earlier, this news story makes a blatant pitch for medical autonomy over euthanasia decisions (Tifft 1983, 68). It does so, first, by depicting doctors as stymied by federal regulations in caring for their patients ("the new regulations . . . may thus make doctors more hesitant to take what many had considered the more humane course"; and "few medical professionals or lawyers welcome the second guessing of the legal system"). Second, it suggests openly that the legal system is incapable of sorting out the morally and medically complex issues informing the debate.

The article depicts legal solutions to the euthanasia controversy as inappropriate in five ways: (1) as making matters worse (adding "further uncertainty to an already complex situation"); (2) as "mischievous and intrusive": ("[A medical commission] urges courts and legislatures for the most part to stay away. 'The resolution of these issues . . . should be left to . . . the patients, their families, and health-care professionals'"; and "legislation diminishing the privacy of the patient-physician relationship 'would be mischievous and intrusive.'"); (3) as inconsistent (Legal solutions are "inconsistent policymaking . . . at best"); (4) as inflexible (The "absolute rule" of laws governing medical profession would be "undesirable"); and (5) as ill suited to such an emotionally fraught area of medical practice ("No judge in the land can adjudicate this type of human suffering"; " I cannot imaging anything worse that relying on a lawyer standing by the bedside leafing through papers to determine what treatment should be administered.") (Tifft 1983, 68).

In summary, news framing of passive euthanasia in the first framing stage reflects both medicalization of euthanasia and overall support for legal and social acceptance of passive euthanasia. By the mid-1980s withdrawal of medical treatments and life-support systems from seriously ill and comatose patients is no longer framed as debatable, but as a taken-for-granted, routine practice. Framing the issue as having reached such a consensus is significant, not only in view of the strength of opposition to passive euthanasia from organized religion, disabilities groups, and other pro-life activists, but in the context of the many troubling and unresolved questions remaining at this incipient stage in euthanasia discourse.[18]

STAGE TWO: EXPANSION OF THE DEBATE OVER PASSIVE EUTHANASIA (REMOVAL OF FOOD AND HYDRATION), 1984–90

As mentioned above, by the end of the first framing stage, the debate over removal of respirators and withholding of medical treatments is portrayed in the news articles in this study as having shifted largely from conflict to consensus. A new wrinkle in the passive euthanasia debate awaited journalists, however, that would soon galvanize opponents of passive euthanasia and provide a fresh source of conflict for the news media. This new controversy—over whether removing food and water from comatose or mortally ill patients should be considered an acceptable form of passive euthanasia—raised disturbing new concerns about the moral and legal limits of passive euthanasia. The dimensions of this new "feeding-tube controversy" were summarized in the following passage from a second-stage news story:

Many Americans have come to view kidney dialysis, cancer chemotherapy and the use of respirators as treatments that can be halted if they become too burdensome physically, emotionally and financially . . . But feeding may present a different issue . . . Is a surgically implanted nourishment tube similar to optional forms of medical technology, or is it more akin to the simple providing of food and water for the sick, which is a moral requirement for everyone. (Ostling 1987, 71)

Notice, first, this passage's articulation of the consensus frame on passive euthanasia mentioned above ("many Americans have come to view"). The "feeding" controversy, however, is constructed as a "different issue." The pro-life concern fueling the controversy over what this passage euphemistically refers to as the removal of a "nourishment tube" was that "starving" and withholding liquids from comatose and mortally ill patients not only constituted "killing" and, as such, defied Biblical law (a pro-life argument articulated through the *Sanctity of Life* religious subframe), but caused extreme physical discomfort even in comatose patients (a pro-life argument articulated through the *Causes Worse Suffering* medical subframe). As such, pro-life activists (including some medical ethicists) argued that "starvation" violated the oath taken by medical practitioners to relieve rather than exacerbate patients' suffering (a pro-life argument articulated through the *Contaminates Medicine* subframe).[19]

Although journalists in the second framing stage use a number of legal disputes to interpret the euthanasia controversy, the primary focus is on two high-profile cases: *Bouvia*[20] and *Cruzan*.[21] News framing of the *Bouvia* case proves particularly instructive in shedding light on a central contradiction of news framing: how it is that news frames simultaneously promote pro-RTD arguments and positions while framing the individuals or activists who embody pro-RTD ideologies unsympathetically.

Framing of Elizabeth Bouvia

The most heated "feeding tube" dispute involved Elizabeth Bouvia, a woman in her twenties with cerebral palsy who demanded to be allowed to die via starvation in the hospital where she had been admitted for psychiatric problems. What was unusual—and most alarming to pro-life and disabilities groups about her case—was that she was neither dying nor in physical pain. Instead, her request to die was almost certainly fueled by clinical depression. Although she had been mobile much of her life and had even married and attended college, a series of psychological episodes culminated in her being hospitalized for depression and suicidal impulses. The hospital, instead of yielding to her demand to die via starvation, obtained a court order to surgically implant a feeding tube in her body and began force-feeding her. She sued to have the feeding tube removed, and in 1986 an appellate court ruled in her favor, reasoning that her "life has been physically destroyed and its quality, dignity and purpose gone" (Reitman 1995, 299, quoting from Bouvia).[22]

What is most interesting about the *Bouvia* case is that of all the legal disputes covered in the articles in this investigation, it was clearly the most potentially damaging to the RTD movement's goals. This is because although the *Bouvia* court decision clearly represented an expansion of the legal "right to die," Bouvia herself was far from an ideal model for the RTD campaign. An enduring concern of both religious and secular opponents of legalized PAS and passive euthanasia is that it is clinical depression—rather than intolerable pain—that motivates most individuals to seek voluntary euthanasia, an anxiety unambiguously supported by the *Bouvia* case. In light of the fact that depression figured so centrally in her desire to die, journalists covering the case might logically have used Bouvia to illustrate this particular drawback of the legalized, routinized practice of passive euthanasia—specifically by addressing the role of depression in euthanasia requests. Her case may, for example, have prompted journalists to interpret the feeding-tube controversy through the *Slippery Slope* frame—a pro-life frame that, among other things, argues that once society embarks on the path of legalizing euthanasia for certain "rational" or "common sense" cases, it will thereafter be used in increasingly unjustified and inappropriate circumstances.

Neither this frame nor the role of depression in euthanasia requests, however, is given more than the most superficial attention in the articles in this study. Moreover, analysis of second-stage framing reveals that Bouvia's case failed to alter in any perceptible way journalists' basic pro-euthanasia, medical framing of the debate. This analysis reveals that while Bouvia herself is cast as troublesome and emotionally unstable in news coverage in this study, she is depicted as a unique case—an anomaly among the vast majority of cases in which withdrawal of food and water is warranted. By functioning symbolically as the exception that "proves the rule" that withholding food and water from dying and comatose individuals is generally appropriate, she functions as little more than a counterargument in the overall promotional framing of euthanasia.

Another way in which subtle promotion of social acceptance of withholding food and water manifests itself in news framing in the second stage involves the euphemistic characterization of this practice as removal of "nutrition and hydration," "nourishment tubes," or "feeding tubes." Once again, although these characterizations seem natural or logical on their face, it is significant that journalists generally avoided more vivid constructions like, "starve to death," "starvation," or "selective starvation"—terms and phrases that pervade pro-life articles on euthanasia obtained from sources outside this study. When the word "starvation" appears in news reports in this study, it tends to appear either in relation to the unsympathetic Bouvia (see, e.g., Gelman and Pedersen 1984, 72; Wallis 1986, 60) or, ironically, to marginalize pro-life views, as this passage from a 1987 article demonstrates: The controversy over feeding tubes . . . is especially thorny for Roman Catholic institutions, because many right-to-lifers are demanding new laws against what they see as killing by 'starvation.' Aiming occasional barbs at the strict pro-life stance, most of those [attending a meeting of health-care administrators] insisted that Catholic tradition accepts an end to feeding in medically hopeless cases" (Ostling 1987, 71).

Note how the word "starvation" is linked to the pro-life movement in this passage and the way in which this usage conveys extremism. Use of quotation marks to enclose "starvation" is a rhetorical device that signals the journalist's discomfort or even disagreement with this particular characterization. The phrase, "what they see as killing by" that proceeds the word "starvation" also has the effect of mitigating the impact of this pro-life view. The suggestion that opposition to withholding food and water from patients is radical and rigid is further underscored by the characterization, "strict pro-life stance," and assignment of the label "right-to-lifers" to opponents of euthanasia. And finally, consensus-building for the practice is evident in the passage's reference to the fact that even "Catholic tradition" condones removal of food and water from "hopelessly" ill individuals.

Framing of Conflict in Stage Two

Both friction between doctors and dying patients (or their surrogates) and the power struggle between the medical and legal professions continue through the second framing stage. A close reading of these conflicts, however, reveals a noticeable decline in intensity compared to stage one. Although articles in the second stage still frequently depict physicians and their patients as at odds, these disagreements—such as that between Elizabeth Bouvia and her doctors—center on unusual cases or those in which doctors feel pressured in unprecedented ways to act against established medical principles (e.g., in Bouvia's case helping a patient die who suffered from depression, but was neither dying nor in physical agony). Similarly, whereas doctors were often portrayed as complaining about the laws regulating euthanasia and fearful of legal reprisals for participating (or refusing to participate) in passive euthanasia in this stage, the bitterness and resentment toward "legal interference" characterizing the first stage is less in evidence. In their place is a sense of resignation and acceptance by the medical profession of legal oversight of euthanasia along with residual anxiety about the threat of lawsuits.

One obvious explanation for the relaxation of conflict between the medical community, patients, and the legal system reflected in this framing stage is that by the mid-1980s doctors had come to accept—and even join to some extent—the groundswell of legal, legislative, and public support for passive euthanasia in the United States. Also relieving some of the animosity were new laws in some states designed to protect doctors from euthanasia-related litigation. Perhaps the most important factor contributing to the easing of conflict between doctors and the legal system, however, concerns the revolutionary economic changes that had transformed the practice of medicine by the mid-1980s. Mergers and acquisitions in the medical industry heightened the focus on bottom-line profits. Meanwhile, managed care, caps on Medicaid and Medicare payments, and tightened restrictions on insurance reimbursements for hospitalized patients meant dwindling financial incentives previously attached to long-term hospitalization of dying and comatose patients. Whatever the source, it is clear that the medical community—which had fought bitterly in court to keep Quinlan on her respirator—made an abrupt about-face by the mid 1980s. By this stage medical authorities had begun actively supporting patients' "right to die" in court.[23]

Although a clear diminution in conflict is apparent between doctors and the legal system and between doctors and patients, internecine clashes among medical professionals over active euthanasia (PAS) were more in evidence in the second framing stage than the first. In the handful of news reports during this period that deal directly with PAS (rather than the feeding-tube controversy), there is new emphasis on conflict between doctors—virtually always over PAS. For example, publication of the aforementioned "It's Over Debbie" ignited a fusillade of criticism from doctors against both the author of the confessional piece and colleagues practicing PAS in secret. Clearly, by the end of the second major framing period, the stage was set for the heightened conflict between medical professionals that would characterize the next framing stage—that featuring Kevorkian's efforts to push PAS out of the closet and into mainstream medicine and society.

NOTES

1. When used alone, the term "euthanasia" refers to both passive and active euthanasia, including physician-assisted suicide (PAS).

2. Two of these medical frames, *No Legal Interference* and *Criminalizes Doctors*, have obvious legal, as well as medical associations. Because they reflect the interests of doctors and orthodox medicine rather than the legal system, however, they are considered medical frames in this study.

3. Because stories occasionally contained more than one dominant frame (e.g., medical and legal frames were equally strong), percentages and totals exceed the total number of stories analyzed.

4. As one euthanasia advocate writes, "The most compelling argument in favor of physician-assisted suicide has always been the one . . . that some conditions are so intolerable that the only relief is death" (Hall 1994, 12). Examples of such conditions include "severe instances of amyotrophic lateral sclerosis [Lou Gehrig's disease],

multiple scleroses, Parkinson's disease, Lupus, end-stage lung disease, and perhaps advanced brain cancer or gastric cancer."

5. Quality of life arguments draw on pragmatic justifications such as the notion that euthanasia candidates are "as good as dead anyway." The U.S. Supreme Court in *Quinlan*, in ruling that euthanasia is appropriate for a suffering or dying individual whose "life is without quality, purpose, or contribution and instead is filled with anxiety and pain," imbued the *Humane Treatment* frame—and its components, "death with dignity" and "quality of life"—with legal authority (*In re Quinlan*, 355 A.2d at 644. 1976 "The State's interest [in protecting life] weakens and the individual's right to privacy grows . . . as the prognosis dims. Ultimately there comes a point when the individual's rights overcome the State's interest.").

6. As suggested by this discussion, the *Humane Treatment* medical subframe also contains the argument that severe psychological pain justifies both passive euthanasia and PAS. Individuals with terminal or catastrophic medical conditions may suffer emotional distress stemming from loss of privacy and autonomy, physical immobility, lack of control over bodily functions, isolation from friends and family, loss of familiar daily routines, awareness of increasing dependence on medical technology, feelings of hopelessness and powerlessness, realization of mental and physical deterioration, anxiety about future pain, and the dread of burdening loved ones financially and emotionally. RTD advocates argue that legalizing euthanasia—including PAS—relieves such sources of psychological pain.

Even if patients never actually avail themselves of assisted suicide, RTD proponents argue that merely knowing they had this option would ease their psychological discomfort. Refuting the counterargument that better palliative care would render euthanasia unnecessary, RTD advocates stress that PAS remains the most compassionate action even for those patients who are in no physical pain, but whose gradual deterioration has so lessened their powers and autonomy that they are no longer "human" in any meaningful sense.

7. According to Gamson (1988a), counterframes circulated by challenger social movements such as the pro-life movement in the euthanasia controversy seldom if ever achieve dominance in news coverage unless major events provide an opening for them.

8. Specifically, American society recognizes the right of individuals to "life, liberty, and the pursuit of happiness." Euthanasia advocates argue that this means not only the freedom to make choices about marriage, careers, child-rearing, and education, but also about the circumstances surrounding death. Indeed, they argue, the fact that society grants individuals the right to refuse medical treatment or life-support systems provides evidence of Constitutional recognition of a "good death" as an integral part of the overall pursuit of happiness. Moreover, it is only the dying who are qualified to determine whether their lives are worth living.

9. The right to both passive and active forms of euthanasia—as well as DNR orders, living wills, and advance medical directives—are all based on the individual-autonomy frame.

10. As one Catholic theologian elaborating on the "duty to die" theme writes, the "autonomous" choice of PAS or passive euthanasia is seldom if ever made by individuals, but rather is "subtly or not so subtly influenced by others: This notion of the isolated, self-sufficient individual endowed with the right to privacy is a fiction. There is the fallacious implication that the isolated individual possesses a freedom that has no inherent connect to an order of truth that transcends the self. The radical rights rhetoric promotes an ethical relativism that is destructive of the common bonds necessary for maintaining human dignity and social order" (Bernardi 1995, 14).

11. It is important to note that although issue stages may be rather clearly delineated,

they typically proceed neither linearly nor without overlap. In many ways framing stages (and the issue cycles within which they operate) exemplify what physicists refer to as "highly complex systems." Like the weather and similar natural phenomena, framing patterns are affected by relatively small and unpredictable forces and are shaped by a plethora of variables. As such, they defy researchers' attempts to pin down their precise beginnings and endings, much less make accurate predictions about their future paths. Out of the "chaos" of news frame dynamics, however, definite patterns are discernible. Although framing stages typically proceed nonsequentially, it is possible with careful, systematic analysis to isolate and extract specific patterns or motifs from the stream of news discourse in order to evaluate their meanings and significance.

12. The phrase "right to die" was surprisingly common in *New York Times* headlines in the years leading up to the *Quinlan* case. For example, in 1968 the paper published an article with the headline, "The Right of a Patient to Die Stressed to Medical Graduates" (2 June 1968, 57). In 1972, an op/ed piece appeared with the headline, "The Right to Die with Dignity" (Josephs, 25 Sept. 1971, 31). And three headlines containing the phrase appeared in 1973 alone ("Physicians Back the Right to Die," 26 Apr. 1973; "A Patient's 'Right to Die' Upheld in Suit on Surgery," 8 June 1973; "The Right to Die," 3 July 1973).

13. Predicting that the show would "touch off a heated controversy," a *New York Times* article declared that "in allowing a doctor to practice euthanasia, the segment has not only broken new ground for a television series, it had gone beyond the Hollywood movie-code, which is generally more liberal than television's code." According to the article, Dr. Kildare switched off life-support equipment keeping a "patient in a terminal coma" alive. The show was "subjected to considerable discussion" and obtained the approval of the AMA before being filmed (Schumach 1963, 7).

14. "Master frames" are highly resonant frames such as "individual rights" used by a spectrum of related social movements to mobilize activists (Snow and Benford 1992). It is in the initial stage of news coverage that the discursive boundaries of a new social problem or issue is fixed; journalists select among master frames distributed by social activists and interest groups early in an issue's cycle. The *Right to Die* master frame is part of a larger rights discourse that has mobilized social movements since the 1950s Civil Rights movement. Abortion discourse appears to have played a particularly strong role in shaping both RTD activists' and the news media's choice of the "rights" master frame for the euthanasia controversy (see, e.g., Condit 1990; Grindstaff 1994). Euthanasia and abortion share a number of common traits: Both are opposed by the same religious groups (e.g., the Roman Catholic Church and fundamentalist Christian organizations); both consist of "pro-life" factions that draw primarily on religious frames and "pro-choice" factions that draw primarily on "rights" rhetoric to advance their respective ideologies; both are fundamentally concerned with questions involving the relationship of the human body to major institutions of control (specifically established medicine and government); both are fueled by (largely unspoken) economic considerations; and the courts have used similar legal justifications in ruling on both controversies.

15. It is telling, for instance, that both the first story included in this research (Clark and Agrest 1975) and a story published twenty-two years later (Van Biema 1997) use the identical headline: "Is There a Right to Die?" A number of synonyms for the "right to die" also appear consistently in all stages of coverage, including "the right of self-determination," "the guarantee of liberty," "patient sovereignty," "self-deliverance," "the right to decide when to die," and "the right to control the circumstances of death." Another RTD catchphrase, "death with dignity," is also a staple of all framing stages, although it appears less frequently than "right to die." Somewhat surprisingly, the

appearance of a third common catchphrase used by RTD supporters—"quality of life"—is relatively rare in news stories in this study, although its message (that comatose or dying patients connected to life support systems have lost the essence of what it means to be "alive") is an underlying theme of most news articles on euthanasia and is a particularly strong subtext of anecdotes journalists selected to personalize and dramatize the euthanasia controversy.

16. Two explanations exist for the drop in frequency of these terms by the third framing stage in the 1990s: First, it is possible that the concept of "heroic" or "extraordinary measures" was sufficiently ingrained in public awareness by the early 1990s that journalists no longer felt the need to use these terms. The second—and more reasonable explanation—is that by the early 1990s these procedures had become "ordinary" rather than "extraordinary" in most hospitals in the United States. Most hospitals by this time also had policies in place by this time officially recognizing advance directives (e.g., living wills). The Patient Self-Determination Act of 1990, which went into effect in 1991, required all hospitals to ask Medicare and Medicaid patients about their end-of-life preferences. These developments undoubtedly resulted in fewer complaints—and hence fewer anecdotes to include in news stories—about hospitals and doctors extending the lives of dying patients through "extraordinary" or "heroic" measures.

17. Although the repetitive use of these terms might also simply be considered yet another example of journalists resorting to "lazy" or shopworn phrases under deadline pressures. Even if this is the case, clearly the cognitive effect on readers remains the same.

18. For example, among the most vocal opponents of legalized euthanasia and PAS have been disability-rights groups, such as Not Dead Yet, which argue against legalized euthanasia on the basis that it would increase pressure on disabled individuals to "take the so-called option of [euthanasia] when they're denied the healthcare treatments and supports they deserve" (Coleman 1999).

19. This is yet another example that illustrates how various medical   subframes are typically interwoven in news stories in this analysis.

20. *Bouvia v. Superior Court*, 179 Cal. App. 3d 1127; 225 Cal. Rptr. 297 (1986).

21. *Cruzan v. Director, Missouri Department of Health*, 110 S. Ct. 2841 (1990).

22. As it turned out, Bouvia did not go through with her suicide plan.

23. As an early reviewer of this book pointed out, the early 1980s also witnessed an increased willingness on the part of physicians to recognize patients' "right to know" their medical prognoses. Before the 1980s, according to the reviewer, the AMA's position was that it was up to doctors to decide whether to reveal the "truth" about their patients' medical conditions. As the reviewer suggests, these related trends—increased support by physicians both for a "right to die" and for a "right to know"—are likely outgrowths of the broader consumer-rights movement led by Ralph Nader in the United States in the 1970s.

CHAPTER 5

THE "BAD DOCTOR" AND THE "GOOD DEATH": NEWS FRAMING OF KEVORKIAN

> Society is and always has been...a symbolic action system, a
> structure of statuses and roles, customs and rules for behavior,
> designed to serve as a vehicle for earthly heroism.
> —Becker (1973, 4–5)

At the same time that social movements rely on the press to call attention to their agendas, the news media rely on protest movements to "help fill the daily news hole and aid the medium in its key business of selling attentive audiences to advertisers" (Molotch 1979, 71). Within this ritualistic exchange, journalists frequently focus on individual activists to drive the news narrative, infuse stories with novelty, conflict, drama, and action, and imbue events and issues with symbolic meaning. News coverage of Dr. Jack Kevorkian, the right-to-die (RTD) activist and retired pathologist whose exploits dominated news coverage of euthanasia throughout most of the 1990s, offers a case study of this dynamic.

Kevorkian's activities, meanwhile, provide a primer on the successful exploitation of the news media by a single social movement actor. Casting himself in the role of provocateur, Kevorkian put his subversive "suicide machine" and guerrilla-style tactics to impressive use, accomplishing in the space of a few years what had eluded generations of RTD activists before him. Kevorkian initially made national headlines on 4 June 1990, after he used a drug-dispensing device to assist in the suicide of Janet Adkins, a fifty-four-year-old Oregon woman diagnosed with Alzheimer's. During the eight years following this openly transgressive act, he launched an unprecedented assault on the medical establishment, Michigan law, and the sensibilities of everyone from religious and political leaders to philosophers and medical ethicists. By 1999, when Michigan prosecutors finally convicted him (after three failed attempts), he had assisted in some 130 suicides, exposed the medical establishment's widespread, clandestine use of physician-assisted suicide (PAS), thrust the issue of PAS onto the national agenda, and forced the American public to confront the stark exigencies of medicalized and technologized death.

The purpose of this chapter is two-fold. First, it offers a discussion of a major contribution of this book—the advancement of a theory about the role news "frame eruptions" play in social change. In addition, chapter 5 offers insights into the ways in which news framing of Kevorkian helped shape public consensus on the euthanasia debate during perhaps the most critical period in the controversial issue's cycle—the first half of the 1990s, when the country awaited the U.S. Supreme Court's first ruling on the constitutionality of a "right to die."[1] Freighted with symbolic and ideological meaning, the national debate over Kevorkian's activities and—more broadly—over social and legal recognition of a "right to die," represents a site of cultural contestation, renegotiation, and redefinition. As Nakagawa (1993) observes, "Stories that describe or account for a social crisis, that is, when a community's fundamental beliefs and values are challenged or called into question, provide perhaps the best opportunity to examine underlying systems of coherence and sense making" (p. 146).

FRAMING STAGES, SOCIAL CHANGE, AND THE ROLE OF "FRAME ERUPTIONS"

A fundamental catalyst for this book concerns the question of how public debate on euthanasia advanced in such a rapid, and yet unheralded manner, completing the cycle from "Should we pull the plug?" to "Should we allow physicians to inject dying individuals with lethal drugs?" in less than two decades. Of particular interest are the mechanisms that allow major social shifts to take place behind a cultural "shroud" that camouflages their precise steps and—more importantly—masks emerging dominant ideologies and positions. To express this in another way, how is it that social change tends to unfold on a largely invisible plane, with its specific constituents remaining largely opaque to average Americans?

Because the answers to these questions rest on the interaction of a highly complex set of forces, they are essentially unanswerable. Analysis of the specific framing stages that mark news coverage, however, provides valuable insights into social change processes. A major contribution of this research is the notion of "frame eruption"—conceptualized as a break in the "stream" of news initiated by the unexpected introduction of a (usually sensational) news story that not only disrupts the pattern of framing in process, but presages, foreshadows, or perhaps even serves as a catalyst for fully articulated future frames. Such a frame eruption occurred in the late 1980s, a framing stage devoted primarily to questions involving passive euthanasia—specifically, removal of food and hydration from comatose and gravely ill patients to expedite death. During this framing stage occasional news articles addressing active euthanasia appeared—such as when a celebrity obtained PAS to avoid a prolonged hospital death or a physician who helped a patient die was charged with murder (see, e.g., Jacoby and Miller 1988, 101). The result of such incidents was the brief foregrounding of active euthanasia in a primarily passive stage. It is hypothesized here that the more "shocking" or fundamentally disruptive the nature of these frame anomalies, the greater their potential to accelerate the movement of issues across frame-stage boundaries. Of course, the more rapid the movement of an issue such as the euthanasia controversy across frame-stage borders, the more expedited the social change process.

In addition to illuminating some of the elements driving the speed and direction of social change, observation of journalists' attempts to deal with "frame eruptions" in the stories investigated for this book affords insights into the news media's role in mystifying the mechanisms of social change. As reporters and editors struggled to contain disparate and contradictory euthanasia-related developments into the existing "package" of news frames, they were faced with the task of planing off rough edges and inconsistencies to create a fluid narrative. Part of the job of telling news stories, in fact, may well involve the largely unconscious task of smoothing over the "seams" caused by the constant incorporation of novel events, facts, and other developments into news about social issues. Journalists weave the new with the old and the disruptive with the routine for several reasons: (1) to preserve the illusion of narrative or frame fidelity—the sense of "flow" that characterizes news coverage (see, e.g., Williams 1975); (2) to maintain a sense of social stability or order (the social control function of the news media); and (3) to enhance their own credibility by avoiding the appearance of confusion or disorientation.[2] The notion of frame eruptions helps explain why social change, as both filtered by and manifested through news frames, is often simultaneously dramatic and yet "commonsensical." Frame eruptions and journalists' reactions to them, then, offer a partial explanation of how the news media facilitate social change while simultaneously effacing or obscuring their own role in the process.

An example of a particularly jarring (and hence change-accelerating) frame eruption occurred with the 1988 publication of the provocative article "It's Over Debbie" in a major medical journal (Anonymous 1988). As discussed at the end of the previous chapter, this article was written by a physician who admitted practicing PAS on a patient who had given less than overt consent. Highly controversial, the article triggered intensive news coverage of *active euthanasia* during a *passive euthanasia* frame stage. The fact that the article was written by a physician—a member of the elite group of institutional and official sources that journalists rely on most heavily in covering the news—compounded its ultimate impact on framing of the euthanasia controversy. Despite the ethically questionable nature of the anonymous physician's actions and the fact that reporters were still in the midst of grappling with passive euthanasia at the time the article was published, reporters were forced by journalistic norms to grant immediate respectability not only to the doctor who authored this article, but to his justifications and arguments supporting PAS. The interjection of "It's Over Debbie" into the passive-euthanasia news stream forced journalists to circulate new pro-PAS arguments from a credible source and, in doing so, challenge established cultural norms and images of physicians as healers.

Consequently, "It's Over Debbie" may be understood as fundamentally disrupting the passive-euthanasia framing cycle in progress. As such, it played a critical role in preparing the ideological and discursive ground for the emergence of a crucial frame shift. Two years later, when images of Kevorkian's subversive "suicide machine" and guerrilla-style PAS fixed the issue of active euthanasia indelibly into the American psyche, what appears to have been an immediate shift in news frame focus from passive to active euthanasia occurred. Based on the "frame eruption" hypothesis advanced above, however, it is unlikely that Kevorkian's impact on news media framing would have been as profound had "It's Over Debbie" not already primed the news media and sowed the ideological seeds for future frames.

STAGE THREE: DEBATE OVER ACTIVE EUTHANASIA (PAS), 1990–97

With the dramatic entry of Dr. Jack Kevorkian onto the media stage in June 1990, framing of euthanasia in the nationally distributed news media sources in this study shifted rapidly from an emphasis on passive euthanasia to preoccupation with active euthanasia (PAS). News discourse previously devoted to questions related to "pulling the plug" or the feeding-tube controversy now focused on "whether doctors . . . should be allowed to prescribe lethal doses of medication or actively help mortally ill patients end their lives" (van Biema 1997, 149). Although, as discussed in chapter 4, the ground had previously been prepared for this transition, what is most remarkable about Kevorkian's rise to media prominence is the speed with which he and PAS-related stories supplanted discourse on passive euthanasia. By the mid 1990s, based on investigation of the articles in this study, journalists considered passive euthanasia—including the "feeding tube" controversy—a *fait accompli*, a taken-for-granted aspect of modern death and dying that had all but completed its discursive life cycle.[3]

In little more than a decade, then, the mainstream, national news media included in this analysis had virtually dispensed with passive euthanasia as the focus of thoughtful debate. By framing passive euthanasia initially as a medical problem, then as a routine medical practice fully integrated into the American way of death, and finally as an individual rights issue, journalists effectively polished over the rough, contradictory edges of what remains a morally complex, ambiguous, and highly consequential social problem. By 1990 passive euthanasia had become what Butler (1999) refers to as an ideology that passes for common sense. News reports in the third framing stage—when they mentioned passive euthanasia at all—depict the medical community as having reached broad consensus on "pulling the plug," withholding nutrition and hydration, DNRs, and other practices that come under the rubric of passive euthanasia. As one 1990 article summarizes, the medical community had by this time come "to accept the view that terminally ill patients should not be kept alive by technological intervention" (Beck et al. 1990, 46). In a rather remarkable attempt not only to establish passive euthanasia as a non-issue, but to redefine its meaning, another reporter deemed the practice, "not suicide, or euthanasia, for both of those mean ending life. It is rather, a desire to end dying, to pass gently into the night without tubes running down the nose and a

ventilator insistently inflating lungs that have grown weary from the insult."
Representing euthanasia as a simple medical option, the reporter later added that
"just as tubal feeding, or surgery or a ventilator is a medical option, so is death"
(Begley and Starr 1991, 42).

Even more striking, however, are the many examples in this stage of
journalists' efforts to represent active euthanasia (PAS) as having achieved
widespread consensus among both medical professionals and the public.
Statistics on public support for euthanasia—relatively rare in the first framing
stage—became a common feature of third-stage news reports. In addition to
citing an opinion poll to buttress the claim that "Assisted suicide appears to be
gaining public support," one article, for example, offered statistics on the
dramatic rise in RTD organization membership. The same story also cited
survey results showing that over half of American lawyers "thought that giving
lethal injections to terminal patients who request it should be legal" (Beck 1990,
46).

Along with consensus-building for PAS, journalists brought a variety of other
framing strategies to bear on the subtle promotion of PAS that characterizes
third-stage framing in this study. One technique involved the pro-RTD wording
of headlines such as "Should We Not Go Gentle?" (1994), "A Lesson in Dying
Well" (1994); and "I Want to Draw the Line Myself" (1997). Other headlines
were equally clear on the directionality of the frame being advanced. The
headline, "Defining the Right to Die," for instance, reflects the pro-PAS position
that the debate has moved beyond questions of the suitability of PAS to the need
for standards to control its use (Lemonick 1996, 82). Articulated through the
pro-RTD medical subframe, *Standards Needed*, this headline (and the news text
itself) strongly suggests that PAS—much like passive euthanasia during the
second framing stage—had already progressed from the exploratory stage to the
regulatory phase. The implication of both headline and news text is that the only
substantive question remaining—within a mere half dozen years after
Kevorkian's first assisted suicide—is how best to fine-tune the procedure to
avoid abuses and protect "good," compassionate physicians from lawsuits.

The *Standards Needed* subframe is dominant in other third-stage articles, as
well, including a 1997 *Time* magazine story that attempts to apply lessons about
PAS learned in the Netherlands to the United States. Like the article discussed
above, this news story argues that American society should move beyond
discussions of the pros and cons of active euthanasia and begin establishing
"strict safeguards to any law legalizing voluntary euthanasia" (Branegan 1997,
31). In the Netherlands, it instructs, "there is an acceptance of the phenomenon
. . . . There's less discussion of the pros and cons, and more about how to control
it." The story's clear support of the Netherlands' pragmatic approach to PAS is
also evident in its concluding paragraphs:

When Hink [a Dutch PAS recipient] first asked to be put to death, the doctors refused, but
after a few more months and more requests, . . . the doctor administered the poison. "He
just faded away," [his wife said]. "I'm convinced we did the right thing. He died a good
death."

That's what euthanasia means in Greek, good death. For the Netherlands, it's also good policy. Other countries will have to decide for themselves, but surely the Dutch style of open debate about a painful and difficult topic is the best way to do so. (Branegan 1997, 31)

The pro-PAS framing of this passage is evident from its lead sentence, which constructs Dutch physicians as rational and cautious in prescribing lethal drugs to patients requesting PAS ("the doctor refused, but after a few more months and more requests . . . "). Next, through a quote by the dead patient's wife, the passage links PAS to a "good death." The phrase, "That's what euthanasia means in Greek, good death. For the Netherlands, its also good policy," further cements the marriage of these ideas. Finally, although the reporter tacks on the caveat, "Other countries will have to decide for themselves," the undeniable message is that what is "good policy" for the Netherlands is also "good policy" for the United States.

Framing of Kevorkian

Although this study's results show that journalists in the third framing stage used a variety of framing strategies to promote social and legal acceptance of PAS, this favorable framing clearly does not extend to Kevorkian himself—the RTD movement's most visible, notorious, and some would say, effective spokesperson. Even the most untrained observer scanning news accounts of Kevorkian during the first three years following his first assisted suicide is likely to conclude he was the target of caustic character assaults. Indeed, this is the finding of the present analysis, which concludes that framing of Kevorkian is overtly derogatory in the first three years following his 1990 assisted suicide of Alzheimer's patient Janet Adkins. This, of course, raises the question of how news frames can simultaneously promote PAS while denigrating its key spokesperson. Given the press's unflattering treatment of Kevorkian, he seems an unlikely catalyst for social acceptance of PAS. In the eyes of many Americans, however, he was a national hero who not only forced the issue of PAS out of the "closet" and onto the public forum, but will likely be remembered as one of the most powerful change agents in recent history. What these incongruities and the results of this analysis suggest is that Kevorkian's role in news framing of PAS is considerably more nuanced than it appears on the surface.

There is no doubt that Kevorkian was greeted by a hostile press when he burst onto the media stage in 1990. Kevorkian himself, in a speech before the American Humanist Association in 1994, had this to say about his treatment in the press: "You must understand that the entire mainstream media, especially in the first year or two, were totally against what I'm doing. Entirely! It was unanimous. They tried to make my work look very negative . . . They insulted and denigrated me . . . Now isn't it strange that on a controversial subject of this magnitude—one that cuts across many disciplines—the entire editorial policy of the country is on one side?" (p. 7).

Responding to his assisted suicide of Adkins in the back of a rusting van, the press dubbed Kevorkian "Dr. Death" and framed him as an aberrant and vaguely menacing presence. The first article about Kevorkian in *Time*, for example, depicts him as "a pugnacious maverick" with questionable motives—including a macabre interest in "harvesting" body parts from the deceased. Elaborating on this theme, the author states that "among other things" Kevorkian had once concocted "a scheme whereby doctors would render death-row patients unconscious so their living bodies could be used for medical experiments" (Gibbs June 1990, 69). An article titled, "The Odd Odyssey of 'Dr. Death,'" published in *USNWR* the same year describes Kevorkian as a "once promising pathologist" who is now "more aptly cast as the lonely monster than the benevolent doctor" (Borger 1990, 27–28). Another early Kevorkian story stresses his "long history of controversial views includ[ing] advocating that death-row prisoners be rendered unconscious and used for medical experiments" (Beck et al. 1990, 46). A story published the following year depicts him as a zealot, a "cheap purveyor of easy death," and "a man more obsessed with the justice of his cause than with the interests of his patients" (Gibbs 1991, 78).

As might be expected of the nation's "paper of record," *The New York Times* coverage of Kevorkian is more nuanced than that of the national news magazines examined in this research. The *Times*, however, also framed Kevorkian as something of a freak, an outsider with dark motivations and a shadowy past. The first story the *Times* ran on Kevorkian, which appeared on page one, represented Kevorkian's assisted suicide of Adkins not as an act of compassion or commitment to an ethical cause, but within the context of similar "clashes" he had had with the medical establishment in the past, including being fired after proposing that death row inmates be used for medical experiments (Belkin 1990, A1). In a story published the next day, the *Times* elaborated on Kevorkian's "outcast" status, portraying him as a man whose "renegade ideas on such things as euthanasia and medical experimentation on death-row prisoners have frightened hospitals" and made him all but unemployable. This story also focuses on the idiosyncracies of Kevorkian's lifestyle, including details about his apartment that create a less-than-flattering image: "It is here amid meager furnishings, including a light fixture dangling from the ceiling by a coat hanger and a chair covered with fabric tacked on with safety pins, that Dr. Kevorkian came up with the suicide device that has been widely criticized by physicians and medical ethicists" (Wilkerson 1990, A16). An article by the same reporter published the following year in the *Times* includes quotes describing Kevorkian as "Dr. Death . . . somebody who wants to be Dr. God" and as "a man with a cause, and the cause is immoral, unethical and very dangerous" (Wilkerson 1991, A10).

The pattern of abandonment of objectivity on the part of reporters covering Kevorkian remains in evidence three years later in articles such as one that inventories his creepy past, suspicious motives, "checkered" career as a pathologist, and bizarre obsessions. "Kevorkian's obsession with death goes beyond his self-appointed missions of mercy to an enthusiasm for the macabre," this article states, including a "fascination with the mechanics of capital punishment," an interest in "experimenting on people while they are still alive—particularly on their brains," and a proposal to allow "condemned convicts to volunteer for 'painless' medical experiments that would begin while they were alive but which would eventually be fatal" (Hosenball 1993, 28). Another 1993 article refers to Kevorkian as "a mad scientist," "a walking advertisement for designer death," "the devil that doctors deserve," "Death's Impresario," and America's "most prominent 'obitiatrist'" (Gibbs 1993, 34).

Nowhere does coverage of Kevorkian stray farther from journalistic norms of "objectivity," however, than in a 1992 article that enumerates Kevorkian's grotesque array of "pathological interests" and "surreal" artistic pursuits, including paintings that use "actual human blood that Kevorkian salvaged from outdated samples at the local blood band, and from his own arm" (Gibbs 1992, 36). The following passage from this article provides a dramatic demonstration of the pejorative depths to which journalists sometimes sank in framing Kevorkian in the early 1990s:

Dr. Jack Kevorkian has spent much of his medical life searching for ways to make better use of human bodies, especially dead ones. Thirty years ago, as a young pathologist . . . he became the first doctor to transfuse blood directly from a corpse into a live patient. He marveled at the possible uses—on battlefields, for instance, or during a natural disaster—and lamented the fact that a public distaste for the procedure would probably preclude its clinical acceptance.

Over time he turned his attention to patients who were soon to be dead, looking to salvage whatever he could. The execution of condemned murders seemed an extravagant waste, since controversial drugs and surgical techniques could be tested on criminal volunteers. (Gibbs 1992, 36)

What explains the overtly negative way in which Kevorkian was represented in the news stories in this study? And how does this lack of objectivity in coverage of an RTD activist square with this study's overall finding that news stories as a whole overwhelmingly promoted pro-RTD frames and ideologies? Schudson (1995) offers insights to the first of these questions. Reporters, he observes, feel justified in vacating their vaunted journalistic obligations to fairness and accuracy when covering social movements or movement activists—such as Kevorkian—whom they consider inhabitants of the "zone of deviance." Movements and activists deemed outside the mainstream "can be ridiculed, marginalized, or trivialized without giving a hearing to 'both sides' because reporters instinctively realize that they are beyond the pale—like the women's movement in its earliest years" (p. 13).[4]

The response to the second question is a bit more complex. Given the numerous examples of hostile framing of Kevorkian in the first several years after his initial assisted suicide, a reasonable conclusion might be that he represented a liability rather than an asset to the RTD movement and its agenda. Ironically, however, in much the same way that negative news framing of Bouvia failed to hurt the RTD cause, the beating Kevorkian took in the press failed to sway the public against him—and more importantly—against PAS. As he notes in the speech cited earlier, the insults and ridicule heaped upon him by the press "didn't work . . . According to the polls, people may be split 50–50 on what they think of me, but they are three-to-one in favor of [PAS], and that's never changed" (Kevorkian 1994, 7).

The disparity between the press's negative framing of Kevorkian and the public's growing acceptance of PAS offers insights into the way in which contested meanings are negotiated in news stories. One way to explain this incongruity is that, paralleling the media's unflattering framing of Kevorkian, is a contradictory frame rooted in invisible "deep structure" cultural forces. Here, the concept of "pentimento"—the layering of one painting over another in a way that both are revealed—proves instructive (Arney and Bergen 1984). In this alternate, parallel framing, Kevorkian is not the ghoulish "Dr. Death" whose interest in the macabre approaches the pathological. Instead, subtextual references evoke the unspoken yet powerful mythos of the "lone gunslinger," the anti-hero whose outsider status and eccentricities not only fail to mitigate his power, but give him special license to confront the mammoth institutions of law and medicine on behalf of the "common" man and woman.[5] Evoking just such a one-man crusade, a 1996 article analyzed in this study concludes that "Dr. Death's . . . relations with organized medicine have always been as mutually contemptuous as his relations with courts, churches, and anything else that's organized" (Sheed 1996, 80). As manifest in such characters as Jimmy Stewart in "Mr. Smith Goes to Washington," Sylvester Stallone in "Rambo," or a host of similar popular culture icons, this highly resonant myth calls forth the penultimate American values of individualism and human rights, as well as outrage at the offenses committed by impersonal institutions.[6]

The archetype of the social outcast who lobs grenades over the walls of injustice—among the most powerful frames available to activists and journalists in constructing social problems—helps shed light on two enigmas concerning PAS. The first is the question of why—given consistent negative framing of Kevorkian in the media—he was able to achieve the status of a populist hero. And the second is how a man dubbed "Dr. Death," portrayed as a ghoulish, death-obsessed, sensation-seeking zealot who flouts both deeply rooted cultural taboos and the law, was so successful in creating support for PAS as an appropriate alternative for painful, prolonged, "technologized" death in a hospital.

Recognizing Kevorkian's mythic status as part of a rival script or frame opens interesting possibilities. In essence, the heroic individualism inadvertently conferred on Kevorkian by journalists conflicted with and may well have overridden the press's negative portrait of him. Under this theory the outlaw image and underworld sensibilities attributed to the Kevorkian character actually lent authenticity to his mythic hero status. As it turns out, the brand of distorted heroism he represented, as well as the news media's portrayal of him as an anti-hero, proved remarkably in sync with the zeitgeist of late-twentieth-century America. This help explains the contradiction between Kevorkian's resonance and appeal with the public and journalists' contemptuous treatment of him.

There is yet another explanation, however, for the paradoxical nature of Kevorkian's role in the PAS debate. In a way that is uncannily similar to framing of Elizabeth Bouvia during the second framing stage, Kevorkian functions in euthanasia news coverage as a symbol or boundary marker who, rather than mitigating arguments for social and legal acceptance of PAS, bolsters them by marking out the parameters of "good" versus "bad" PAS. Just as Bouvia was framed as an exception to the general rule that withdrawing food and water "makes sense" as an end-of-life option for individuals whose "quality of life" is diminished beyond repair, Kevorkian proves the exception to rule that the practice of PAS under normal circumstances (read: by "good doctors") deserves social and legal support. Cast in the role of the "fallen" healer, Kevorkian stands in stark relief to "humane" doctors who have for decades risked their professional careers and criminal prosecution to relieve their patients' pain and suffering by administering overdoses of narcotics to end their lives.

As if to underscore this very theme, journalists in the news articles investigated in this study strived to distance Kevorkian from other doctors who practice PAS. When the American Medical Association (AMA)—America's most powerful physicians' organization—affirmed its opposition to PAS in 1983 and again in 1996, one AMA member told a group of delegates that his colleagues "fear speaking out [about the pervasive practice of PAS among physicians] because we don't want to be painted with the same brush as Dr. Kevorkian" (Stern 1996, 1). Given the dominance of medical sources in euthanasia coverage, it is not surprising that journalists would mirror the concerns of the medical establishment by attempting to set Kevorkian apart from the rest of the medical community. One of the first stories on Kevorkian in this study, for instance, offered the assessment that "Kevorkian is not like other doctors . . . [M]uch of the medical community would . . . reject Kevorkian's solution, fearing the damage that would be done if doctors routinely acted as executioners" (Gibbs 18 June 1990, 69). Another news story titled "The Real Jack Kevorkian," struggled to position Kevorkian relative to other doctors, locating him finally "on the far-out fringe, not just of medicine but of American culture" (Hosenball 1993, 28).

It is also not unexpected that journalists covering PAS would attempt to repair and restore the reputations of medical professionals possibly tarnished by Kevorkian by carving out a deep divide between "good" and "bad" PAS practitioners. Two articles were chosen as examples of this phenomenon. The first is a 1996 article in *Time* magazine that features a prototypical "good doctor" who practices PAS. Like Kevorkian, the doctor at the center of this news story believes passionately that PAS is the most compassionate solution for patients "in terrible agony." But unlike Kevorkian, this doctor is a benign, avuncular family physician who has performed PAS in private for twenty-five years (Lemonick 1996, 82). It is difficult to imagine this wholly sympathetic depiction of a "good doctor" who practices PAS—which was published some six years after Kevorkian's first assisted suicide—without Kevorkian's contribution to public understanding of what a "bad" doctor who practices PAS looks like. In this context, perhaps Kevorkian's most enduring and profound impact is not the way in which he forced the truth about the practice of PAS into public discourse, but the means he provided the news media to define "bad" PAS—and hence make the notion of "good" PAS possible.

The effort to reconstruct the image of both the medical profession and "good" doctors who practice PAS is also apparent in a *New York Times* profile of Dr. Timothy Quill (the physician who made national headlines after he published a 1992 article in *The New England Journal of Medicine* describing his use of PAS to end a patient's life). The *Times* article repeatedly contrasts the "quiet," "thoughtful," and respected Quill (referred to in the story's lead sentence as "more Marcus Welby than Jack Kevorkian") with the self-serving, publicity-seeking Kevorkian, portrayed as a medical outcast who forges short-term, impersonal relationships with the "clients" whose deaths he brings about with his crudely built device. Both Quill's "long, rich doctor-patient relationship[s]" and his previous experience running a hospice for the dying, the article notes, set "Dr. Quill apart from Dr. Kevorkian, the Michigan pathologist who first meets his clients when they request help in dying . . . " (Gross 1997, A12). Also note in the following passage how the article contrasts Quill with Kevorkian, a framing technique that not only effectively establishes Quill as a "good doctor," but promotes PAS, which Quill openly advocates:

Even the fiercest critics of assisted suicide say Dr. Quill's approach is thoughtful and his credentials are impeccable. He is a professor of medicine and psychiatry at the University of Rochester, the associate director of medicine at the Genesee Hospital and a general practitioner . . . .

"He is a good representative of what ought to happen [with PAS], because death is not his subspecialty but an integrated part of his practice . . . He treats someone as a whole person, not an anticipatory corpse," as opposed to Dr. Kevorkian and others "who have a stake in finding clients and justifying their own existence." (Gross 1997, A12)

Kevorkian is not used solely by the news media in this study to promote PAS by distinguishing "good" from "bad" PAS, however. Equally significant is the role journalists assign him in redefining and repositioning the RTD movement itself as a mainstream organization. For example, Derek Humphry—the founder of the Hemlock Society and the RTD leader who before Kevorkian was depicted as on the outermost fringes of the movement—comes across as positively respectable compared to Kevorkian. Several articles about Kevorkian include quotes from RTD spokespeople, including Humphry, who openly criticize Kevorkian. One, for example, quotes Humphry as saying, "We're not lawbreakers [like Kevorkian], we're law reformers" (Gibbs 1992, 36). Another story includes a quote by a Hemlock Society official who describes Kevorkian's methods as "ad hoc," "wide open for abuse," and the reason right-to-die laws are needed (Wilkerson 1991, A10). After asserting that Kevorkian does not work "very well as a symbol for the euthanasia debate," yet another news report contrasts Kevorkian's goals and tactics with those of the "death with dignity" movement: "Even groups that sponsor 'death with dignity' legislation were careful to include safeguards to prevent the laws from being abused . . . ' Even the staunchest proponents of physician-assisted suicide should be horrified at [the Janet Adkins] case because there were no procedural protections'" (Gibbs 18 June 1990, 69). An even more obvious effort to distinguish Kevorkian from the larger RTD movement was made in another lengthy story in-depth story (Belkin 1990, 50). This article's lead contrasts the methods, motivations, and temperament of Kevorkian with those of Ralph Mero, the co-founder of the RTD organization Compassion in Dying. Whereas Kevorkian is characterized as "strange . . . reckless, unrestrained, flagrant," Mero is described as "cautious, a deliberate man who . . . speaks with quiet understatement." Observe how the reporter further applies the good-guy/bad-guy model to the two RTD activists and, in the process, simultaneously champions Mero's brand of PAS and discredits Kevorkian's:

Mero and other members of Compassion have set up . . . written guidelines that cover every detail, from how patients are chosen to how many Compassion members will attend an assisted death. Almost everything about the rules, in fact the very existence of the rules, can be seen as a determined contrast to Jack Kevorkian . . . "Dr. Kevorkian provides no information about how he selects the patients he chooses to help, no overall framework or guidelines. To many people, his penchant for publicity appears unseemly, and appears designed to focus attention on him rather than on the greater issue, that suffering people have the right to choose." (Belkin 1990, 50)

Although stories in the third framing stage show clear signs of journalists' efforts to restore the medical establishment's authority and credibility in the aftermath of Kevorkian, an intriguing finding of this study is that doctors themselves came under harsher treatment in the third stage than in the two previous framing stages. Accompanying the promotional framing of PAS in the third stage is a subtle, yet discernible chill in depictions of doctors and established medicine generally. It is almost as if the news media, as a primary institution for the maintenance of social control in American society, reacted to the social disruption caused by Kevorkian by lashing out at the medical community, whose unchecked technologies and insensitivity to patient needs effectively spawned "Dr. Death." As discussed earlier in this chapter, reporters and editors in early-stage articles maintained a careful distinction between blaming medical technology and blaming doctors and the medical establishment for the euthanasia "problem." In contrast, reporters in the third stage were noticeably less reticent about assigning responsibility for Kevorkian (and the havoc he wreaked in the legal, judicial, and medical realms) to doctors and medicine generally.

A particularly strong example of this is found in a news story that directly blames the increased demand for PAS on doctors' "mistreatment" of their patients. This article employs a quote from a doctor to provide evidence of medicine's culpability in the rise of Kevorkian as an American hero: "'We don't treat [patients] well, and they know it.' This mistreatment . . . is a combination of deceit, insensitivity and neglect," the doctor admits. "[D]octors ignore their patients' suffering." Faced with such mishandling of patients, the article continues, "Is it any wonder Kevorkian has hundreds of letters from people who want him to help them die?" (Gibbs 1993, 34). Equally condemning of the medical profession is the news story's suggestion that healthcare workers are out of touch not only with their patients' wishes, but with important legal developments affecting patients:

Many health-care workers knew little about new laws that allowed them to withhold or withdraw machines like respirators and kidney machines or even feeding tubes, Many rejected the idea that once a treatment is started, it can still be dropped, even though the law upholds a patient's right to do so. Though the courts have recognized the right of patients to refuse food and water, 42 percent of health-care workers rejected that option . . . One study found that in 25 of 71 cases, when patients were moved from nursing homes to hospitals, their living wills never made it into hospital charts. (Gibbs 1993, 34)

This same article also portrays doctors as placing their own interests above those of their patients: "Even when patients go to the trouble of expressing their wishes, the doctor's values may prevail." Still more incriminating is the article's depiction of doctors as ignorant and indifferent about pain management: "The vast majority [of doctors] simply don't know how to treat pain, and they don't think it's important . . . Surveys of doctors . . . show how many are unaware of their patients' options or are unwilling to respect them" (Gibbs 1993, 34). Yet, at the same time, the news report suggests that there is something a little dirty, illicit, or clandestine about the fact that many physicians have hastened patients' deaths in secret for decades. As one passage states, "No one knows how often doctors write the prescription and whisper the recipe for a deadly overdose; but one informal survey of internists last year found that one in five say they have helped cause the death of a patient" (Gibbs 1993, 34). In essence, doctors are condemned both for keeping their patients alive and for killing them in secret.

Other news stories in the third framing stage echo this pattern of assigning greater blame for the PAS controversy—and particularly for creating "Dr. Death"—on physicians and a medical establishment reluctant or unwilling to listen to patients and heed their requests for aid in dying. A 1991 news story, for instance, traces PAS requests to the "extraordinary decline in trust between physicians and patients and patients and hospitals" (Ames et al. 1991, 40). A 1994 news report suggests that doctors—and not machines—are "out of control," comparing the typical doctor to a "precocious child no one ever scolds." Reprimanding physicians for neglecting their duty to the dying, this article concludes that "Doctors have forgotten their 'pastoral function': to minister to the dying, not simply to stave off death at any cost . . . Doctors are so unrelenting in their pursuit of a diagnosis and cure . . . that they forget what's best for the patient" (Ingrassia 1994, 54). A 1994 article depicts physicians as having been rigid and overly aggressive in "trying to keep death at bay," as failing to understand their patients' priorities, and as lacking trust in their patients' families and loved ones (Gorman 1994, 65). Another story published in 1994 provides a laundry list of physicians' failures: "Doctors don't listen to what patients want; they aren't honest with bad news; they manage pain poorly, and their decisions leave an alarming number of families broke or near broke" (Brink 1995, 70).

Additional news narratives go even further, such as one that blames the demand for PAS on doctors' greed and discomfort with death. Doctors, according to this article, have little incentive to pay attention "to matters of dying and providing simply comfort care," the article states, because "they aren't reimbursed . . . [and] they are . . . extremely uncomfortable about death" (Beck 1994, 58). A news report in *USNWR* is equally harsh, accusing doctors of "ignoring the wishes of their patients and families, using extraordinary measures to keep the terminally ill alive—often only out of fear of being sued"—and portraying them as untrustworthy and likely to abuse PAS if it were legalized (Shapiro 1991, 32).

Given journalists' focus on restoring and repairing some of the damage inflicted by Kevorkian on the medical establishment, the relatively negative portrayal of doctors and the medical profession found in news stories in the third framing stage appears contradictory. Once again, however, it is important to distinguish news representations of "bad" doctors and medical establishments—those depicted as deaf to patient's requests for assistance in dying—from depictions of "good" doctors and medical establishments—those who practice PAS out of compassion even at the risk of legal penalties, lawsuits, and loss of careers. This is similar to the way in which negative framing of Kevorkian was used to offset the efforts of "good" doctors—such as Dr. Timothy Quill—who practice PAS.

As this discussion makes clear, the idea of a "good death" promoted in the third framing stage was overwhelmingly one in which individuals not only have the "right to die"—the freedom to "choose" the time, place, and circumstances of their deaths—but are entitled to aid in dying from a caring physician. In the third framing stage's version of a "good death," individuals die peacefully and without pain. Loved ones gather around the deathbed to share final farewells with the dying person—who, although unable to prevent death, is deeply grateful and relieved to be able to control the time and manner in which it occurs. This scenario, played out ritualistically in anecdotes in the news reports in this study, stands in stark relief to the counternarrative of the "bad death" offered in the same news coverage. A "bad death" in the articles analyzed here is a desperate affair that unfolds in a sterile hospital setting amid the existential drone of life-support machines. Occurring only after a protracted, anguished, debilitating, dehumanizing, and expensive illness, it includes the singular horror of watching a loved one's "quality of life" ebb slowly away.

NOTES

1. *Washington v. Glucksberg*, 117 S.Ct. 2258 (1997); *Vacco, Attorney General of New York v. Quill*, 117 S.Ct. 2293 (1997). (In this combined ruling on two lower-court decisions, the U.S. Supreme Court upheld two laws banning PAS on the basis that no fundamental constitutional "right to die" exists.)

2. Indeed, certain events may be so "shocking" or unprecedented that they render journalists incapable of performing these three functions and hence unable to report on certain phenomena. This may help explain why AIDS was not covered in the mainstream news media until a full decade after it initially struck the gay and intravenous-drug

communities. As it was, when it finally attracted news media attention, AIDS created a major frame eruption in the ongoing coverage of a spectrum of issues ranging from homosexuality and sexually transmitted diseases (STDs) to health risks associated with blood transfusions and intravenous drug use.

3. Although a handful of passive euthanasia stories appear in stage three, they generally concern: (1) legal cases brought before the courts in the 1980s and ruled on in the 1990s (e.g., *Cruzan*); (2) new legal wrinkles in previously resolved passive euthanasia issues (e.g., a controversy over whether a school nurse should be asked to resuscitate a disabled child with serious health problems); or (3) a celebrity death involving passive euthanasia (e.g., former president Richard Nixon).

4. This is true even when the frames of unpopular movements or activists are the only alternative frames available; the journalistic balancing norm is "rarely interpreted" to include protest-movement frames (Gamson 1988a, 227). And even when alternative (read: non-official) frames make it into print, they are often distorted and/or sandwiched between official rebuttals of activists' positions. In this way, what appears to be "balanced" reporting actually masks a strong status quo bias.

5. As a testament to his "hero" status, Kevorkian was given the Humanist Hero Award in 1994 from the American Humanist Association.

6. The "gunslinger" image of Kevorkian occasionally appeared overtly in articles about him, such as a *Newsweek* story that referred to his enemies "closing in" on him, his "showdown in court," and his sweeping into court with "his posse of close friends" (Cohen 1998, 46–47).

CHAPTER 6

RESULTS ON THE IDEOLOGY OF EUTHANASIA NEWS FRAMES

The events through which we live are forever outrunning the power
of our ordinary, everyday moral, emotional, and intellectual concepts
to construe them, leaving us, as a Javanese image has it, like a water
buffalo listening to an orchestra.
—Geertz (1968, 101)

This chapter presents the second half of this study's findings on framing of the euthanasia debate in the national press. Whereas the previous two chapters focused on conclusions concerning general framing characteristics, coverage of Kevorkian, and shifts in framing stages over time, here findings related to the ideological nature of euthanasia news frames are presented, including: the framing strategies used by journalists to promote pro-RTD frames and weaken pro-life frames; the ideological role of medical, legal, and economic frames in euthanasia discourse; and omitted or marginalized frames.

IDEOLOGY OF NEWS FRAMING OF EUTHANASIA

As discussed in the previous chapter, the national news magazines in this analysis reflected overwhelming support for pro-RTD frames. Stories in *Newsweek, Time, USNWR*, and *The New York Times* used news frames to construct a favorable image of passive euthanasia and PAS in two major ways: (1) through use of specific framing elements or "condensing symbols" (e.g., catchphrases, metaphors, descriptors, anecdotes, visual images, etc.) to construct euthanasia as an appropriate end-of-life option; and (2) through marginalization or omission of frames articulating anti-euthanasia views. Although the first of these is addressed to some degree in the previous chapter, this chapter elaborates and expands on journalists' selection of framing elements to promote pro-RTD and pro-medical ideologies and explores the incidence of frame omission and marginalization.

FRAMES PROMOTING PRO-RTD IDEOLOGIES

Intensifiers and Modifiers

In addition to the intensifiers and loaded modifiers such as "extraordinary measures" discussed in chapter 4, a persistent feature of euthanasia stories in all framing stages is pervasive stress on the pain and suffering experienced by patients (or their surrogates) who seek passive or active euthanasia. Depictions of the anguish endured by "hopelessly ill" patients, including vivid details of their physical deterioration and diminished "quality of life" are among the strongest currents flowing through news stories in this research. Terms such as "suffering," in "misery," and "in anguish" are routinely used to describe individuals (or their surrogates) who request or obtain euthanasia. For example, an early article describes a patient as "totally crippled and in constant pain" (Clark and Agrest 1975, 58).

Other depictions are even more graphic, such as: "a physician crawling on the chest of a patient to cram a tube down his throat" (Gelman and Pedersen 1984, 72); the "thicket of tubes and life-extending apparatus" that attend death in institutional settings (Wallis 1986, 60); "the nausea and other side effects" often suffered by the dying (Clark et al. 1981); a patient "struggling to breathe, vomiting repeatedly from a drug meant to sedate her" (Grady 1988, 88); a dying man, whose "feet had turned the color of overripe eggplants, their mottled purple black an unmistakable sign of gangrene" (Begley and Starr 1991, 42); references to "a life ground down by pain" and "death in a high-tech hell" (Gibbs 1992, 36); and a particularly disturbing depiction of dying patients "fighting for oxygen and clawing at their masks" (O'Neill 1995, 28).

Considered cumulatively, these graphic, highly detailed images of human anguish unmistakably create identification with and sympathy for those desiring passive or active euthanasia. The following passage is typical of the level of medical and technical detail employed by journalists to express the torment endured by patients whose lives have become a cruel joke—and death a salvation:

His gangrenous bladder had been removed, his kidneys had completely collapsed, his lungs were laboring to inflate on their own his heart was weakened by a coronary during or after the gallbladder surgery . . . His body could not tolerate more surgery. Although poisonous wastes were building in his system, dialysis had to be halted because it triggered his angina. He was slipping in and out of consciousness; soon his lungs would be no more able to gather in oxygen than a punctured balloon. (Begley and Starr 1991, 42)

As is the case with virtually every depiction of pain and suffering in the articles in this study, relief for the tormented man in the above anecdote comes via euthanasia (in this case passive euthanasia, in the form of removal of a life support system). Such representations—particularly when incorporated into highly emotional anecdotes that dramatize the pain and desperation of dying individuals and their families—foster support for the choices of these "victims" of medicalized death—which generally involve assisted suicide. Most news articles implicitly or explicitly state through anecdotes, quotes, and journalists' observations that it is abject misery—sometimes exacerbated by the insensitivity of medical professionals—that drives ordinary or "good" citizens and their families to seek passive euthanasia or PAS, or—if unable to obtain these—to commit suicide on their own, often in collusion with loved ones. The particular news frame through which this ideology is enacted is *Humane Treatment*, a pro-RTD medical frame that argues that the most compassionate course is to allow patients who are "hopelessly" ill and suffering to die. As one journalist who articulates the "problem" of euthanasia through the *Humane Treatment* frame explains, "the dread of unrelenting pain is one factor that may encourage patients and doctors alike to blur the line between letting death occur and causing it" (Grady 1988, 88).

Related to frames that emphasize pain and suffering is stress on the hopelessness of euthanasia candidates' medical prognoses. An early euthanasia article, for instance, draws on an extensive arsenal of modifiers to describe Quinlan's condition, including: "hopeless," a "hopeless case," "no hope," "without hope," "in any technical sense already dead," "lost her consciousness of life," "no known treatment," "desperately ill," "there's just no chance for her," "without a chance of recovery," "incurable," and "going progressively downhill" (Clark and Agrest 1975, 58). A second news story on Quinlan—along with characterizing her as "hopelessly ill"—uses the following depictions to interpret her condition: "shows slight signs of life"; "inevitable death"; "kept alive by a respirator"; and "practically speaking, Karen Ann is *dead already*" (Sheils and Agrest 1975, 76, emphasis added). Fifteen years following publication of these stories, reporters make use of virtually the same vocabulary to represent the controversy surrounding Nancy Cruzan,[1] another comatose patient whose relatives battled all the way to the United States Supreme Court to remove her from life-support (Gibbs 19 Mar. 1990). It is significant that news framing of Cruzan—whose case followed Quinlan's by a decade and a half—was almost identical to that of Quinlan. In both cases journalists employed a combination of *Humane Treatment* and the *Economic/Pragmatic* frame, which, as mentioned earlier, argues that when death is inevitable, keeping individuals alive on life support or denying them PAS places an undue financial burden on their families, the medical system, and society as a whole.

Another consistent feature of euthanasia coverage through the full period of analysis concerns use of the terms "vegetative state" or "persistent vegetative state." Although these are medical terms used by physicians and other healthcare professionals to describe specific physical conditions and prognoses, they take on their own unmistakable meanings and significance when used in news stories outside their original, clinical contexts. Appearing alongside loaded modifiers such as "extraordinary means" are frequent references to comatose patients as "vegetables." These depictions communicate the tacit, "common sense" notion that such patients have no life in any meaningful sense and hence should be "allowed" to die via euthanasia. This is the point of one article, for instance, that not only depicts a patient as a "human vegetable," but uses the depictions:

"hopelessly ill," "with no hope of living individual lives," "doomed to a blighted life" "to prolong life if no real hope exists," "to prolong lives that can't be saved," and "carrying heroic measures too far." Other examples include: "[the] patient was 'maintaining his existence but not his life'" (Malcolm 1985, 1); "the motionless man's condition worsening by the day, despite all the machines, wire, and tubes that were feeding him and monitoring him and draining him and even breathing for him" (Clark and Agrest 1981); "a 'vegetative' patient whom doctors refused to disconnect from a life-support system even after the family obtained a court order" (Press et al. 1985, 18); an accident victim who, "for the past 17 years, . . . has not moved voluntarily, spoken a single word or responded in any way to light, sound our touch" (Rosellini 1994, 67); dying individuals trapped in a "hopeless twilight known to doctors as a 'persistent vegetative state'" with no chance "of regaining the essence of being human" (Wallis 1986, 60); and this quote from a *New York Times* article: "'Annabelle,' the patient cried as her daughter entered the room, 'how can you do this to me? Don't' let me live like a vegetable!'" (Malcolm 1985).

The "human vegetable" metaphor also shows up in articles in middle- and late-stage coverage, such as a 1989 news story that refers to Nancy Cruzan as "stiff and severely contracted, her knees and arms drawn into a fetal position," "oblivious," "totally unaware," and in "a persistent vegetative state" (Sanders 1989, 80). A 1990 story uses both "persistent vegetative state" and "to be kept alive as a 'vegetable'" to describe a patient's condition (Kaplan and McDaniel 1990, 22). At other times, journalists use synonyms for "human vegetable" to suggest the futility of keeping such patients alive, as in this provocative passage: "The doctors, too, emphasized the uselessness of it all. 'It's a question of futility . . . We don't keep corpses on ventilators" (Begley and Starr 1991, 42).

A brief reflection on the ideological function of the "human vegetable" metaphor is warranted here to explain and underscore its role and significance in euthanasia coverage in this research. Like all metaphors, the persuasive potency of this particular example resides in its power to define reality while seeming utterly natural (Chilton and Lakoff 1995). Here, Kaplan's (1990) insight that metaphors used in news stories "conventionalize unfamiliar or controversial values and practices, rendering them less vulnerable to scrutiny and criticism" proves germane (p. 38). Metaphors such as "human vegetable" are not simple or inconsequential language selections, but are concrete expressions of abstract ideas and problems, as well as implied conclusions and solutions to these problems (Schaffner 1995). They symbolize important cognitive processes involving logic, reason, and justification for action. In this sense, the "commonsensical" appeal and familiarity of the vegetable metaphor mask its ideological message, thereby intensifying its persuasive power: Given the "lifelessness" or "uselessness" of individuals whose physical conditions have rendered their lives as meaningless as that of turnips or potatoes, euthanasia becomes a highly practical and reasonable option. Stripping it to its core meaning, "human vegetable" connotes that such patients are no longer human. Dehumanized, they may be disposed of with minimal anxiety or guilt.

Syntactical Structures

Because of the cognitive associations headlines, subheads, and leads activate in readers, these syntactical elements are considered particularly powerful framing devices (see, e.g., Pan and Kosicki 1993). News readers are increasingly "headline consumers" who only occasionally read the full text of news stories (Roeh and Nir 1993). (Arguably, because editors select headlines, they may be considered representative of the ideological position of the news publication) Hence, headlines and subheads, which encapsulate a news story's main topic and theme, have been singled out as key structures in news framing. For this reason it is important to examine these syntactical structures as part of news story frames.

Overall, this study's results show that headlines, subheads, and leads both implicitly and explicitly promote pro-RTD arguments and agendas. Although some headlines dealing with Kevorkian are clearly disparaging in tone (e.g., "Dr. Death Strikes Again"; "Dr. Kevorkian's Death Wish"; "Dr. Death: A '90s Celebrity"), most are either neutral or slightly supportive of euthanasia. One obvious way in which pro-RTD ideology manifests itself is through pervasive use of the pro-RTD catchphrase "right to die." It is significant, in this context, that more than a quarter of all headlines in the study use this RTD anthem.[2]

Another notable way news reports' syntactical structures promote pro-RTD ideologies is through the use of (rhetorical) question headlines and subheads. What is most significant about question headlines in this study is that they operate as signs of balance and objectivity rather than actual manifestations or reflections of these vaunted journalistic conventions. In this sense, question headlines may be seen as counterframes or condensed versions of opposing points of views. Appearing in nearly a third of all articles in the study, question headlines and subheads serve two key ideological functions: First, they situate the euthanasia debate squarely within the conflict model favored by commercial American news media. For example, a headline that asks, "Who Will Play God?" (*Time* 9 April 1984, 68), identifies not only the terms of the dispute (who should decide whether euthanasia is appropriate), but the major adversaries in the battle (medical science versus the legal system). More critically, however, question headlines are often used in the news articles in this study to disguise or neutralize pro-life counterarguments while preserving the outward appearance of objectivity. For example, the headline "Is it Wrong to Cut Off Feeding?" implicitly suggests the counterargument, "It is Wrong to Cut Off Feeding" (Ostling 1987, 71). Here, presentation of a potentially damaging pro-life argument as a question helps maintain the external appearance of neutrality in an article that clearly supports removal of feeding tubes from comatose patients to hasten their deaths. Along with depicting opponents of this form of passive euthanasia as "contentious . . . right-to-lifers" departing from their own religious traditions, the article marshals facts and statistics—such as the thousands of comatose patients currently being "kept alive by feeding tubes" and the "many Americans" and organizations (including the AMA) that have "endorsed . . . the right to halt nutrition"—to make the case that withdrawal of food and hydration is a reasonable course of action (Ostling 1987, 71).

This function is also exemplified by the headline "Mercy—or Murder?,," which serves to mask the news story's support for the unstated (pro-RTD) argument "Euthanasia is mercy." The pro-life counterargument "Euthanasia is Murder" is dispensed with through numerous details and depictions, including a highly sympathetic portrait of Roswell Gilbert, a 76-year-old Florida man imprisoned for shooting his wife, who is portrayed in the article not as a murder victim, but as "an Alzheimer's disease sufferer [who] pleaded with her husband to 'please, let me die'" (Givens et al. 1985, 25). Although the counterargument equating euthanasia with murder is never made explicit, it is also discredited by the article's depiction of laws against euthanasia as unfair and inconsistent from state to state.

Anecdotes

Because they organize information and interpret the meaning of issues and events according to personal experience, anecdotes are considered key framing elements. As episodic rather than thematic framing devices, anecdotes are believed to enhance "frame resonance"—the alignment of a news frame with readers' pre-existing perceptions, experiences, and myths (Iyengar 1990). By imbuing news stories with dramatic and narrative meaning, anecdotes also represent causes and solutions more persuasively than other rhetorical elements (Snow et al. 1986; Snow and Benford 1988).

Given the important role of anecdotes in news framing, it is significant that in euthanasia stories in this analysis, they are used overwhelmingly to promote pro-RTD ideologies. The following example, typical of anecdotes found in this research, illustrates their use in the framing of euthanasia as a humane end-of-life option and an individual "right":

Marie was dying. Her 69-year-old body, wasted by incurable emphysema and inoperable lung cancer, could no longer function on its own. As her family stood by her hospital bedside on a hot summer morning, the doctor suggested hooking her up to life-sustaining equipment. Marie looked beseechingly at her daughter Rose. "What do you think?" she asked. "No, Mom," Rose answered. Marie nodded. The doctor bristled. 'If that were my mother, I'd do it," he said. But the family stood firm. The following day Marie died quietly, without the shirs, clicks and high-tech hums that form an electronic dirge for so many Americans. Last week Rose explained why she was buying "Final Exit," Derek Humphry's' controversial new best-selling guide to suicide. "I don't want what happened to me to happen to my children, to have a doctor try to dictate to them," she said. "It's an outrage. When I'm dying, I want to be in control." Whose death is it anyway? (Ames 1991, 40)

Several details of this anecdote warrant attention. First, note how within the first two sentences the author successfully communicates the "hopelessness" of Marie's case. Not content with the word "dying," the reporter enlists other modifiers, including "wasted," "incurable," and "inoperable" to communicate the idea that Marie is as good as "dead already." As discussed earlier, the repetition and intensity of these descriptors suggests the inevitability of death (and hence the futility of using "life-sustaining equipment").

Even more significant, however, is the anecdote's association of a "good death" with passive euthanasia. After Marie and her family stand "firm" in the face of pressure from the doctor to place Marie on life-support, she is rewarded by being allowed to die "quietly, without the shirs, clicks and high-tech hums that form an electronic dirge for so many Americans." Although "shirs and high-tech hums" is not as pejorative as some depictions of mechanized death, the image is nevertheless far from appealing. These points—which provide support for acceptance of passive euthanasia and give dramatic voice to the right of patients and their relatives to control the circumstances of death—are reinforced in the next few sentences: "'When I'm dying, I want to be in control.' Whose death is it anyway?" and by what amounts to a plug for the best-selling, do-it-yourself suicide manual by Derek Humphry, *Final Exit*. What is striking about this anecdote's reference to *Final Exit*, which provides detailed instructions for assisting or committing suicide, is its inclusion in an anecdote that is essentially about passive euthanasia—removing Marie from life support. The ease and "naturalness" with which the author conflates passive and active euthanasia—two markedly different practices—is significant. It can safely be assumed that in 1991 most Americans were more likely to approve of passive euthanasia than active euthanasia in a case like Marie's. By creating a cognitive link between the two practices, this anecdote effectively blurs the boundaries between these two types of euthanasia in the minds of readers, something that almost certainly promotes acceptance of active euthanasia and provides a possible clue to the public's rapid (less than two-decade) move from acceptance of passive euthanasia to PAS.

Other anecdotes in articles in the study promote pro-RTD ideology by advancing pro-life viewpoints as "straw-man" arguments—easily disputed oppositional views offered primarily to demonstrate their weaknesses. For example, an anecdote about an eighty-three-year-old woman whose nephew wants to remove her feeding tube introduces the pro-life, religious frame, *Divine Authority* (Tifft 1983, 68). The journalist refutes this frame in two powerful but subtle ways. First, he uses highly persuasive quotes, including a Superior Court judge's pronouncement that "'There is a point at which a patient, or someone acting for him if he is incompetent, has the right to refuse treatment.'" Second, the journalist casts as the antagonist in the anecdote an uncompromising doctor who balks at the nephew's request to have his aunt's feeding tube removed. "You can't play God," the doctor informs the nephew. Angry, the nephew turns on the doctor: "'What are you doing? God's will is that this woman is ready to go. You're the one holding her back.'" In the end, the nephew triumphs over the doctor in court, and the hospital is forced to expedite the aunt's death by removing her feeding and hydration tubes. Here the straw-man argument that patients and their surrogates "can't play God" is refuted by the counterargument that doctors play God everyday by extending the lives of mortally ill individuals.

Although both of the above anecdotes portray doctors as aggressively pushing life-extension therapies onto reluctant patients and/or their relatives, anecdotes that cast physicians in the role of advocates of passive euthanasia who persuade and sometimes even pressure patients and their families to refuse or withdraw life-sustaining treatments are even more common in the articles in this study. Typical of this form of pro-RTD ideology is an anecdote about a woman who is informed by her dying husband's doctors that without "massive and heroic intervention, [he] would almost certainly die within 48 hours." The man's doctor's "counseled her not to request any extraordinary measures that, as they put it, would only prolong his misery." Here, as in the first anecdote, the inevitability of the patient's death is underscored through starkly vivid descriptions of his physical deterioration. But in this example the loaded modifiers "massive and heroic" and "extraordinary" are used to show the fragile hold the patient has on life. Once again, the underlying message is the inevitability of death (and hence the rationality of passive euthanasia). Eventually, although the dying man's wife objects to passive euthanasia for her husband, the doctors convince her that he has "no reasonable medical options," and she reluctantly yields to their judgment. Observe in the following passage from this news story how the resolution of this tale not only links euthanasia with a "good death," but makes use of fictional devices to suggest the righteousness of the woman's decision to allow passive euthanasia for her husband:

Early the next morning, the cloud seemed to lift from Ponzo's mind, and for a brief few moments he saw his wife, and perhaps his end, with a calm lucidity. They exchanged final "I love yous." "I just held him in my arms," Mrs. Ponzo said. "I took off his [oxygen] mask—he didn't need it anymore—and held him and held him until his final breath." It was a good way to die, as dying goes, for sometimes it goes horribly. "A peaceful death," [the doctor] said softly as he led his interns and residents past Ponzo's closed door on morning rounds a few hours later. It could even be counted as sort of a success. Ponzo did not suffer the outrage of "people sticking needles in [him] and thumping on [his] chest. That's a violent and brutal way to depart this world," said Weiss to the interns and residents gathered around. (Begley and Starr 1991, 42)

It is difficult to miss the message conveyed by the apocryphal quality of the opening sentence's, "a cloud seemed to lift." Only after Mrs. Ponzo accepts the doctor's recommendation of passive euthanasia does her husband experience "calm lucidity," and "a peaceful death" in her loving arms. Here, the refrain of the inevitability of death (and hence the rationality of passive euthanasia) is spelled out unambiguously in the anecdote's conclusion: "It was a good way to die . . .'A peaceful death . . . Ponzo did not suffer the outrage of 'people sticking needles in [him] and thumping on [his] chest. That's a violent and brutal way to depart this world'" (Begley and Starr 1991, 42).

What makes this—and other anecdotes used in euthanasia coverage in this study so potent—is their "naturalness" or sense of inevitability. Like photographs, anecdotes project a strong sense of reality—a phenomenon that makes them less likely to raise questions in the minds of readers. As Bruner (2002) writes, "Stories are surely not innocent: they always have a message, most often so well concealed that even the teller knows not what ax he may be grinding. For example, stories typically begin by taking for granted (and asking the hearer or reader to take for granted) the ordinariness or normality of a given state of things in the world—what *ought* to prevail" (pp. 5–6). Moreover, partly because they are interwoven so seamlessly with facts, quotes, and other types of evidentiary material in news stories and because of their innate drama and immediacy, anecdotes assert themselves with a cognitive force that makes it difficult to imagine alternative narratives. For this reason, it is instructive to contrast the pro-RTD anecdotes offered in the above discussion with anecdotes promoting pro-life arguments and ideologies.

Unfortunately, this task is hampered by the scarcity of pro-life anecdotes in the euthanasia articles in this study. Among the handful of examples is one from a story about the practice of euthanasia in the Netherlands (Branagan 1997). Although presumably meant to communicate the potential for abuse if PAS were legalized in the United States (*Slippery Slope* frame), it falls significantly short of that goal.

Inevitably, of course, there are abuses, and flagrant ones are prosecuted. Sippe Schat, a doctor from northern Friesland, goes on trial later this month for the alleged murder of a 72-year-old cancer patient who had seemed in good spirits just before she died in a nursing home. According to prosecutors, Schat simply gave her a lethal shot of insulin without consulting anyone and left her to die alone, allegedly telling a nurse as he left, "If she hasn't died by 7 a.m. tomorrow, give me a call." (p. 149)

While attempting to illustrate the dangers of legalizing PAS, the woman portrayed as a PAS victim inspires little righteous indignation or concern about PAS. First, the fact that she is a "72-year-old cancer patient" lying near death in a nursing home almost certainly undermines the narrative's supposedly anti-euthanasia message. Moreover, considered in the context of the rest of the article's pro-RTD framing, it is difficult to imagine that this brief anecdote—which lacks lurid or alarming details to support its anti-PAS claim—has the resonance of the typical pro-RTD anecdote found in this study. Pro-RTD anecdotes tend to be longer, offer more detail, and present more vivid and emotionally provocative images and scenarios as "evidence" of the pain and suffering endured by patients requesting PAS.

Two notable pro-life anecdotes appearing in different USNWR stories are significant, not only for their brevity relative to typical pro-RTD anecdotes, but for the weakness of their anti-euthanasia arguments, which risk inadvertent support for euthanasia. Note especially the disclaimer that "such cases are rare," which precedes the first of the following two anecdotes, as well as the advanced age of the patients involved in both examples. Also notice the relatively short span of time the second patient remained on life support (12 days) compared to the years and even decades of extended life on respirators and other machines patients in this study's pro-RTD anecdotes tend to endure:

Right-to-life advocates buttress their arguments by pointing to patients given up for dead who inexplicably survived, even if such cases are rare. Carrie Coons, 86, fell unconscious in Albany, N.Y., a year ago after a stroke. One Friday last April, a judge heeded pleas from her doctors and sister, who described her condition as 'hopeless, and authorized the removal of a feeding tube. That weekend, Coons began talking and eating, prompting the judge to quickly reverse himself. (Gest and Burke 1989, 35)

And "One 80-year-old woman had repeatedly denounced extraordinary treatment if she were in a hopeless condition. Then she slipped into a coma after a cerebral hemorrhage. Last week, after 12 days of artificial feeding, her family was about to remove the tube when she unexpectedly regained consciousness and began to take food. (Gest et al 1990, 22)

Another pro-life anecdote published in 1993 about a man whose support for passive euthanasia diminishes after his wife's death in a hospice, also lacks persuasive muscle (Gibbs 1993): "I can still intellectualize why people seek out a person like Kevorkian. But I've come to understand that the lives of even the terminally ill are precious and matter, right up to the last second of breath. There is such a thing as dying with grace, dignity, compassion and support, and there are alternatives to the kind of suicide Kevorkian proposes" (p. 34).

The failing of this brief anecdote is that its notion that "the lives of even the terminally ill are precious and matter, right up to the last second of breath," could as easily apply to a patient whose life-support equipment is removed or who is assisted "peacefully" and painlessly to her death by a physician. Additionally, use of the phrase, "dying with grace, dignity, compassion and support" might have been extracted verbatim from an RTD brochure.

Based on this analysis, reporters covering euthanasia seem unable or unwilling to articulate the case against social and legal acceptance of the practice. Because of the dearth of pro-life anecdotes in the news articles in this research, it is necessary to turn to an outside publication to find an appropriate example of what a pro-life anecdote might look like. For this purpose an anecdote was chosen from the Roman Catholic publication *America*, excerpted here:

A telling example of how easily the right to die can change into the duty to die appeared in a letter published in The Santa Rosa (California) Press Democrat...from an 84-year-old woman who had been living with her daughter for 20 years. "Everything went fine for many years," the woman wrote, "but when I started to lose my hearing about three years ago, it irritated my daughter . . . She began to question me about my financial matters and apparently feels I won't leave much of an estate for her . . . She became very rude to me . . . Then suddenly, one evening, my daughter said very cautiously she thought it was O.K. for older people to commit suicide if they cannot take care of themselves." After recounting the ways in which her daughter has reinforced this message, the woman commented: "So here I sit, day after day, knowing what I am expected to do when I need a little help." (Bernardi 1995, 14)

In contrast to three examples of pro-life anecdotes above, this one articulates the pro-life counterframe, "The right to die will become the duty to die" in a dramatic, resonant manner. Anecdotes expressing pro-life ideologies in an equally persuasive way are virtually nonexistent in the articles investigated in this research.

Depictions and Images

Although the previous chapter addressed the role of depictions and images in the ideological framing of euthanasia, this topic is revisited briefly to underscore the breadth of framing strategies used to promote acceptance of euthanasia and PAS in the news reports in this study. An article that exemplifies this is one mentioned in chapter 4 titled "Defining the Right to Die" about an elderly doctor who practices PAS. Accompanying this article is a photograph of the doctor profiled in the piece. Smiling beneficently in this picture is a kindly, white-haired gentleman with a gentle smile, a stethoscope curled around his neck, an illuminated x-ray hanging behind him on the wall, and an open book laying before him on his desk. A rosy glow bathes the scene. The image evoked is that of the sweet family doctor of old, an idealized physician who personifies the myth of the healer devoted not only to the physical but the emotional health of his patients. The cutline next to the photo states in bold type, "Assisting Suicide: Dr. Bry Benjamin has aided terminally ill patients for 25 years." What the euphemistic "aided terminally ill" actually means, the article's text reveals, is prescribing lethal drugs to patients who are in pain and dying. For nearly a quarter of a century, it turns out, the amicable doctor in the photograph has engaged in criminal behavior. He has been forced to practice PAS surreptitiously, the article informs readers, because, "The law forbade him" to provide his patients with medications for this purpose, and "doctors didn't even whisper among themselves about assisted suicide, much less debate it in medical journals" (Lemonick 1996, 82).

In addition to promoting PAS through the depiction of its practice by a quintessentially "good doctor," the article makes an overt pitch for legalized, regulated PAS. This is demonstrated in the following passage, which openly argues it is time to move beyond discussion of the appropriateness of PAS to working out proper standards for its use. Note the consensus-building function of the first two sentences, which imply that since PAS is already widely practiced by physicians, it may as well be made legal.

The law is finally catching up to what some physicians have been doing quietly all along. In a survey of Oregon doctors published in the *New England Journal of Medicine* . . . 60 percent said they should be able to help some terminal patients die, and 7 percent admitted to having done so. The actual number, say ethicists, may be much higher. Yet because the practice has been carried out in private, the medical establishment has yet to develop a consensus on how and when to help a patient die.

The use of the word "finally" in this passage suggests that the legal system has been sluggish in approving PAS. The statistics on the number of doctors supporting PAS is an example of the use of concrete details to promote news frames—in this case the medical subframe, *Standards Needed*. Since so many doctors are already practicing PAS with (and without) the direct consent of their patients, the story suggests through this frame that it makes sense to legalize (and regulate) the practice. After detailing some of the dangers facing the medical community as a result of lack of regulation of PAS (e.g., "doctors may become more vulnerable to lawsuits"), the article concludes by presenting a final argument for legalization and regulation of PAS. Depicting Benjamin as reluctant to "give pills to someone [who] decided to commit suicide on Tuesday and on Wednesday would have changed his mind," the author asks, "Is that a good argument for keeping the practice illegal? No, says [another physician]. 'It's incredibly arrogant to say nobody's going to be careful so we shouldn't let patients make this decision for themselves. What doctors do need is a set of standards that make clear the role a physician should play in letting a patient go" (Lemonick 1996, 82.).

OMISSION AND MARGINALIZATION OF PRO-LIFE FRAMES

Medical Frames

As detailed throughout this and the previous two chapters, the major way in which journalists covering euthanasia in this research advanced pro-RTD ideologies was by emphasizing pro-RTD frames and omitting or marginalizing pro-life frames. It is significant that of the 121 news stories this study analyzed, only eight were coded as pro-life. Although this finding is addressed in chapter 4, a more in-depth explanation of marginalization of pro-life medical frames is provided here to demonstrate the specific arguments that did not make their way into news coverage of euthanasia in this research.

Among the most important pro-life medical frames, *Contaminates Medicine* is given scant attention in the articles in this analysis, despite the fact that it is among the most frequent medical frames appearing in anti-euthanasia literature. This frame—which fundamentally argues that legalization of PAS will lead to the gradual deterioration of medical standards, medical professionalism, and doctor-patient trust—contains a number of cogent arguments. Key among these is the notion that doctors who assist suicides will undergo a transformation from "agents of death" to "angels of mercy" in the eyes of society. As articulated by one anti-euthanasia spokesperson, "It is destructive to the public good to make people worry that when they go to a hospital the doctor is thinking about whether to allow them to live or die" (Stone 1988, 642). Also contained in this frame are the arguments that: (a) physicians who assist in suicides help "sanitize" the act by lending it the stamp of medical respectability; (b) legalizing euthanasia will inevitably lead to the breakdown of medical standards generally; (c) euthanasia will eventually be conflated with "healing"—something that pro-life activists claim has already occurred in Holland (Emanuel 1994, 1890); and (d) doctors and hospital administrators burdened with chronic or severely debilitated patients might find euthanasia an attractive alternative to devoting the considerable time, attention, and economic resources such patients require. In the end, as a physician who opposes legalized euthanasia argues, doctors, rather than the dying, will ultimately be the ones who are "empowered" and who benefit most from legalized euthanasia (Hendin 1996).

As this lengthy description indicates, many of the ideas articulated through *Contaminates Medicine* are not only reasonable, but may be crucial to understanding the full ramifications of legalization of PAS. Clearly, the American public, as well as policymakers, would have benefited from inclusion of these and other pro-life arguments in media discourse on euthanasia.

Another pro-life medical frame—*Alternatives Exist*—fares only somewhat better in euthanasia coverage in this study, although it, too, is presented most often as a marginalized counterframe. This frame, common in the discourse of hospice organizations and others who oppose legalization of PAS, argues that PAS would be unnecessary if doctors provided adequate palliative care for the dying. Those who argue that better pain medications would eliminate the need for euthanasia and PAS point to studies that show medical institutions deficient in providing effective pain care: For example, one study found that 40 percent of 4,000 patients who died following medical interventions were in "severe pain most of the time" prior to their deaths (Keenen 1998, 14). Figures like these, however strongly their suggestion that improved palliative care would eliminate most euthanasia requests, are extremely rare in the news articles in this study.

Economic/Pragmatic Framing

Although ideology permeates all media content, it is clearly more relevant in news coverage of some issues than in others (Barkin and Gurevitch 1987). Because they figure heavily in relations of power, for example, economically related issues are particularly freighted with ideological meaning. A significant finding of this research was that journalists covering euthanasia promoted the ideologically charged *Economic/Pragmatic* frame while simultaneously masking its presence. The results show that this frame—which argues that euthanasia is justified on the basis that it preserves human and economic resources that might better be spent elsewhere—is expressed implicitly, as a subtextual rather than fully articulated frame. In this sense its function is similar to what rhetoricians refer to as a "warrant"—an underlying assertion that links evidence to a claim (see, e.g., Condit 1987; following Toulmin 1958). Here, the "evidence"—emphasis on the high costs and wastefulness of prolonging the lives of individuals who are virtually "dead already"—supports the "claim" that euthanasia is a practical solution in such cases. The following excerpt from the lead of a news story on Nancy Cruzan is emblematic of the way journalists in this investigation both promote and obscure what might be considered a potentially "dangerous" frame:

Nancy Cruzan, now 32, has done nothing for the past seven years . . . She has not hugged her mother or gazed out the window or played with her nieces. She has neither laughed nor wept . . . nor spoken a word . . . [S]he has lain so still for so long that her hands have curled into claws; nurses wedge napkins under her fingers to prevent the nails from piercing her wrists. "She would hate being like this,' says her mother, Joyce. "It took a long time to accept she wasn't getting better" . . . Nancy's 'life' is so faint that it does not meet a minimum standard of protection under the law; . . . unaware as she is, she has none of those qualities and prospects and experiences that give life its value. (Gibbs 19 Mar. 1990, 62)

As with depictions of Quinlan in earlier coverage, the image of Cruzan as "already dead" is starkly evident in this passage. The characterization of her hands as "curled into claws," and her life as "so faint that it does not meet a minimum standard of protection under the law . . ." strongly suggest that keeping her alive constitutes a drain on her family. Less explicit, but also conveyed in this passage, is the idea that preserving her useless life, which has "none of those qualities and prospects and experiences that give life its value," represents a misuse of economic resources. The *Economic/Pragmatic* frame is also promoted subtly yet distinctly in subsequent paragraphs, in which the reporter characterizes the medical costs associated with keeping Cruzan and similar patients alive as "crushing" and rising "annually at double and triple the rate of inflation" (Gibbs 19 Mar. 1990, 62).

Although the author of this news story never actually spells out the relationship between the exorbitant medical costs of keeping Cruzan alive and the need for euthanasia, references to the high costs of caring for such patients, combined with ritualistic emphasis on the "hopelessness" and "lifelessness" of such individuals, suggest the practicality of the euthanasia "solution." The clear implication is that economically, at any rate, euthanasia "makes sense." This point is underscored in another passage in the same article: "[D]oes it make sense for taxpayers to spend tens of thousands of dollars a year to keep each unconscious patient alive?" Answering this question through the voices of medical authorities, the reporter concludes that "Overtreatment of the terminally ill strikes physicians as both wasteful and inhumane." Next, stressing the psychological burden borne by terminally ill patients denied passive euthanasia, the reporter observes that "it was not so much the pain of the cancer that plagued him; it was the mental burden of a lingering illness" (Gibb 19 Mar. 1990, 62). The unmistakable message of this and similar statements is that for individuals labeled "hopeless," "incurable," "comatose," or in some other sense, "dead already," euthanasia is not only humane, but the only economically sane solution.

One obvious explanation for the indirect or tangential way in which journalists in this study employ the *Economic/Pragmatic* frame involves the negative historical associations that pro-life activists have attempted to attach to euthanasia. The grimmest of these include references to the Nazi "euthanasia" program used in the 1930s and 1940s to purge Germany of scores of unwanted and unproductive citizens, including the mentally and physically disabled. Pro-life activists, through the *Slippery Slope* frame, frequently invoke euthanasia practices in Nazi Germany to discredit the RTD movement, warning of the inevitable erosion of cultural and moral standards that will occur once society ventures down the dark path toward legal and social acceptance of euthanasia. For some pro-life activists, America's own brief but intense infatuation with eugenics also offers an object lesson in the potential for abuse should PAS—like passive euthanasia before it—become legal in the United States. The eugenics movement, referred to by one historian as "the most enduring aspect of Social Darwinism," prospered in the United States from about 1885 to 1920 (Hofstadter 1983, 161).[3]

Of course, the fact that the *Economic/Pragmatic* frame is never dominant and is rarely evoked directly in stories in this investigation is unlikely related to journalists' knowledge of Nazi euthanasia or of United States society's almost four-decade embrace of eugenics. The frame's inherent contradictions and tensions are more than sufficient to reign in journalists who might consider using it. Economic arguments for the legalization of PAS come into direct conflict with well-established and highly resonant American beliefs, myths, and ideographs, such as the triumph of justice and democracy over capitalism and equal treatment under the law for all Americans regardless of age, mental debilitation, or physical condition. Equally hampering the full articulation of this frame are the incongruities it exposes in the image of medicine in contemporary society. Journalists in the articles in this study are silent on the major conflicts of interest that plague our healthcare system, such as the expectation on the one hand that hospitals will turn a blind eye to economics when it comes to treating patients while, in reality, their status as profiteers places them under constant pressure from stockholders to prevent the hemorrhaging of revenues caused by expensive high-tech medical care and long-term hospitalization of dying elderly and comatose individuals. As mentioned earlier in this chapter, patients who languish in hospitals represent a serious financial liability for profit-driven medical institutions and their parent companies.

In light of these and other economic exigencies, only the most naive observer would deny that a relationship exists between the dramatic shifts in medical economics over the past several decades and the breathtaking speed with which euthanasia was incorporated into medicalized care of the dying between the mid-1970s and the end of the twentieth century. It was in the 1970s that the reality of the impact of America's growing population of elderly and longer life spans first hit the medical community. During this decade demographers began "producing a gloomy 'standard model' of aging" that predicted "an accumulation, a pandemic of people in worse and worse shape" who would remain alive with chronic diseases that doctors could not cure. This model—which predicted massive drains on medical resources as the population of elderly continued to soar—has been the dominant paradigm among gerontologists and demographers for the past twenty years (Hilts 1999, D7).

Of course, these facts and relationships hardly constitute evidence of a "conspiracy of silence" on the part of reporters writing about euthanasia in the publications analyzed here. Nevertheless, it is indisputable that the medical establishment and other institutions of power in the United States have much to gain from social and legal acceptance of euthanasia. It may be that mainstream journalists and editors feel this relationship must remain cloaked to some degree in order to preserve social order by protecting established medicine's image and credibility with the American public. If so, the most predictable impulse for both journalists and their (mostly medical) sources would be to avoid direct use of an economic frame to construct public knowledge about the euthanasia issue. This sheds light on why, despite the fact that doctors and their patients are increasingly forced to make end-of-life decisions in the harsh glare of bottom-line medical economics, discussion of the financial incentives motivating acceptance of euthanasia are for the most part underplayed or invisible in the stories in this analysis. By employing the highly resonant but risk-laden *Economic/Pragmatic* frame in a way that promotes its arguments while obscuring its presence, journalists covering euthanasia offer strong justification for social and legal acceptance of euthanasia. They are mute, however, on the groups or institutions that will benefit most from American society's sanctioning of this practice. As such, their coverage of a social issue with critical consequences to the elderly, disabled, and terminally ill is deeply ideological. It not only promotes and legitimates the interests of one of the nation's most powerful institutions, but does so in a way that unequivocally masks these interests.

Religious/Ethical Frames

Religious/ethical frames—which are pervasive in the discourse of pro-life activists—were especially underrepresented in the news coverage examined in this study. Included in this category are four subframes: *Divine Authority* (Only God has the authority to determine the time of death); *Sanctity of Life* (Life is precious and hence to be preserved at all cost); *Murder is a Sin* (Euthanasia is murder and hence violates the Fourth Commandment); and *Suffering is Positive* (Suffering fosters spiritual growth).

Given the news media's commercial interests and characteristics,[4] it is unreasonable to expect religious framing to dominate euthanasia coverage. It makes sense, however, given the opposition of nearly all organized religious organizations to legalization of PAS, that religious frames would at least play a moderate role in coverage. Yet this is not the case. For example, *Sanctity of Life* is dominant in only one of the 121 stories analyzed in this investigation. It seems even more likely that religious frames would prevail in the handful of articles in this study in which pro-life frames dominate. Of the eight stories in which pro-life frames are dominant, however, religious/ethical frames are privileged in only one—an article that blends the *Suffering is Positive* religious subframe and popular psychology to urge Americans to face the "problem of death . . . rather than being assisted to kill themselves in order to avoid it" (Peck 1997, 18).

It is telling that the strongest example of a story with a dominant religious/ethical frame is one in which pro-RTD rather than pro-life ideologies dominate. Titled "Sisters of Mercy" (van Biema 31 May 1993), this news report—which focuses on the reaction of a group of Catholic nuns to the assisted suicide of a nun in their order—is significant for two reasons: First, it is one of the few stories in the study that addresses contradictions in religious attitudes toward euthanasia (e.g., religious proscriptions against euthanasia versus religious support for compassion for the sick and suffering). And second, it serves as an example of the use of religious sources to promote PAS, a practice almost universally condemned by organized religion in the United States. In this news story, a group of nuns, whose religious beliefs would normally lead them to oppose euthanasia, are depicted as condoning their colleague's choice of PAS. Although the novelty of this news angle almost certainly informed the reporters' choice of religious sources to express support for PAS, this usage must also be seen as a rhetorical strategy with powerful persuasive appeal: If Catholic nuns support PAS, it suggests, how wrong could it be?

Slippery Slope

Journalists covering euthanasia in the news magazines in this analysis also omitted other major pro-life frames. The most notable is the *Slippery Slope* frame, which "warns against the potentially disastrous consequences of stepping over the boundary that separates 'allowing to die' from active killing" (Bernardi 1995, 14). The logical end point of the moral and medical decay set into motion by legalizing euthanasia, according to this common anti-euthanasia argument, is both mass "killing" or "extermination" of the elderly, handicapped, and other burdensome groups and erosion of public trust in medical professionals. Although the news stories in the study frequently raise the *Slippery Slope* frame, it is virtually always used in a way that mitigates its persuasive impact.

Typical of the framing strategies mitigating its effectiveness are those in a 1986 news story titled, "To Feed or Not to Feed?" The article begins with a compelling, emotional anecdote about a comatose patient named Nancy who is in a "persistent vegetative state" and whose husband is fighting to have her feeding tube disconnected (e.g., "'There is no quality of life,' he insists. 'Nancy would not want to be in this state'") (Wallis 1986, 60). This pro-RTD anecdote is followed by five paragraphs supporting removal of feeding and hydration through various framing strategies, including concrete details, statistics, and depictions. (e.g., "There are about 10,000 other Americans in Nancy Jobes' predicament" and "Public opinion surveys suggest that most Americans fear and oppose this invasion of one of life's most private moments"). Quotes from medical authorities are also used to support removal of food and water from dying patients (e.g., "'We're not talking about going into Granny's room and taking away her water pitcher.' Granny benefits from such care . . . , but the comatose patient derives no comfort, no improvement, no hope of improvement' [from being fed and hydrated intravenously]").

Significantly, it is not until the end of the article that the author introduces a pro-life counterframe in an attempt to mask the article's almost blatant pro-RTD tone. After mentioning that some critics consider "dehydration . . . a gruesome way to die" (an articulation of the *Causes Worse Suffering* medical subframe), however, the reporter weakens this frame's message with the disclaimer, "(though just how much comatose patients feel is not known)." Next comes a paragraph articulating the *Slippery Slope* frame:

Some raised concerns about the so-called slippery slope toward wholesale euthanasia. Said Dr. Mark Siegler, director of the Center of Clinical Medical Ethics . . . "We start off with dispatching the terminally ill and the hopelessly comatose, and then perhaps our guidelines might be extended to the severely senile, the very old and decrepit and maybe even young, profoundly retarded children." Adding to such worries is the current era of medical cost cutting. "That's what this is all about, to get rid of people who are a burden to their families and the state," warned St. Louis Pediatrician Ann Bannon, president of Doctors for Life. (Wallis 1986, 60)

Notice the modifier "so-called" the reporter attaches to "slippery slope," signaling the questionable merits of this frame. Additionally, although the article as a whole offers two quotes from doctors who argue persuasively that removing food and hydration from comatose patients sets a dangerous precedent, it is remarkable for what it does not offer—namely an anecdote to provide dramatic evidence rather than facts and statistics to support the meager pro-life arguments included in the report. In order to appreciate just how little credence the article gives the *Slippery Slope* frame, it is useful to imagine the presentation of the pro-RTD and pro-life arguments in reverse: What impression would this article leave about the appropriateness of the practice of withholding food and water if the lead contained a dramatic anecdote illustrating how the practice might be used inappropriately rather than the anecdote about Nancy, whose "permanent vegetative state" has placed "a tremendous financial burden" on her husband? And how persuasive would the argument for removal of food and water be if it were confined to a little more than a paragraph near the end of the article and included only after six full paragraphs of arguments and evidence supporting the *Slippery Slope* frame?

Based on this analysis, euthanasia framing in the two national news magazines in the investigation not only privileged medical positions and promoted pro-RTD ideologies, but was dangerously superficial. News consumers relying on these national publications for information on the euthanasia controversy were provided a remarkably narrow selection of perspectives and positions from which to evaluate this controversial issue. The next chapter explores some of the implications of the findings presented in this chapter, including the systematic dominance of medical and "rights" frames to construct this highly complex social problem.

NOTES

1. In 1983 Cruzan suffered severe head injuries in an automobile accident that left her with serious brain damage. Her doctors considered her beyond recovery. Although her parents determined she would have wanted to die rather than live in a "persistent vegetative state" (PVS), hospital officials refused to withdraw feeding and hydration. Cruzan's parents brought suit, and the case went before the U.S. Supreme Court, which ruled in 1990 that although the Fourteenth Amendment grants patients the liberty to refuse medical intervention, this right is not a basic constitutional one. The Court upheld a Missouri statute requiring individuals to provide sufficient evidence of their end-of-life wishes before they could exercise the liberty to refuse treatment.

2. In addition to stories using the "right to die" catchphrase alone in the title, a number of variations appear, including: "Arguing the Right to Die"; "Whose Right to Die?"; "The Right to Die in Dignity"; "A Limited Right to Die"; "Fasting for the Right to Die"; "Defining the Right to Die"; "Expanding a Right to Die"; "Defending the Right to

Die"; "Is There a Right to Die?"; "Doctors, Patients and the Right to Die"; "Judges Who Support the Right to Die," and "Weighing the Right to Die?" Other headlines offer novel catchphrases that are overtly or subtly pro-RTD in tone, including, "Death with More Dignity"; "Many see Mercy in Ending Empty Lives"; "Love and Let Die"; "Should We Not Go Gentle?"; and "A Lesson in Dying Well."

3. The movement—which involved forced sterilization and restrictions on marriage for criminals, the mentally ill, and the "most dangerous and hurtful class[es]" (Conrad and Schneider 1992, 12–13)—had become a "fad" by 1915 in America (Hofstadter 1983, 161). One historian writes that, "[A]side from public education, sterilization was the only state-sponsored social improvement in which America led the world" (Katz 1986, 184). Although use of eugenics in American society stopped short of eradicating unproductive or unwanted populations, some euthanasia opponents see disturbing parallels between eugenics and euthanasia. Both, they contend, are motivated by the same economic imperatives, and their potential consequences are alarmingly similar: unequal treatment or even elimination of citizens considered a drain on society, such as the elderly, the mentally deficient, the emotionally unstable, and the physically disabled. And both invite class-based discrimination. Whereas the American eugenics movement was motivated by a desire to eliminate the "unfit"—generally identified with the lower classes—from the gene pool (Katz 1986), euthanasia has most often been used in the United States to hasten the deaths of the elderly poor in America—and specifically women (see, e.g., Osgood 1995).

4. Journalists' lack of attention to religious themes arises from a number of factors, including fear of offending readers. Other possible causes include reporters' generally weak religious affiliations and reluctance to cross religious-secular boundaries. The factor that best explains omission of religious perspectives on social issues, however, is the high value placed on "objectivity," a vaunted convention that arose in response to nineteenth-century commercialization and nationalization of news (see, e.g., Schudson).

CHAPTER 7

THE "RIGHT TO DIE" AS "GOOD DEATH": IMPLICATIONS AND CONCLUSIONS

> Humanity doesn't suffer from its questions, but from its answers.
> —Niedelmann (1999)

> The media operate from a set of assumptions, biases [and] attitudes
> that, for them, are implicit, not explicit. When there is bias in media
> reporting, it is because these underlying assumptions go
> unquestioned, unnoticed, and unexamined.
> —Goldman (1999)

As the results presented in chapters 4 through 6 show, journalists brought a host of unexamined assumptions and biases to their coverage of the euthanasia debate in the nearly twenty-five years between Karen Ann Quinlan's coma and Kevorkian's murder conviction. The purpose of this chapter is to tease out some of these assumptions and evaluate their consequences. The articles in the national news media investigated in this longitudinal study not only privileged pro-RTD frames and marginalized or omitted pro-life frames, but represented the issue almost entirely from the perspectives of two powerful institutions—medicine and law. How does framing euthanasia primarily as a medical and legal issue impact public perceptions of its meaning and consequences? What conclusions may be drawn from the results of this analysis about the news media's role in promoting the agendas of particular movements and institutions while thwarting those of others? What do the findings convey about the links between news, ideology, and social change—including evolving definitions of a "good death?" And finally, what do the results suggest about the mainstream news media's ability to facilitate public engagement in complex social problems with serious moral, economic, cultural, and political repercussions?

The framing patterns this study identified—including the dominance of medical and legal frames—are in no way "neutral" or ideology-free. Choice comes into play at every stage of news creation, particularly in "what is included and what is excluded, what is made explicit or left implicit, what is foregrounded and what is backgrounded, what is thematized and what is unthematized . . . " (Fairclough 1995, 104). In this context journalists' emphasis on medical and legal frames may be seen as having a dual function: It preserves the illusion of news media objectivity, authority, and "balance" while serving the news media's widely recognized function of maintaining and reinforcing the status quo by advancing institutional values, viewpoints, and definitions of social problems (see, e.g., Hall 1977).

NEWS CONSTRUCTION OF "A GOOD DEATH"

As discussed in chapter 5, the idea of a "good death" the news articles in this study promoted is overwhelmingly one in which individuals have the "right to die," and since the early 1990s (third framing stage), to do so with the active intervention of a caring physician. The news narratives' persistent stress on choice, freedom, and autonomy at life's end undoubtedly resonate with long-established American values including individualism, liberty, economic pragmatism, and aversion to death and its discomforts. Also highly persuasive are the news stories' repeated images of loving deathbed rituals—virtually all of which feature the practice of passive or active euthanasia. Found in anecdote after anecdote in news reports in this study, they function to advance the utility of euthanasia as a "solution" to the problem of a protracted, painful death.

Closer scrutiny of the "good death" sold to the American public in these narratives, however, reveals a number of contradictions. Questions about its validity arise, for example, when one considers who is likely to take advantage of the "good death" promoted here. Prime candidates for euthanasia are overwhelmingly poor and elderly and most likely female. Frequently widowed and alone, women, in particular, face the prospect of dying isolated in institutional settings in circumstances far removed from those depicted in the "good death" anecdotes found in news coverage of PAS. Most disturbing, a "good death" via PAS may eventually become something less than a true choice for elderly poor and disabled individuals whose consumption of medical and economic resources is highly restricted, if available at all. Diane Coleman, the president of the disability rights group, Not Dead Yet, has expressed anxiety about the threat normalization of PAS poses to disabled Americans. The greatest fear disabilities groups share, she states, is the supposed "voluntary" status of euthanasia (Coleman 1999). She sees so-called "futility guidelines"—which allow medical professionals to remove or withhold medical treatments from disabled patients against their own or their surrogates' wishes—as the first step toward mandatory or routine PAS for such individuals.

Accompanying this darker version of the consequences of a "right to die" are predictions of explosive growth in the number of elderly citizens in the United States in the twenty-first century. The concern among advocates of the aged is that the burden of caring for this expanding population will lead to increased pressure on the elderly to "choose" passive euthanasia or PAS (Longino 1988). As Osgood (1995) writes, it is members of this group (whom she refers to as the "oldest old") "who, in the future, will demand the most health care resources and who have the least to offer society in terms of labor, productive work, and economic benefits" (p. 415). Compounding these economic pressures, rapid cultural changes, along with the "cult of youth," denial of death, and the ageism that pervades American society, promise further marginalization of members of this group.

IMPLICATIONS OF MEDICAL AND LEGAL FRAMING OF EUTHANASIA

Dominance of Medical Frames

It is significant that medical frames were found to be equally dominant in both pro- and anti-euthanasia news coverage. Moreover, even those articles criticizing specific medical practices functioned overall to preserve and reinforce the institutional power of medicine. Although journalists may have employed medical frames to question the appropriateness of particular medical practices—such as doctors' overuse of life-extension technologies or even PAS itself—the question of whether the medical establishment is the most suitable arena for debating euthanasia was never raised. Similarly, while facts, quotes, and viewpoints sometimes reflected theological, ethical, philosophical, or sociological perspectives, these arguments were mere volleys exchanged on an essentially medical battleground. The story journalists told about euthanasia in this investigation was overwhelmingly a medical narrative (albeit with legal complications driving the plot).

On the surface, it may seem quite logical that medical frames should dominate news coverage of euthanasia. After all, the modern phase of the RTD movement arose as a direct result of advances in medical technology allowing doctors to extend the lives of the mortally ill and incapacitated. The vast majority of Americans also die in medical institutions, and both passive and active euthanasia are still largely carried out in hospitals. Moreover, who better than medical sources to speak to the issue of PAS—which by definition involves doctors' participation? Given the links between euthanasia and established medicine, then, there is some justification for journalists' framing of euthanasia primarily through the discourse of orthodox medicine.

Something that is often overlooked, however, perhaps in part as a result of the news media's medicalization of euthanasia—is that suicide does not intrinsically require medical intervention at all (Kalwinsky 1998). Although institutionalized medicine exercises control over virtually all aspects of death and dying in America, medicine's authority in this area is a relatively recent phenomenon (see chapter 3). In fact, a primary goal of the RTD movement since its inception has been to wrest control over the dying process from the medical establishment. Were Americans granted direct access to the lethal drugs needed to end their lives, or if most people simply chose to die via assisted suicide at home or in hospices, euthanasia would move outside the auspices of mainstream medicine and could no longer be defined as a medical issue.

Far from benign, the news media's promotion of medical authority in American society has broad implications. Among the most serious is its contribution to "medical imperialism," defined by Strong (1979) as the "increasing and illegitimate medicalization of the social world" (pp. 199–200). Critics of medicalization cite the growing trend in American society of explaining diverse social problems (e.g., substance abuse) in terms of the medical or "disease" model. The drawback of this approach is its marginalization of alternative models. As Conrad and Schneider (1992) note, "When medical perspectives of problems and their solutions become dominant, they diminish competing definitions" (p. 242). This is certainly supported by the results of this research, which shows that except for legal frames, medical constructions overwhelmed alternative interpretations of the euthanasia controversy. Ethics and religion, two areas of discourse with more than a passing interest in death, in the quality and sanctity of life, and in the meaning of suffering, were largely marginalized in the news stories analyzed here. Had this not been the case—for example, had journalists instead chosen to interpret the controversy primarily through the *Sanctity of Life* or *Divine Authority* frames—an vastly different "dominant reading" of the euthanasia issue would most certainly have resulted.

In addition to limiting the full range of discourse and perspectives on an issue of considerable social import, the news coverage of euthanasia examined in this study masked the medical industry's financial interest in promoting social and legal acceptance of euthanasia and interest in ensuring that the issue continues to be interpreted as a medical procedure. This study's conclusion that journalists reporting on euthanasia marginalized the Economic/Pragmatic frame means that they effectively obscured the financial considerations driving the RTD campaign. As discussed in the previous chapter, the articles in this analysis gave scant attention to economic incentives—particularly those fueling the medical industry's stake in social acceptance of euthanasia as a routinized aspect of medical care. This century's stunning technological developments, combined with an increasingly nonregulatory, probusiness political climate, have proven enormously beneficial for hospitals and their parent corporations, which have enjoyed unprecedented medical expansion and monopolization as a result. Along with its business partners—health insurance, medical research, and drug companies—mainstream medicine is among the most profitable United States industries (Conrad and Schneider 1992).

An even more profound consequence of medicalization of euthanasia, however, relates to its shaping influence on cultural attitudes toward death and suicide in American culture. Interpreting the issues surrounding death and dying primarily as clinical or medical problems divests them of their natural and human dimensions—which, in turn, reinforces the denial of death that cultural scholars have identified as a pervasive (and unwholesome) aspect of American society. More serious, medicalization of euthanasia imbues suicide and "mercy killing" with a moral neutrality or even validity denied to "mercy killing" throughout centuries of Western history. Carried out under the guise of "science," medical practices are perceived as objective, rational, and ideology-free. Although this perception may be deeply flawed, these values are nevertheless extended to assisted suicide by virtue of its categorization as a medical question and its association with medical professionals (see, e.g., Zola 1972; Conrad and Schneider 1992). As Emanuel (1994) notes, medicalization of euthanasia—and particularly PAS—effectively sanitizes the practice.

By defining euthanasia fundamentally as a medical practice requiring medical expertise and medical technologies, then, journalists covering euthanasia in the news sources in this investigation not only helped secure medical hegemony over death and dying and expanded the medical establishment's economic "market," but helped lend passive euthanasia and PAS the stamp of scientific and medical legitimacy. Whatever the ultimate cultural costs of news media emphasis on medical frames to represent euthanasia to the American public, this framing choice unquestionably means the sacrifice of a host of alternative constructions of a social issue with significant, long-term consequences. Equally important, news reporting that promotes medical hegemony over such a central and personal aspect of human experience necessarily means the denial of this same authority to society's elderly, severely disabled, and terminally ill—those most affected by the outcome of the debate over euthanasia.

DOMINANCE OF LEGAL FRAMES

The dominance of legal frames in euthanasia coverage found in this research has its own set of serious ideological and societal implications. As the mainstream news media have become less willing or able to challenge institutional authority or to cover morally complex topics in a way that stimulates rather than hampers public debate, it is left to the legal system to address society's ethically complex, technology-related controversies. Indeed, the past century has witnessed an increasing trend in the United States toward allowing the courts to address technologically related social controversies, in particular. In addition to handling disputes over passive and active euthanasia, the courts function as the nation's primary clearinghouse for an array of thorny issues spawned by medical technology ranging from abortion and human gene mapping to cloning and the use of fetal cell tissues for medical research. This dependence on legal solutions, however, comes at a stiff price; there are significant dangers in giving the courts sweeping powers to define and "solve" issues such as whether PAS should be socially sanctioned or whether a "right to die" properly exists.

Located at the intersection of the personal and the political, the acknowledged and disavowed, the real and the metaphysical, the debate over euthanasia is singularly problematic where the law is concerned. As Nuland (1997) writes, it makes little sense "to legislate or have the courts impose a rationality" on such an inherently irrational and anxiety-inducing issue (A15). Like a host of similarly emotionally fraught social issues, euthanasia is value-laden, rich in complexity, and deeply intertwined with core personal, philosophical, and metaphysical beliefs and meanings. When such complex issues are dispatched to the legal system before being subjected to extensive public debate, they risk being straitjacketed into narrow mandates or edicts and stripped of their nuances and ethical dimensions. As might be expected, the results are demoralizing to those left out of the decision-making process—often the very groups and individuals most passionate about and most likely to be affected by the issues in question. Denying these groups a voice, of course, in no way sidesteps or defuses dissent, as the past several decades of abortion-related violence, including clinic bombings and the murder of abortion workers, amply demonstrates.[1] As First Amendment scholar Rodney Smolla (1995) reminds us, "Squelching speech . . . simply redirects it, drives it underground, where it festers into more dangerous hysterias" (p. 95).

The urge to seek legal answers to highly complex social problems—while more rapid and less "messy" than protracted, divisive public debate—not only tends to accelerate social change, but does so in unpredictable and disruptive ways. It is not merely that the court's ham-fisted approach to solving such issues ensures a backlash from disaffected citizens and groups. Moreover, the problem goes beyond the law's detached realism, codified language, and formulaic remedies—none of which are equipped to wrestle with issues deeply embedded in cultural and personal beliefs, meanings, emotions, and ritualistic practices. The most serious consequence of the news media's increasingly "thin" public discourse on ethically dimensional issues is that it robs Americans of the opportunity to use such debates to redefine their core cultural values, refocus their objectives and goals, and reestablish their sense of themselves as active participants in the public sphere. This is not to say that the legal system has no place in resolving ethical dilemmas; rather it is that the law—with its detached realism, codified language, and formulaic remedies—simply lacks the depth or breadth to grapple with issues elementally embedded in cultural and personal beliefs, meanings, emotions, and ritualistic practices.

Much better suited for this role in many ways are the mainstream news media, which have been granted broad freedoms in exchange for providing an open forum for public debate on just such issues. In modern mass societies the national news media are the closest approximation of the traditional public forum, the intellectual marketplace where citizens encounter a broad spectrum of speakers engaged in robust debate on issues of cultural significance (Habermas 1989).

Unfortunately, based on the results of this study, the news media fall considerably short of the "public forum" ideal. Nowhere is this more evident than in journalists' privileging of the "right to die" frame to represent euthanasia in the articles in this research. Of course, rights discourses have always enjoyed a high level of resonance in American culture. As Tarrow (1994, 129) observes, "It is striking how naturally Americans frame their demands in terms of rights—whether they be the rights of minorities, women, gay men and lesbians, animals or the unborn. European movements are far less likely to employ a rights discourse, even when their goals and constituencies are similar." News media scholars have found legal rights to be an integral part of news media coverage of the women's movement, the civil rights crusade, the campaign for animal rights, and the abortion debate, among other issues (see, e.g., Condit 1990; Silverstein 1992; Patterson and Hall 1998).

In its implicit promotion of RTD goals and agendas, the "right to die" frame clearly functions in an ideological capacity. This framing choice, however, raises concerns that go beyond ideology to the viability of American democracy itself. Rights rhetoric is attractive to movement activists and the press because it resonates strongly with classical liberal ideals in the United States that falsely equate liberty with individual autonomy. Although "rights" frames offer journalists "a convenient political shorthand . . . valuable in the era of thirty-second TV news clips" (Silverstein 1992, 125), the danger of interpreting complex issues in terms of rights is that it not only oversimplifies and distorts social problems, but places too much emphasis on rights at the expense of morality and responsibility.[2] In addition to promoting conflict and thwarting consensus, philosopher Mary Ann Glendon (1991) contends that the "relentless individualism" associated with rights rhetoric squelches other viewpoints. Rights talk silences discourse about personal responsibility, ethics, and communitarian ideals. In doing so, she argues, it "seems to condone acceptance of the benefits of living in a democratic social welfare state without accepting the corresponding personal and civic obligations" (p. 15). Ironically, arguments steeped in individual rights often prove counter-productive to the very groups most likely to articulate them—the poor, minorities, and other powerless individuals. Whereas rights rhetoric has enabled marginalized groups to gain the respect and attention of those in power, it is also the powerful who are most likely to manipulate rights frames in their favor. Rights rhetoric "fosters a climate that is inhospitable to society's losers, and that systematically disadvantages caretakers and dependents, young and old. In its neglect of civil society, it undermines the principal seedbeds of civic and personal virtue" (p. 14).

As an antidote to news media discourse emphasizing individual rights frames—which Glendon sees as promoting "the short-run over the long-term, sporadic crisis intervention over systematic preventive measures, and particular interests over the common good"—she suggests enriching public dialog with "the more carefully nuanced languages that many Americans still speak in their kitchens, neighborhoods, workplaces, religious communities, and union halls" (Glendon 1991, 15). Following her prescription would require the news media to choose frames that not only invite reason and stir compassion, but reflect a broad diversity of perspectives. If journalists followed these guidelines—for example, showing greater sensitivity to and respect for diverse viewpoints on issues like euthanasia—what kinds of policy decisions might result? Political representatives exposed to coverage reflecting a full range of interpretations might choose to support alternative ways of dying, allocating increased funds for hospice and in-home care of the terminally ill. Other outcomes might include renewed efforts to improve end-of-life pain management, recognition of the role depression plays in older Americans' choice of suicide, or greater commitment to the general needs of disabled, elderly, and other citizens most affected by euthanasia decisions. Following another track, honest discussion of the economic costs associated with America's burgeoning elderly population might steer society to an understanding and acceptance of the limits of its financial obligations to severely disabled and dying individuals. Whatever its specific consequences, news coverage reflecting diverse viewpoints and voices is considerably more likely than either adjudication or emphasis on rights frames to foster a decision-making process that is inclusive rather than exclusive, grounded in equitable distribution of resources rather than in the protection of state and economic interests, and informed by the ideal of the marketplace of ideas rather than newsroom conventions that privilege institutional sources.

Yet another price Americans pay for the convenience and ease of relying on the courts for short-term solutions to complex social problems is loss of a sense of community—the notion that America as a culture is capable of taking full responsibility for its manifest and hidden political policies and social agendas, including the way in which technological and economic imperatives drive virtually every aspect of contemporary life in the United States. In packing our most difficult dilemmas off to the courts without sustained public discussion and only the barest of news "coverage," the media forfeit Americans' democratic birthright: that of confronting and coming to terms with past choices and fully imagining the unintended consequences of future decisions.

IMPLICATIONS OF OMISSION AND MARGINALIZATION OF RELIGIOUS AND ETHICAL FRAMES

As Parenti (1996) reminds us, "The media's most common method of distortion is omission. We are misled not only by what is reported but by what is left unmentioned." Of the various frame omissions this study identifies, the absence or marginalization of religious, theological, and ethical frames is perhaps the most limiting. In the news stories in this analysis, metaphysics and medicine inhabit distinctly different spheres, with religion, philosophy—and medical ethics to a lesser extent—shunted off to the margins.

On one level this moral and metaphysical void in euthanasia coverage may be regarded as simply another manifestation of the secularization of public discourse dating back in Western civilizations to the Reformation (see, e.g., chapter 3). The virtual absence of metaphysical or religious framing of a topic as deeply situated within the realm of meaning and values as euthanasia, however, should not be so easily excused. More than a mere symptom of the "crisis of legitimacy" facing religions since the dawn of modernity, the news media's failure to address the moral dimensions of euthanasia and PAS amounts to an abdication of what Weber calls society's "ultimate and most sublime values" (Hoover and Venturelli 1996, citing Weber 1968, 260). Although journalists take pride in the "objectivity" this approach affords, their reluctance to enter the turgid waters of ethical and moral debate has a number of troubling implications.

First, as discussed earlier, rationalistic, legalistic solutions to social problems—which seek to draw unambiguous lines between "right" and "wrong" and "legal" and "illegal"—are simply too heavy-handed to produce satisfying answers to dilemmas as meaning-laden and complex as those raised by the euthanasia debate (Hoefler and Kamoie 1994). As Glendon (1991, 15) argues, relying overmuch on legal rather than philosophical or theological frameworks underestimates the public's "capacity for reason and the richness and diversity of moral sentiments that exist in American society." Second, by framing death and dying primarily as either a medical or individual rights issue, the news media devalue the meaning of death by commodifying and politicizing it. So entrenched and normalized has this mode of reporting become in American society that we not only fail to notice the absence of what Hoover and Venturelli (1996, 263) refer to as "the sacred spheres of life" in public debate, but would be hard-pressed to imagine news coverage that draws from a rich vein of moral, religious, and ethical frames to help contextualize and humanize public debate over thorny issues like euthanasia.

Although journalists covering euthanasia in the articles in this research were careful to include quotes from medical ethicists and clerics who articulated (however superficially) ethical and religious principles, almost without exception these were presented within the context of larger legalistic and/or medicalized frames. When religious or ethical considerations were included (such as the Vatican's stand on euthanasia), this material was often presented in a sidebar or as verbatim text, with no comment or attempt at integration or interpretation. In contrast, meanwhile, legal and medical frames were powerfully articulated in emotionally compelling anecdotes, in pointed quotes by experts, and through other sophisticated discursive devices.[3]

The effect of this type of distortion is that religious or ethical arguments functioned in the articles analyzed as mere "signs" of conflict in the Sausseurian sense, as obstacles standing in the way of the "right to die," or as cursory acknowledgment by journalists of the existence of a collective moral conscience. The result in any case is that reporters, in ticking off alternative frames or counterarguments, are ultimately able to keep these unwieldy, complex areas of discourse from serious consideration.

It is perhaps too much to expect journalists to *foreground* overtly religious frames. In ignoring aspects of social issues such as religion, considered fundamental to significant numbers of Americans, however, the news media intensify cultural combat over conflicting ways of knowing, such as science versus spirituality, reason versus myth, and intellect versus emotion. Calling for a reexamination of the "rationalist approach to understanding contemporary life," Hoover and Venturelli (1996) warn that "the eclipse of 'the religious' within media discourse" endangers the public sphere—and hence democratic freedom. In abdicating the responsibility to address the mythical and moral as well as the legal and rational dimensions of public life, the news media lay alms before the altar of America's preeminent "secularized religion"—individualism, a cult that de Tocqueville (1835/1966), with astonishing prescience, recognized in his book *Democracy in America* more than a century ago as intrinsically antithetical to the welfare of society as a whole. As he believed, a major advantage of including religious or morally centered discourse in public debate is its potential to temper the political, "to bond the category of political freedom to an ethical foundation" (Hoover and Venturelli 1996, 262). Without an ethical foundation, "democracy" is little more than rhetoric—a hollow shell used by politicians to advance their agendas, but devoid of the lifeblood of the people.

De Tocqueville issued his warning against allowing individualism to erode the nation's ethical foundation—which, as it happens, was built on a strong sense of religious conviction and communitarian ideals—with France's political upheaval fresh in mind. Arriving on America's shores in 1831 in the wake of the French Revolution, de Tocqueville observed the new nation with an eye toward assessing the aftermath of the American Revolution, which, like its French counterpart, was expressly fought to wrest power from the elite and return it to the people in the form of democracy. What de Tocqueville recognized was the uniqueness with which the political was married to the religious in the United States. In American democracy—unlike European political systems—liberty was infused with, and hence indistinguishable from, morality. As de Tocqueville recognized, the resulting government was more likely to act on the principles that what affects one affects all, and the powerless must be protected from the powerful. In the American society he witnessed, the self was not truncated from the body politic, but irrevocably fused with it through the coupling of political and religious ideals.

Unfortunately, in the century and a half since de Tocqueville offered his astute observations, the United States has experienced a steep decline—if not outright debasement—of many of the ideals he singled out for praise. Individualism, which he noted as a potential threat to the young democracy, has today risen to cult status in American society. As he understood, the American ethos of individualism—which is reproduced and reinforced in mass media messages in the twenty-first century on a scale unimaginable in his time—conflicts with many of the fundamental goals and needs of members of a pluralistic society. Moreover, since de Tocqueville's visit, economic pressures have not only led to the institutionalization of news media conventions that privilege the secular over the ethical and moral (hence splitting the self from the body politic), but to the news media's ritualistic privileging of interpretive frames that reflect the interests of the corporate elite and wealthy. This study's results—which show medical and legal frames to dominate all other viewpoints and interpretations of the euthanasia debate—clearly support this contention.

If American society expects to make decisions about tough social issues that foster rather than destroy social equilibrium, the news media must become more integrative and inclusive. Blaming American society's "atrophied political processes" on its impoverished public discourse and narrow framing of social problems, Glendon (1991) argues that the survival of a heterogenous society depends on the open exchange of ideas—even those like religion and ethics that seem out of place in a secularized society (p. 181). "At the grassroots level," she warns, "men and women of widely varying backgrounds are increasingly manifesting their discontent with . . . an unwritten law that morally or religiously grounded viewpoints are out of bounds in public dialogue." Far from undermining public discourse, she argues, on the few occasions in which religious and moral views have been given legitimacy (e.g., the speeches of

Martin Luther King), the results have mitigated rather than increased "fear, suspicion, divisiveness, and intolerance" in American society (p. 181).

Finally, in addition to the need for a diversity of viewpoints and voices in the news, more time must be set aside for public deliberation on divisive social issues like euthanasia. As policymakers and the public struggle over the question of granting social sanction to PAS—a practice that promises long-term, unpredictable consequences for millions of Americans—it is vital that the news media heed this counsel. The low quality of public discussion identified in this study, however, is not the news media's problem alone. Rather, it is reflective of the broad impulse in American society to "come to answers too quickly" and, in the process, ignore some of the more crucial philosophical aspects of life (Niedelmann 1999). Americans—perhaps the most action- and solution-oriented people in the world—are impatient with long-term controversies, failing to appreciate the time and energy needed to confront and find solutions to complex social dilemmas. As Niedelmann argues, "The great issues of human life have to be seen as questions that we live with, that we ponder, that we try to open our hearts and minds to. There are no answers in that sense. There are just states of confronting realities . . . and contradictions."

If the nation's mainstream news media fails to recognize the relationship between aborted public discussions and unsuccessful social policies, they risk becoming increasingly irrelevant and untrustworthy in the eyes of the public. The more news organizations consolidate power, trim news budgets, and focus on economic exigencies rather than carrying out their civic obligations, the tighter their yoke to coercive state and economic institutions. The closer the unholy union between the news media and institutional interests, the more citizens are squeezed out of policy decisions affecting their personal, day-to-day lives. Some news scholars, including Hallin (1994), argue that the commercial news media in this nation have already reached the point where they are incapable of acting as representatives and commissioners of the public interest. Unfortunately, the results of this study do nothing to contradict this thesis. As long as newsroom conventions and ideological ties to state, institutional, and economic interests continue to shape the contours of national news coverage, there is little hope that the news media will fulfill their responsibility to invite and engage the public in vigorous debate over crucial social issues (Hallin 1994).

NOTES

1. A good illustration is the speed with which the legal system dispensed with abortion, which, after truncated public discussion, was referred to the courts for hasty resolution. Almost four decades after *Roe v. Wade*, the ruling continues to fragment and tear at the fabric of society in the form of litigation, legislation, protest demonstrations, violence, and the deep disenfranchisement of an angry, vocal segment of the population. The nation seems to have learned little from the abortion controversy. The course of the euthanasia debate followed a similar trajectory: Passive euthanasia received the sanction

of the courts and the public in remarkably short order. By 1990—only a decade and a half after *Quinlan*—news media discourse (and by extension public discussion) of the divisive issue had all but ended.

2. Glendon (1991) warns against American culture's "increasing tendency to speak of what is most important to us in terms of rights, and to frame nearly every social controversy as a clash of rights" (p. 4). She identifies America's rights obsession—which she maintains is a recent historical trend—as both a consequence and cause of the expanded role given to the courts. Referring to the explosion of legal rights as "the central legal drama of the times," she argues that rights rhetoric, with its assumption that individuals are entitled to inherent benefits and may demand legal enforcement to receive them, undermines social harmony. Aside from creating "unrealistic expectations," the quest for rights is never exhausted. Once rights rhetoric is given legitimacy through news media circulation of rights frames, it tends to take on a life of its own. The prevailing attitude becomes, "if rights are good, more rights must be even better" (p. 16). The problem with the ratcheting up of rights is that in a pluralistic society liberties are always in conflict. As she notes, "there is very little agreement regarding which needs, goods, interests, or values should be characterized as 'rights' or concerning what should be done when, as is usually the case, various rights are in tension or collision with one another" (p. 16). Rights rhetoric—in this study exemplified by journalists' privileging of the "right to die" frame—"inhibits dialogue that might lead toward consensus, accommodation, or at least the discovery of common ground" (p. 14).

3. This pattern is exemplified by a *New York Times* article featuring an emotionally provocative pro-RTD anecdote about a comatose patient kept alive for eighteen years at a cost of $6 million. Accompanying this compelling story was a sidebar that excerpted—without comment or elaboration—Pope John Paul II's 1980 "Declaration on Euthanasia" ("Doctors, Patients and the Right to Die" 1984).

What's in a Name? Definitions and Terms Used in the Debate over Euthanasia

> A definition is not, as conventional wisdom assumes, the set of
> necessary and sufficient conditions that constitute a known, fixed,
> starting point for political, economic, and ideological struggles.
> Rather a definition represents the outcome of such
> struggles—unstable, negotiated, and often quite temporary.
> —Treichler (1989, 449)

Of all the elements of social conflict, none tends to be more problematic—or more fiercely contested—than the definitions and terms social activists use to frame the discursive boundaries of public debate on controversial issues. As Treichler's quote above implies, even the most rudimentary definitions and terms used by claims-makers can profoundly shape cultural values, beliefs, and actions. Language is never neutral. Naming or defining a problem not only privileges certain interpretations, but establishes the existence of a social problem and, once established, determines its relevancy or irrelevancy (see, e.g., Toulmin 1958; Gusfield 1981; Lake 1986; Zarefsky 1986; Best 1987).

Nowhere is the battle over the naming of social problems and their solutions more in evidence than in the struggle over the definitions and terms social movement actors use, including those involved in the debate over euthanasia—an issue that rivals abortion as one of the most contentious and polarizing in recent American history. As is frequently the case in contests over the construction of social issues, each side in the euthanasia conflict brings its own preferred terms and definitions to the discursive arena. The result in the case of euthanasia is something of a terminological quagmire.

The first challenge for anyone wishing to investigate euthanasia discourse is how to refer to the opponents in the conflict. The countermovement formed to oppose legal and social acceptance of euthanasia goes by no formal name, although movement activists generally refer to themselves as "pro-life" or "anti-euthanasia."[1] Not coincidentally, the "pro-life" label is also used by abortion opponents, many of whom also oppose euthanasia. For purposes of clarity and consistency, groups opposed to euthanasia in any of its forms are referred to in this book by this label. On the other side of the debate, those advocating legal and social acceptance of euthanasia are referred to as RTD or pro-RTD in this book. The rationale for the RTD label, which evokes the ideologically laden "rights" frame, is that euthanasia supporters commonly identify themselves in this way (e.g., The Society for the Right to Die). Hence, the RTD label is used in this book to refer to both the general campaign to legalize euthanasia and to formal organizations—such as the Hemlock Society—dedicated to promoting social and legal acceptance of euthanasia.

Unfortunately, proper labeling of the groups involved in the euthanasia conflict is not the only semantic obstacle plaguing this issue. Not even the word "euthanasia" itself is free from ambiguity. According to one commentator, "Even when one has an overriding aim of neutrality and precision, it is difficult to define, accurately and clearly, which interventions on noninterventions should and which should not be regarded as constituting euthanasia" (Somerville 1993, 2). A broad spectrum of meanings and definitions have been attached to the word "euthanasia" throughout history:

In ancient Greece it simply referred to a good death, whatever the cause. By the end of the nineteenth century it referred to the manner of death, the taking of life in order to end suffering. By the end of World War II it had come to mean the taking of life without permission. Since then the word has been avoided by many right-to-die advocates who prefer phrases like "self-deliverance," "accelerated death," "death by design," "self-termination," "elective death," and "the final freedom." (Colt 1991, 358)

In seventeenth- and eighteenth-century England, terms for euthanasia included "self murder" and "self-killing," both of which were later supplanted by the Latin construct "suicide." A long list of terms have been used synonymously with euthanasia in the twentieth century, including: "assisted suicide," "aid-in-dying," "therapeutic euthanasia," justifiable suicide," "rational suicide," "hastened death," "merciful release," and "auto-euthanasia." The exact meaning of yet another popular word for euthanasia—"mercy killing"—remains obscure, and, for obvious reasons, is rejected by the pro-life movement.[2]

Then there is the somewhat thorny problem of distinguishing "euthanasia" from "suicide," two overlapping terms that are often used interchangeably. In both suicide and euthanasia, individuals decide to die and take steps to do so. Distinctions between the two are usually grounded in social and legal considerations, such as "the means by which death is achieved, that is, who delivers the fatal stroke, and . . . the physical and mental state of the person who dies or wishes to die" (Fairbairn 1995, 121). This rather vague distinction does more to illuminate the ideological struggle to define the terms of the euthanasia debate than to establish the boundaries between "suicide" and "euthanasia." While pro-life activists often conflate the two constructs on the basis that all suicide—including euthanasia—violates the "sanctity of life" and is therefore immoral, RTD activists frequently stress the opposing purposes of each: Whereas suicide results from emotional or psychological illness, RTD activists regard euthanasia as a "rational" attempt to alleviate suffering when "no hope" of recovery remains.

Uncertainty also shadows discussions about the precise categories euthanasia encompasses. One writer, for example, has identified no fewer than six types of euthanasia: (1) passive, (2) semipassive, (3) semiactive, (4) accidental, (5) suicidal, and (6) active (Lundberg 1988, 2142–43). Interest in the relative merits and drawbacks of the minute variations in euthanasia practice has spawned something of a cottage industry for bioethicists, legal scholars, and medical authorities (see, e.g., Rachels 1979; Hauerwas 1986; Wennberg 1990; Somerville 1993). Moreover, as discussed more fully below, controversy exists over the meaning of "voluntary" versus "involuntary" euthanasia.

The inability of the two sides in the conflict to agree on particular terms, definitions, or even on a common meaning of "euthanasia" is indicative of both the technological complexity and deep divisiveness of the issue. For example, depending on the context and the point of view of the speaker, "euthanasia" encompasses everything from the removal of life-support systems and failure to administer medical treatments to injecting patients with lethal drugs. Adding to this problem is disagreement over whether and to what extent other activities—such as declaring patients "brain dead" for organ transplants—qualify as forms of "involuntary" euthanasia.[3]

Then there is the ambiguity of the phrase "right to die," which pro-life activists object to on principle. As one commentator observes,

This foggy phrase could mean the right of competent patients to refuse extraordinary means of medical treatment. It could also signify an unconditional right to suicide. More radically, it could denote the right of an individual to be killed by another or even the right of the state to kill certain individuals deemed unfit. The precise understanding of this right stands at the heart of the current euthanasia debate, where one party adamantly defends the restricted sense of this right as one of rational refusal and where the other party ardently support extension of this right to include active euthanasia and suicide. (Conley 1994, 9)

In order to untangle some of the semantic complexities obscuring euthanasia discourse, it is helpful to address the precise end-of-life activities that each side of the euthanasia controversy supports and opposes. Both pro-life activists and RTD supporters tend to define euthanasia broadly—although for dramatically different reasons (Somerville 1993, 2–3). While pro-life groups advocate a definition of euthanasia inclusive of all interventions and noninterventions that *shorten or fail to prolong* life, RTD activists argue for a definition commodious enough to allow all interventions or noninterventions that allow individuals *death with dignity*—by which they generally mean the right "to control the time and manner of death" (Beschle 1988–89, 321). To buttress their position, RTD activists point to the etymological roots of "euthanasia," which—roughly translated from Greek—means "good death." They therefore promote the legalization of any activity—medical or otherwise—that fosters this ideal.[4]

In pursuing their general goal of a "good" or "dignified" death for all individuals, RTD supporters favor *active euthanasia*, defined as "the administration of any means intended to produce death, such as the deliberate injection of a lethal dose of morphine" (Schanker 1993, 983).[5] An apparently widely practiced variation of active euthanasia is the "double effect" phenomenon, which refers to the administration of narcotic drugs to terminally ill patients—ostensibly to relieve pain, but also, in actuality, to suppress respiration and cause death (see, e.g., Hall 1994; Newman 1991; Emanuel 1994; Meier and Cassel 1983; and Lundberg 1988).[6] Hall (1994) describes the "double effect" in this way:

An increasingly common practice in the United States today is to relieve distress with the use of narcotics which have the effect of inhibiting breathing. A typical case might be a terminal cancer patient whose breathing is assisted by a ventilator. The time comes when deterioration has progressed to a point where . . . the decision is made to turn the ventilator off. The patient may then experience severe distress, which can be relieved with narcotics, but the narcotics may also hasten the patient's death by depressing respiration. In cases such as this, the argument is often made that, if a physician acts to relieve the distress but the treatment also shortens the patient's life or 'hastens' his or her death, this is ethically acceptable because the death of the patient was an unintended consequence, a secondary effect in a double-effect situation. (p. 11)

Of course, this rationale troubles some medical ethicists, doctors, and pro-life supporters who point out that by calibrating the dosages carefully, doctors can easily use the technique purposefully to cause death. Indeed, writes Newman (1991, 165), "If dosages of narcotic drugs are sufficiently high and the patient's respiration is poor, death is a virtual certainty."

In addition to active euthanasia, RTD supporters advocate the legalization of *passive* euthanasia, defined as "the withdrawal of life-sustaining care, such as artificially supplied nutrition and hydration or a respirator" (Schanker 1993, 983). It is important to stress, however, that euthanasia supporters consider the distinction between "active" and "passive" euthanasia "arbitrary and morally irrelevant . . . since the lethal injection or the withdrawal of treatment both result in the patient's death" (p. 984). As Newman (1991) argues,

It is sometimes claimed that the "passive" techniques are morally acceptable because they allow for a natural death, while "active" techniques independently cause death. But in the modern medical setting, these terms and distinctions are ephemeral. The concept of natural death in the hospital has lost its meaning. "If you want to have a natural death," says Dr. Alan Stone, "you have to stay out of the doctor's hands." If you make it alive to the hospital, medical technology derails nature and alters the course, experience and timing of death. (p. 164, quoting Stone 1988, 636)

The rationale for "letting" patients die is that the actual cause of death "is not the withdrawal of life support, but the underlying disease that made such support necessary" (Newman 1991, 164). Burnell (1993) notes that "passive euthanasia" is also referred to as "euthanasia by omission." As he explains, "Passive euthanasia is usually requested by the person dying, either verbally or through a written document such as a living will. In passive euthanasia, by withholding intravenous feedings, medications, surgery, a pacemaker, or a respirator, the doctor can let the patient die of the underlying disease." (p. 248). In terms of these activities, RTD proponents favor both what they label "voluntary" euthanasia (carried out with the informed consent of a patient) and "involuntary" euthanasia (performed without the consent of the patient). Written requests for passive euthanasia are generally made in "advance directives" such as living wills, which specify in writing the specific end-of-life therapies individuals do *not* want in the event that they are unconscious and incapable of expressing their wishes directly.

On the opposite side of the debate, the most conservative pro-life activists oppose any intervention or non-intervention—medical or otherwise—that hastens an individual's death. Many pro-life groups not only express opposition to self-administered or physician-assisted suicide (PAS), but consider refusal of medical treatments—even those with broad legal and medical acceptance—to constitute euthanasia. Like RTD activists, some pro-life groups also dispute the distinction between "passive" and "active" euthanasia, recognizing no moral difference between withholding treatment and directly administering lethal medication—since both result in death. These more conservative members of the pro-life movement consider both active and passive euthanasia practices to violate religious notions of the "sanctity of life" and in that sense to constitute "murder."

It is important to stress, however, that not all pro-life activists oppose those practices generally considered acts of passive euthanasia. In fact, most pro-life activists and many religions that oppose active euthanasia do not object to the withholding of life-extension therapies; not only do they *not* consider such actions to constitute euthanasia, but they object to the nomenclature "passive euthanasia" to refer to the withholding of medical care. Here, however, the distinction between euthanasia as the withholding of *all* medical therapies and only those considered "extraordinary" becomes a crucial one. Often, approval or disapproval of the practice turns on this difference. Except for the most conservative opponents of euthanasia, pro-life supporters generally do not consider disconnecting a patient's artificial respirator passive euthanasia, but simply "allowing nature to take its course." As a rule, then, those opposing euthanasia consider the "active/passive distinction as the most appropriate place to draw the line on how far society can safely go in allowing any form of euthanasia" (Schanker 1993, 984).

The conservative branch of the pro-life movement has also brought its opposition to medical definitions of "brain death" into the debate over euthanasia. Arguing that death only occurs upon the cessation of the heartbeat, they contend that unconscious patients whose organs are removed while their hearts continue to beat are victims of *involuntary* euthanasia. In general, opponents of euthanasia object to the term "voluntary euthanasia" and consider it particularly fraudulent when applied to the disconnection of life-support systems from comatose or gravely ill patients who are unable to express their wishes in this regard.

As this discussion makes clear, both the RTD and the pro-life movements are variously hamstrung by their definitions of euthanasia (Somerville 1993). By using the term to apply to all interventions or noninterventions that shorten life, the pro-life movement gains simplicity, but at the cost of taking an all-or-nothing approach to an issue that most Americans regard as too complex and personal for black-and-white answers. As Somerville writes, "The full spectrum of issues raised by medical intervention or non-intervention in dying, should not be included in one term . . . The terms in this most important, sensitive, nuanced and delicate area need to be precisely used" (pp. 3–4). The same dilemma confronts the RTD movement, which defines euthanasia as all interventions and non-interventions that promote a "good death." Bound to this broad agenda, RTD leaders unilaterally support all such activities rather than accepting certain procedures and interventions and rejecting others.

NOTES

1. For example, one organization opposing euthanasia calls itself the International Anti-Euthanasia Task Force.

2 Although *Black's Law Dictionary* (1990, 988) defines "mercy killing" as "euthanasia [or] the affirmative act of bringing about immediate death allegedly in a painless way and generally administered by one who thinks that the dying person wishes to die because of a terminal or hopeless disease or condition," Burnell argues that the term technically refers to ending one's life by "shooting or strangulation only" (1993, 248).

3. For example, Citizens United Resisting Euthanasia (CURE) equates the harvesting of organs from patients who have been declared "brain dead" with "involuntary" euthanasia—or as CURE's founder describes it—as an example of "checkbook euthanasia" (Appleby 1996).

4. The word "euthanasia" derives from the Greek word *eu*, meaning easy or painless, and *thanatos*, meaning death.

5. A 1997 study reported in *The New England Journal of Medicine* found that 53 percent of 118 physicians polled admitted knowingly prescribing lethal drug doses to AIDS patients who requested assisted suicide. Most of the physicians surveyed had prescribed lethal doses of narcotics at least three times, and one doctor admitted helping 100 patients die (Van Biema 17 Feb. 1997). In a 1998 reported in *The Journal of the American Medical Association* (*JAMA*), roughly one-third of a group of 206 general internists said they would participate in PAS if the patient were terminally ill and "persistently" requested PAS (Sulmasy 1998, 1034).

6. Although the precise number of physicians who help patients die is unknown, a Michigan survey published in 1996 in *JAMA* reported that one in five physicians had helped patients die (Stolberg 1997). A survey of Washington state doctors found that 12 percent had been asked to help patients die and, of these, 25 percent did so (Angell 1997).

APPENDIX B

RESEARCH METHODS

The print media selected for this study are nationally distributed newspapers and news magazines—specifically, *Newsweek, Time, U.S. News & World Report (USNWR)*, and *The New York Times*. The first three of these represent the nation's highest-circulation, weekly news magazines, and *The New York Times* is frequently referred to as the nation's "paper of record." Although the wide variety of news sources available in the United States may initially suggest a rich diversity of voices, viewpoints, readership, and content, scholars have found the mainstream media in reality tend to speak univocally. As one media critic has observed, "Much of what passes for diversity in mass media is largely a matter of packaging designed to deliver a product to market" (Bennett 1988, quoted in Pearson 1993, 17). Framing scholars have found negligible differences in the way television, newspapers, and news magazines frame major news stories. For example, Gitlin (1980) concluded that across newspapers, television networks, and news magazines, "the overall *repertory* of frames [and] . . . their forms of distortion are essentially the same" (p. 301).

Along with offering a representative sample of mainstream news frames, print media such as those used in this study provide special advantages for news researchers. News scholars have found selection, amplification, and systematic distortion to be hallmarks of all news media content (see, e.g., Bennett 1988; and Paletz and Entman 1981). But television news—which risks losing viewers if it strays from its formulaic reliance on stories, video footage, and viewpoints with the broadest possible appeal—tends to condense, oversimplify, and decontextualize news to a greater extent than print media. Unlike broadcast news, print journalism actually stands to gain rather than lose audiences by covering more specialized topics and perspectives (Postman and Powers 1992). News magazines in particular, as Solomon (1992, 57) points out, "offer more of a chance for in-depth reporting than is provided by the few minutes of television newscasts—and minus television's concern with 'good visuals,' which may affect news judgment."

While attracting a smaller audience than television news, *The New York Times* and the weekly news magazines selected for this analysis are among the nation's key "forums for public discourse" (Gamson and Modigliani 1989, 3). A As such, they are considered part of the "inner ring" of United States news organizations—the 11 "top-tier" media outlets with the greatest access to federal officials and hence the most influence (Hess 1984, cited in Solomon 1992, 68). *The New York Times*, unlike most daily newspapers, has a substantial national readership, which is responsible for the paper's growing circulation. By 2001, about half of the newspaper's 1.15 million customers read the national edition (Auletta, 2002). As *Newsweek*'s major role in breaking the Clinton sex scandal of 1998–1999 demonstrates, news magazines play a key agenda-setting role for both the public and for other mainstream news organizations (Kielbowicz and Scherer 1986). This is further supported by a 1986 survey that revealed that roughly half of American journalists read *Time* and *Newsweek* on a regular basis (Solomon 1992, 56, citing Weaver and Wilhoit 1986, 37).

Weekly news magazines offer still other unique advantages for news research using frame analysis. Because *Time, USNWR*, and *Newsweek* present a synthesis of the most important national news on a weekly rather than daily basis, these magazines serve what might be called a "frame condensing" function. By sifting through and selecting from the full array of news stories circulated daily in newspapers and on television, news magazines are more likely to reflect overall dominant frames than the daily news media. As Entman (1991) writes about news magazines, "Their less frequent deadlines usually allow them to canvass official sources (and other media) thoroughly, distilling the results in a narrative reflecting the principal themes in the news" (pp. 8–9, citing Gans 1979). This assertion is supported by the fact that news magazine editors compile their stories from a variety of news bureau sources and are significantly involved in editing and rewriting them (Solomon 1992).

Based on the above justifications, the sample selected for this study consisted of all stories on euthanasia published in *Time, USNWR*, and *Newsweek* over the roughly two-decade period between the *Quinlan* case and Kevorkian's 1999 murder conviction in the nationally televised death of Thomas Youk. A total of 121 news articles stories were included in the study. Only those stories focusing primarily on the topic of euthanasia, PAS, and/or the RTD movement and were of sufficient length to allow identification of clear story frames were included in the analysis. Columns and op-ed articles in *The New York Times* were not included in the study sample, both because of their tendency to be too brief to allow effective framing analysis and because of this study's focus on news reports rather than opinion discourse. Both to supplement this data sample and ensure that the frames found in the publications selected for research were congruent with other mainstream news frames, a representative sample of euthanasia stories from other print sources was also examined, including a regionally diverse selection of daily newspapers obtained from the Lexis-Nexis electronic database. In addition, literature from pro-life and RTD publications, as well as articles from scholarly medical and legal journals was also examined—both to capture the full range of euthanasia frames and to obtain background information on the conflict.

The *Quinlan* case—a watershed event in the long history of conflict over euthanasia—was chosen as the logical starting point for the analysis. This case not only marked the beginning of legally sanctioned euthanasia in the United States, but represented a paradigm shift in moral and medical approaches to care of the suffering and terminally ill. In this sense the *Quinlan* case may be described as a "hot moment" (Levi-Strauss 1966, 259), a "critical incident" (Gerbner 1973, 562), or a "critical event" (Pride 1995), all terms that refer to culturally charged events that serve as catalysts for change.[1] Attracting extensive media coverage, such events tend to open up new discursive arenas in which challenges to existing cultural arrangements, institutional structures, beliefs, and values may be acted out. Pride (1995) theorizes that critical events frequently lead to shifts in dominant news frames.[2]

By attending to two-and-one-half decades of news coverage of the euthanasia debate, this analysis benefits from the many advantages of longitudinal research, including the opportunity to monitor shifts in news framing of euthanasia over an extended period. Although news scholars consistently promote this type of research, relatively few researchers actually conduct long-term media analyses (Carragee 1991). Beginning the analysis in the mid-1970s allows research on the entire modern phase of the RTD movement, which was ignited by the *Quinlan* case.

METHODS

To investigate how the mainstream national news framed the euthanasia debate, a number of steps were systematically followed. First, because past studies have shown that the news media tend to reflect only a small percentage of the available frames in circulation on a given topic, a variety of nonmainstream news sources were examined, including euthanasia-related articles in medical, medical ethics, and legal journals, in religious publications such as *America* (a Jesuit periodical), and RTD movement and pro-life literature published on the Internet and elsewhere. From these readings five broad categories of pro-euthanasia and pro-life frames were identified: Medical, Legal, Social, Economic, and Religious/Ethical. Within these broad categories, more refined frames were then identified, such as the pro-euthanasia frames, *Humane Treatment, Medicine out of Control*, and *Right to Die*, and the pro-life frames, *Sanctity of Life, Slippery Slope*, and *Contaminates Medicine*. The purpose of identifying these framing categories was to discover the spectrum of available frames from which editors and journalists made their selections.

issues and events. These include: (1) story sources; (2) syntactical structure (e.g., headlines, subheads, and leads); (3) condensing symbols (also called referent images), including metaphors, exemplars, catchphrases, depictions, and visual images (Gamson and Modigliani 1989); (4) anecdotes; and (5) causal conclusions or suggestions in news stories (Entman 1991). Each of these is explained in greater detail below.

Sources

Evaluation of story sources (official, non-official, medical, legal, religious, etc.) in news media texts represents a crucial element of news media analysis (Fairclough 1995, 185). The sources used in news stories not only provide clues to the dominant framing of news narratives, but reveal what sources are systematically omitted from news discourse (see, e.g., Hall 1977).

Syntactical Structure

The rationale for analyzing headlines, subheads, and leads euthanasia stories included in the present analysis is based on the observation that readers use headlines both as cues to a story's frame and frequently decide to read or ignore a story based on the headline alone. Additionally, busy news consumers tend to read a news story's headlines, subheads, and perhaps the lead, while only scanning the body of the story. Pan and Kosicki (1993) describe headlines as "the most salient cue to activate certain semantically related concepts in readers' minds [and] . . . thus the most powerful framing device of the syntactical structure" (p. 59). Second in importance to the headline is a news story's lead, which imbues events and issues with a newsworthy angle, and in so doing, provides a specific perspective through which readers interpret social phenomena (Kosicki 1993, 60).

Condensing Symbols

Among the basic elements of the coding strategy used in this study involved identifying the five condensing symbols (metaphors, exemplars, catchphrases, depictions, and visual images) that signal the presence of frames (Gamson and Modigliani 1989). A coding scheme was designed with these framing elements in mind. The assumption on which this aspect of framing analysis is based is that identification of symbolic elements in news stories such as catchphrases (e.g., "right to die," "death with dignity," "she's already dead," "sanctity of life") and depictions (e.g., doctors as saintly; Kevorkian as a deviant; comatose patients as "vegetables") leads the researcher to the overriding or dominant story frame.

Anecdotes

Anecdotes also represent crucial elements in textual analysis (see, e.g., Burke 1969; Greenblatt 1992). These short, pithy stories about individuals designed to personalize and illustrate the characteristics and consequences of social problems and issues not only tend to support dominant news frames, but function as important rhetorical elements in their own right. As "mediators" between the localized and the universal, they have been shown to have a powerful influence on audience perceptions (see, e.g., Iyengar 1991). By condensing arguments into easily digestible narratives or "snapshot" case studies, anecdotes serve as carriers of cultural images and myths. Functioning at times as "morality tales" that instruct audiences on causes and solutions and act as linking agents, anecdotes connect lessons from the past with current problems. Because they are, as Greenblatt (1992) writes, "seized in passing from the swirl of experiences and given some shape," anecdotes are always "available for telling and retelling" (p. 3). Anecdotes are also implicated in distorting and oversimplifying complex issues. Designed to strike an emotional chord with news readers and viewers rather than appealing to reason, anecdotes such as "the wrenching case where a dying person is suffering unavoidable pain" have been linked expressly by some euthanasia opponents to American society's increasing willingness to consider assisted suicide a viable option for the terminally ill (Kamisar 1998, A27).

Causal Analyses and Evaluations

Euthanasia stories in this study were also coded with Entman's (1991) "salient aspects" of news frames in mind. Specifically, attention was paid to how journalists: (1) assigned blame or responsibility; (2) how they used words and images to foster audience identification with particular social actors or ideologies; and (3) how they used depictions or words to label or define the euthanasia issue (p. 11).

NOTES

1. Fiske (1994) uses the term to describe the postmodern blurring of "real" events and their mass-mediated representations. "A media event," he writes, "is not a mere representation of what happened, but it has its own reality, which gathers up into itself the reality of the event that may or may not have preceded it" (p. 2).

2. For example, following the bombing of TWA 800 by terrorists, Pride (1995, 6) found that a shift occurred in dominant media framing of airport security from a "cost is prohibitive" to a "safety is most important" frame.

EUTHANASIA TIMELINE

1884   The first medical reference to euthanasia in the United States appears in the *Boston Medical and Surgical Journal*, the predecessor of the *New England Journal of Medicine*. The article, written by a physician, argues that doctors should be permitted "to stand aside passively and give over any further attempt to prolong a life which had become a torment to its owner" (Emanuel 1994).

1905-6   A bill to legalize euthanasia is introduced in the Ohio legislature and defeated.

1931   The prominent English physician C. Killick Millard makes a widely circulated speech advocating legalized euthanasia.

1935   *The London Daily Mail* publishes a provocative story by an anonymous doctor who confesses to "mercy killing" five patients. The article, picked up by American newspapers, generates an outpouring of mail from patients requesting assisted suicide, from doctors making similar confessions, and from physicians and medical organizations condemning the practice.

1935   The Voluntary Euthanasia Legislation Society, the world's first organization devoted to legalizing euthanasia, is founded in England by Dr. C. Killick Millard, George Bernard Shaw, H. G. Wells, and others.

1936   England's House of Lords rejects the "Voluntary Euthanasia Bill," which would have allowed adult terminally ill patients to obtain aid in dying by signing a consent form.

1937   A bill that would have allowed terminally ill patients to obtain assisted suicide is introduced (and rejected) by the Nebraska legislature.

1938   Three pro-euthanasia groups are founded in the United States: the Euthanasia Society of America (ESA), the Euthanasia Education Council, and the Society for the Right to Die.

1957   In a public statement on the morality of resuscitation, Pope Pius XII declares that use of "ordinary means" only are required to satisfy the Christian mandate to preserve life.

1968   An Ad Hoc Committee of the Harvard Medical School establishes a new definition of "brain death."

1969   Charles Potter founds the Euthanasia Education Council (later changed to Concern for Dying) to distribute information on living wills.

1970   Founding of the Foundation of Thanatology at New York's Columbia University.

Aug. 1972   Physicians testify at hearings on "Death with Dignity" held by Special Senate Committee on Aging.

8 Jan. 1973   The American Hospital Association approves a 12-point "Bill of Rights" that includes the right of individuals to choose death by refusing medical treatment. This marks the first time a national health organization defends what courts have previously ruled—that adult, terminal patients have the right to die without medical intervention.

15 Apr. 1975   Karen Ann Quinlan falls into a coma after a drug overdose and is connected to a respirator.

Sept. 1975   Quinlan's parents seek a court order to withdraw their daughter from her respirator. New Jersey Superior Ct. Judge appoints a public defender for the comatose Quinlan.

31 Mar. 1976   In the first ruling allowing a guardian to disconnect life support on a patient's behalf, a New Jersey Supreme Court judge permits Karen Ann Quinlan's parents to have her respirator removed. Overruling a lower court, the judges declare that no "interest of the State could compel Karen to endure the unendurable, only to vegetate a few measurable

months with no realistic possibility of returning to any semblance of cognitive or sapient life."

30 Sept. 1976   California passes the first "right-to-die" law in the United States. It allows terminally ill patients to direct their doctors to withdraw or withhold medical treatments that "serve only to postpone the moment of death," frees doctors from legal liability in such cases, and prevents insurance companies from denying benefits to survivors on the basis that the insured committed suicide.

1980   Derek Humphry founds the Hemlock Society, a Los Angeles-based organization formed to fight for the right of the terminally ill to obtain assisted suicide.

June 1980   The Vatican distributes a "Declaration on Euthanasia," which condemns "mercy killing," but recognizes the right of individuals to refuse "burdensome" life-sustaining efforts.

1981   The Society for the Right to Die with Dignity publishes the first do-it-yourself suicide manual, *A Guide to Self-Deliverance*, in London.

Apr. 1981   A presidential commission holds hearings on the "right to die"; panel members reach consensus that terminal patients should have the right to refuse life-sustaining medical treatments.

Nov.–Dec. 1983   The U.S. Justice Department (under Reagan) sparks a national debate when it sues a New York hospital for Baby Jane Doe's records, seeking to discover whether the hospital violated the handicapped baby's civil rights when it failed to perform life-saving surgery on the infant. A federal district court rejects the request for Baby Doe's records, holding that her parents had acted in the baby's best interests. (The baby's parents had previously won the right to refuse the surgery in two New York courts—including the state appeals courts.)

20 Jan. 1984   Elizabeth Bouvia loses her court battle to force medical practitioners to help her commit suicide by starvation. The California Supreme Court rules that the twenty-six-year-old quadriplegic has no right to such assistance from society.

Apr. 1984   Colorado Governor Richard Lamm declares in a speech that the terminally ill elderly "have a duty to die." His statements stir widespread media attention and public condemnation.

Dec. 1984   In *Bartling v. Superior Court* (209 Cal. Rptr. 220; Ct. App. 1984), a California appeals court rules that competent, dying adults have a constitutional right to refuse medical treatment.

17 Jan. 1985   For the first time a state supreme court eliminates the distinction between removal of respirators and removal of feeding tubes from dying patients who want—or are believed to want—this action. The decision, made by the New Jersey Supreme Court, is considered precedent-setting because it permits the withholding of all medical therapies from competent terminally ill patients, as well as those in a comatose or persistent vegetative state.

May 1985   Roswell Gilbert, a seventy-five-year-old retired electrical engineer from Florida, is convicted of first-degree murder and given a life sentence for shooting his wife, who had Alzheimer's disease.

11 June 1985   Karen Ann Quinlan dies.

1986   Americans Against Human Suffering is founded (renamed Americans for Death with Dignity in 1993).

Mar. 1986   The American Medical Association (AMA) issues a decision that it is "not unethical" to remove life support—including food and water—from comatose patients "even if death is not imminent" (Wallis 1986, 60).

16 Apr. 1986   Writing that "the right to refuse medical treatment is basic and fundamental." a California appellate court rules in *Bouvia v. Superior Court* (179 Cal. App. 3d 1127, 1137, 225 Cal Rptr. 297, 1986) that even non-terminal, non-vegetative, and non-comatose patients may refuse medical treatment— including forced feeding and hydration.

12 Sept. 1986   The highest Massachusetts court rules that ex-fire fighter Paul Brophy, in a "persistent vegetative state" for three years, has the right to die by having his feeding tube removed. The court holds that Brophy's expressed wish not to be kept alive by artificial means outweighs the state's interest in keeping him alive. Brophy thus becomes the first non-terminal patient to have his feeding tube removed by court order.

June 1987   The N.J. Sup. Ct. expands patients' right to die by ruling that individuals have the right to refuse life-sustaining medical treatment.

8 Jan. 1988*   The *Journal of the American Medical Association* (JAMA) publishes "It's Over, Debbie," written by an anonymous gynecology resident who administered a fatal dose of morphine to a terminally ill patient after hearing her say, "Let's get this over with" (Anonymous 1988, 272).

1988   A California initiative to legalize assisted suicide fails to attract enough signatures to place it on the ballot.

1988   The *New England Journal of Medicine* publishes a statement by 10 doctors from leading medical schools and hospitals that "it is not immoral for a physician to assist in the rational suicide of a terminally ill person" (Wanzer 1989, 848).

1990   Two right-to-die groups, the Society for the Right to Die and Concern for Dying, merge to form Choice in Dying.

4 June 1990   Dr. Jack Kevorkian uses his "suicide machine" for the first time to help Janet Adkins, a 54-year-old woman with Alzheimer's disease, commit suicide.

July 1990   In *Cruzan v. Director, Missouri Dept. of Health* (497 U.S. at 279), the U.S. Supreme Court for the first time establishes a limited constitutional "right to die." Using a liberty-interest argument, the Court holds that "the right of a competent adult patient to refuse medical treatment has its origins in the constitutional right of privacy." However, the Court also rules that Missouri's interest in preserving life gives it the right to require "clear and convincing evidence" of Cruzan's wish to die before allowing her feeding tube to be removed.

Aug. 1991   Derek Humphry's *Final Exit: The Practicalities of Self-Deliverance and Assisted Suicide for the Dying* advances to the top of *The New York Times* best-seller list and attracts intense media attention.

Mar. 1991   Dr. Timothy Quill publishes a controversial essay in the *New England Journal of Medicine* describing how he helped a leukemia patient named "Diane" commit suicide (see Quill 1991).

Nov. 1991   Voters reject Washington's Initiative 119 (a ballot to legalize PAS.

Dec. 1991   The Patient Self-Determination Act of 1990 goes into effect. This federal law requires all hospitals treating adult Medicare or Medicaid patients to ask these patients whether they have advance directives that specify the end-of-life treatments they choose or reject.

Nov. 1992   Voters reject the California Death with Dignity Act (Prop. 161) by a margin of 54 to 46%.

8 Mar. 1993   Michigan jury acquits Dr. Kevorkian in the deaths of two individuals.

8 Nov.1994   Oregon voters pass Measure 16, the Death With Dignity Act (DWDA), the world's first law legalizing PAS for terminally ill adults. Almost immediately, the law is challenged as both unconstitutional and a violation of federal law.

Dec 1994   Federal judge Michael Hogan grants a preliminary injunction blocking the DWDA from implementation "until the constitutional concerns are fully heard and analyzed."

3 Aug. 1995   Federal judge Michael Hogan strikes down the Oregon DWDA as unconstitutional (violates the Equal Protection Clause of the U.S. Constitution). (*Lee v. Oregon*, 891 F. Supp. 1439).

Mar. 1996   In *Compassion in Dying v. the State of Washington*, the U.S. Ninth Circuit Court of Appeals strikes down a law prohibiting doctor-assisted suicide, establishing a Constitutional "right" to assisted suicide. The decision was based on the due process clause of the Fourteenth Amendment—the same clause used by the U.S. Supreme Court to establish abortion rights. The Court held that just as individuals have a right to decide whether to have a child, they have a right to choose the circumstances of their deaths, and the state must have a compelling reason to interfere with this right.

1996   In *Vacco v. Quill*, the U.S. Court of Appeals for the Second Circuit strikes down a New York law prohibiting assisted suicide. In its analysis the court holds that the law violates the equal-protection clause of the Fourteenth Amendment because it treats two classes of the terminally ill differently. Although the law allowed individuals to be removed from life-support (as mandated in *Cruzan*), it prohibited terminally ill people not on life-support systems to hasten their deaths by other means, such as by lethal injection or pills.

Mar., May 1996	Kevorkian is acquitted for the second and third times in two years in Michigan courts.
June 1995	Australia legalizes doctor-assisted suicide. The law, called the Northern Territory Rights of the Terminally Ill Act, allows patients deemed terminally ill by two doctors to request death by lethal injection or pills.
Oct. 1996	The U.S. Supreme Court agrees to consider the constitutionality of two 1996 state appeals court rulings that struck down laws prohibiting assisted suicide. The cases are: *Compassion in Dying v. the State of Washington* and *Vacco v. Quill* (see description, above). At question is whether terminally ill individuals have a Constitutional right to physician-assisted suicide that outweighs the states' interest in protecting life.
8 Jan. 1997	The U.S. Supreme Court hears arguments in *Compassion in Dying v. the State of Washington* and *Vacco v. Quill*.
27 Feb. 1997	The Ninth Circuit Court of Appeals (California) dismisses challenges to Oregon's DWDA, ruling 3-0 that the plaintiffs failed to show immediate threat of harm.
Mar. 1997	The Northern Territory Rights of the Terminally Ill Act is overturned in the Australian legislature.
June 1997	In a pair of unanimous rulings (*Washington v. Glucksberg* and *Vacco v. Quill*), the U.S. Supreme Court upholds state statutes prohibiting PAS. Refusing to rule out the possibility of future recognition of a constitutional "right to die," Chief Justice Rehnquist states that "Our opinion does not absolutely foreclose such a claim" (Greenhouse 1997, A1).
Nov. 1998	Michigan prosecutors bring criminal charges against Dr. Jack Kevorkian after he videotaped himself injecting a fifty-two-year-old man (Thomas Youk) dying of Lou Gehrig's disease with a lethal drug and then allowing CBS News to air the tape on its "60 Minutes" program. The "60 Minutes" broadcast—which showed Youk's actual death—attracted widespread media coverage.

Mar. 1999   After aiding in the suicides of more than 130 individuals and being acquitted in three trials (with a fourth trial ending in a mistrial), Kevorkian is convicted of the murder of Thomas Youk (see Nov. 1998 entry).

Oct. 1999   The Hyde-Nickels bill—which would have nullified the DWDA by banning the use of the lethal drugs required to carry out physician-assisted suicide—is introduced into the U.S. House of Representatives. Although it passes the House by a nearly 2-1 margin in 2000, a similar bill fails to attract sufficient votes in the United States Senate.

Apr. 2002   A U.S. District Court judge blocks a directive issued by United States Attorney General John Ashcroft in Nov. 2002 to allow federal action to be taken against Oregon physicians who prescribe lethal drugs under the DWDA. If the directive had stood, it would have led to the revocation of prescription licenses of doctors involved in PAS. Ashcroft appealed the ruling to the Ninth Circuit Court of Appeals, which was slated to begin hearing oral arguments in May 2003.

May 2003   A New York supreme court judge gives parents the right to withdraw or deny medical care and treatments from their dying offspring. Before the ruling, New York was one of the few remaining states in the country without a law allowing parents to remove children in "a persistent vegetative state" from respirators and other life-support systems.

BIBLIOGRAPHY

Altman, Lawrence K. 21 Mar. 1991. "More Physicians Broach Forbidden Subject of Euthanasia." *The New York Times* C3.

Alvarez, Alfred. 1972. *The Savage God.* New York: Random House.

Ames, Katrina, Larry Wilson, et al. 26 Aug. 1991. "Last Rights." *Newsweek* 40.

Amundsen, D. W. 1989. "Suicide and Early Christian Values." In *Suicide and Euthanasia: Historical and Contemporary Themes.* Edited by Baruch A. Brody. Dordrecht, Netherlands: Kluwer Academic Publishers: 142–44.

"An Appointment for Dr. Death." 28 Dec. 1992. *Time* 36.

Angell, Marcia. 11 Jan. 1997. Jim Lehrer News Hour, PBS (interview).

_____. 1988. Euthanasia. *New England Journal of Medicine* 319: 1348–50.

Anderson, D. C., and W. W. Sharrock. 1979. "Biasing the News: Technical Issues in Media Studies." *Sociology* 13:3: 367–85.

Andsager, J., and L. Smiley. 1998. *Public Relations Review* 24:2: 183–201.

Anonymous. 1988. "It's Over Debbie." JAMA, *Journal of the American Medical Association* 259–272.

Ansen, David. 5 Nov. 1979). "Coming to Grips with Death" *Newsweek* 99.

Appleby, Earl E., Jr. 1996. "Brain Death—The Hoax that Won't Die." LifeNET Euthanasia Roundtable, URL: http://www.awinc.com/partners/bc/compass/lifenet/euthan1.

Aries, Phillippe. 1974. Western Attitudes Toward Death: From the Middle Ages to the Present. Baltimore: John Hopkins University Press.

_____. 1985. *Images of Man and Death.* Cambridge, MA: Harvard University Press.

_____. 1981. *The Hour of Our Death.* New York: Vintage Books.

Arney, William R., and Bernard J. Bergen. 1984. *Medicine and the Management of Living: Taming the Last Great Beast.* The University of Chicago Press.

Associated Press. 11 Nov. 1994. "Voters in Oregon Allow Doctors to Help the Terminally Ill Die." *The New York Times* A28.

Auletta, Ken. 10 June 2002. "The Howell Doctrine." *The New Yorker* 78:15: 48–71.

Ball-Rokeach, S. J., G .J. Power, K. K. Guthrie, and H. R. Waring. 1990. "Value-framing Abortion in the United States: An Application of Media System Dependency Theory." *International Journal of Public Opinion Research* 2: 249–73.

Ball-Rokeach, S. J. and M. Rokeach. 1987. "Contribution to the Future Study of Public Opinion: A Symposium." *Public Opinion Quarterly* 51: 184–85.

Ball-Rokeach, S. J., M. Rokeach, and J. W. Grube. 1984. *The Great American Values Test: Influencing Behavior and Belief Through Television.* New York: Free Press.

Barker-Plummer, Bernadette. Sept. 1995. "News as a Political Resource: Media Strategies and Political Identity in the U.S. Women's Movement, 1966–1975." *Critical Studies in Mass Communication* 12: 306–24.

Barkin, S. M., and M. Gurevitch. 1987. "Out of Work and On the Air: Television News of Unemployment." *Critical Studies in Mass Communication* 4: 1–20.

Barley, Nigel. 1997. *Grave Matters: A Lively History of Death Around the World*. New York: Henry Holt.

Basil, Mitchell. 1990. "The Value of Human Life." *Medicine, Medical Ethics and the Value of Life* 34–46.

Bates, Tom. 12 Nov. 1994. "Oregon Doctors Split Over Suicide Measure; Catholic Run Hospitals Object to State Vote, Won't Help Patients Die." *Rocky Mountain News* 51A.

Bates, Tom, and Mark O'Keefe. 21 Nov. 1994. "Suicide Law Reflects Oregon Politics; Voters Tend to be Quirky but Consistent in Maverick State." *The Plain Dealer* 3E.

Bateson, Gregory. 1972. *Steps to an Ecology of Mind*. New York: Ballantine Books.

Battin, Margaret P. 1994. *The Least Worst Death: Essays in Bioethics on the End of Life*. New York: Oxford University Press.

Baumann, Z. 1993. *Morality, Immortality and Other Life Strategies*. Oxford: Polity Press.

Baylor, Tim. July 1996. "Media Framing of Movement Protest: The Case of American Indian Protest." *The Social Science Journal* 33:3: 241–55.

Beavan, John. 9 Aug. 1959). "The Patient's Right to Live—and Die." *The New York Times* SM14

Beck, Melinda. 16 May 1994. "A Lesson in Dying Well." *Newsweek* 58.

Beck, Melinda, Karen Springer, et al. 18 June 1990. "The Doctor's Suicide Van." *Newsweek* 46.

Becker, Howard S. 1963. *Outsiders: Studies in the Sociology of Deviance*. New York: Free Press.

Begley, Sharon, and Mark Starr. 26 Aug. 1991. "Choosing Death." *Newsweek* 42.

Belkin, Lisa. 6 June 1990. "Doctor Tells of First Death Using His Suicide Device." *The New York Times* A1.

Bell, Allan. 1991. *The Language of News Media*. Cambridge, MA: Blackwell.

Bell, Daniel. 1976. *The Cultural Contradictions of Capitalism*. Basic Books.

Belluck, Pam. 30 Mar. 1999. "Kevorkian Seen as 'Distraction' On Suicide Aid." *The New York Times* A1.

Bennett, T. 1982. "Media, 'Reality,' Signification." In *Culture, Society and the Media*. Edited by M. Gurevitch, T. Bennett, J. Curran, and J. Woollacott. London: Methuen: 287–308.

Bennett, W. Lance. 1975. *The Political Mind and the Political Environment*. Lexington, MA: Heath.

_____. 1982. "Toward of Theory of Press-State Relations in the United States." *Journal of Communication* 40:2: 103–25.

_____. 1988. *News: the Politics of Illusion*. New York: Longman.

Benson, John. Summer 1999. "The Polls—Trends: End-of-Life Issues." *Public Opinion Quarterly* 63:2: 263–77.

Berger, Leslie. 20 May 2003. "Transformation, by Pill or Scalpel." *The New York Times* D7.

Berger, P. and T. Luckmann. 1966. *The Social Construction of Reality*. Garden City, NewYork: Doubleday.

Berk, Kent S. Dec. 1992. "Mercy Killing and the Slayer Rule: Should the Legislatures Change Something?" *Tulane Law Review* 67: 485.

Berman, Marshall.1982. *All That is Solid Melts into Air*. New York: Penguin.

Bernardi, Peter J. 6 May 1995. "The Hidden Engines of the Suicide Rights Movement." *America* 172:16: 14

Beschle, Donald L. 1988–89. "Autonomous Decisionmaking and Social Choice: Examining the Right to Die." *Kentucky Law Journal* 77: 319–67.

Best, Joel. Apr. 1987. "Rhetoric in Claims-Making: Constructing the Missing Children Problem." *Social Problems* 34:2: 101–121.

Binder, Amy. Dec. 1993. "Constructing Racial Rhetoric: Media Depictions of Harm in Heavy Metal and Rap Music." *American Sociological Review* 58: 753–67.

Black's Law Dictionary. 1990. 6th ed.

Blumer, Herbert. 1971. "Social Problems as Collective Behavior." *Social Problems* 18: 298–306.

Borger, Gloria. 27 Aug./3 Sept. 1990. "The Odd Odyssey of 'Dr. Death.'" *U.S. News & World Report* 27–28.

Branegan, Jay. 17 Mar. 1997. "I Want to Draw the Line Myself." *Time* 30.

Breed, Walter. 1955. "Social Control in the Newsroom." *Social Forces* 33: 326–35.

Brink, Susan. 4 Dec. 1995. "The American Way of Dying: Hospital Culture is at War with Patients' Wishes About How They're Treated in Their Final Days." *U.S. News & World Report* 119:22: 70.

Brody, Howard. 1992. "Assisted Death: A Compassionate Response to Medical Failure." *New England Journal of Medicine* 327: 1384.

_____. 1993. "Causing, Intending, and Assisting Death." *Journal of Clinical Ethics* 4: 112–17.

Bruner, Jerome. 2002. *Making Stories: Law, Literature, Life*. New York: Farrar, Straus and Giroux.

Bugen, Larry A.1979. *Death and Dying*. Dubuque, IA: William C. Brown.

Bumgardner, Cynthia M. 2000. "Euthanasia and Physician-Assisted Suicide in the United States and the Netherlands: Paradigms Compared." *Indiana International & Comparative Law Review* 10: 387.

Burke, Kenneth.1969. *A Grammar of Motives*. Berkeley: University of California Press.

Burnell, George M., M.D. 1993. *Final Choices: To Live or Die in an Age of Medical Technology*, New York: Plenum Press.

Burr, Vivien.1995. *An Introduction to Social Constructionism*. New York: Routledge.

Bushong, Stephen K. and Thomas A. Balmer. 22 Dec. 1995. "Breathing Life into the Right to Die: Oregon's Death with Dignity Act." *Issues in Law and Medicine* 11:3: 269.

Butler, Judith. 20 Mar. 1999. "A 'Bad Writer' Bites Back." *The New York Times* A27.

Butler, Robert N. 1968. *Why Survive? Growing Old in America*. New York: Pantheon.

Buzzee, Sarah E. Fall 2001. "The Pain Relief Promotion Act: Congress's Misguided Intervention into End-of-Life Care." *University of Cincinnati Law Review* 70: 217.

Callahan, Daniel. 1990. *What Kind of Life? The Limits of Medical Progress*. New York: Simon & Schuster.

_____. 1993. *The Troubled Dream of Life, Living with Mortality*. New York: Simon & Schuster.

Campbell, Christopher P. 1995. *Race, Myth and the News*. Thousand Oaks, CA: Sage.

Campbell, Tom. 1983. *The Left and Rights: A Conceptual Analysis of the Idea of Socialist Rights*. London: Routledge & Kegan Paul.

Camus, Albert. 1955. *Myth of Sisyphus and Other Stories*. New York: Alfred A. Knopf.

Carey, James W. 1975. A Cultural Approach to Communication, *Communication* 2: 1–22.

_____. 1986. "Why and How? The Dark Continent of American Journalism." In *Reading the News*, pp. 146–96, Edited by R. Manoff and M. Schudson. New York: Pantheon.

_____. 1988, 1989. *Communication as Culture: Essays on Media and Society.* Cambridge, MA: Unwin Hyman.

Carragee, Kevin M. Apr. 1991. "News and Ideology: An Analysis of Coverage of the West German Green Party by The New York Times." *Journalism Monographs* 128.

Carragee, K. and L. Jarrell. Nov. 1987. "Media Frames and the Definition of a Foreign Social Movement." Paper presented to the Speech Communication Association, Boston, MA.

Cartwright, F. F. 1977. *A Social History of Medicine.* New York: Longman.

Cassell, Eric J. 1975. "Dying in a Technological Society." In *Death Inside Out.* Edited by P. Steinfels and R. Veatch. New York: Harper & Row.

Centers for Disease Control. 2001. "Highlights: National Health Expenditures." Downloaded from CDC web site, http://www.cdc.gov/nchs/products/pubs/pubd/hus/heexpend.pdf.

Centers for Medicare & Medicaid Services. 2002. "Number of Medicare Beneficiaries, 1970-2030." Office of the Actuary. Downloaded from CMS web site, http://cmc.hhs.gov/charts/healthcaresystem/chapter3.asp.

Cerminara, Kathy L. and Alan Meisel. *The Right to Die.* Hobeken, NJ: Wiley Law.

Cherlin, Andrew. 27 Mar. 1999. "Caroming Between Extremes, Social Scientists Can Overlook Reality." *The New York Times*, national edition, A19.

Chilton, Paul and George Lakoff. 1995. "Foreign Policy by Metaphor." In *Language and Peace.* Edited by C. Schaffner and A. L. Wenden, Brookfield, VT: Dartmouth Publishing Co.: 37–59.

Chomsky, N., and E. Herman. 1988. *Manufacturing Consent: The Political Economy of the Mass Media.* New York: Pantheon.

Clark, Matt and Susan Agrest. 3 Nov. 1975. "A Right to Die?." *New York Times* 58.

_____. 7 June 1976. "Karen Lives On." *New York Times* 48.

Clark, Matt, Gosnell, Mariana, and Dan Shapiro. 31 Aug. 1981. "When Doctors Play God." *New York Times* 48.

Clay, Joy A. Jul./Aug. 1995. "Death Rights: Difficult Politics and Policy Making." *Public Administration Review* 55:4: 381–84.

Cohen, A., A. Akiba, H. Adoni, and C. Bantz. 1990. *Social Conflict and Television.* vol. 183, Newbury Park, CA: Sage.

Cohen, Roger. 1998. *Hearts Grown Brutal: Sagas of Sarajevo.* New York: Random House.

Cohen, Stanley, and Jock Young, eds. 1972. *The Manufacture of News: A Reader.* Beverly Hills, CA: Sage.

Colt, George H. 1991. *The Enigma of Suicide.* New York: Summit Books.

Coleman, Diane. 28 Mar. 1999. "Talk of the Nation" interview, National Public Radio.

Condit, Celeste M. Mar. 1987. "Democracy and Civil Rights: The Universalizing Influence of Public Argumentation." *Communication Monographs* 54: 1–18.

Condit, Celeste M. and J. Selzer. 1985. "The Rhetoric of Objectivity in the Newspaper Coverage of a Murder Trial." *Critical Studies in Mass Communication* 2:3: 197–216.

Condit, Celeste M. 1990. *Decoding Abortion Rhetoric: Communicating Social Change.* Urbana: University of Illinois Press.

Conley, John J. 1994. "Letting Go." *Society* 31:2: 9.

Conrad, P. and J. W. Schneider. 1992. *Deviance and Medicalization: From Badness to Sickness.* Philadelphia: Temple University Press.

Covert, Catherine L. 1992. "'We May Hear Too Much': American Sensibility and the Response to Radio, 1919–1924, In *Media Voices: An Historical Perspective*. Edited by Jean Folkerts. New York: Macmillan: 300–15.

Cox, Donald W. 1993. *Hemlock's Cup: The Struggle for Death with Dignity*. Buffalo, New York: Prometheus Books.

Daar, Judith F. Summer 1995. "Direct Democracy and Bioethical Choices: Voting Life and Death at the Ballot Box." *University of Michigan Journal of Law* 28: 799.

De Certeau, Michel. 1984. *The Practice of Everyday Life*. Berkeley: The University of California Press.

DeFleur, M. L., and S. J. Ball-Rokeach. 1988. *Theories of Mass Communication*, 5th ed. New York: Longman.

Dempsey, David. 23 June 1974. "The Living Will—and the Will to Live." *The New York Times Magazine*, section 6, 12.

Dewey, John. 1927. *The Public and its Problems*. Chicago: Swallow Press.

"Doctors, Patients and the Right to Die." 23 Sept. 1984, *The New York Times*, Week in Review, 6.

Doerflinger, Richard M. 22 Sept. 1995. "The Good Samaritan and the 'Good Death': Catholic Reflections on Euthanasia." *Issues in Law & Medicine*.

Domke, David. Dec. 1997. "Journalists, Framing, and Discourse About Race Relations." *Journalism & Mass Communication Monographs* 164: 1–54.

Donahue, G. A., P. J. Tichenor, and C. L. Olien. 1973. "Mass Media Functions, Knowledge and Social Control." *Journalism Quarterly* 50: 652–59.

Donati, Paolo R. 1992. "Political Discourse Analysis." In *Studying Collective Action*. Edited by Mario Diani and Ron Eyerman. Newbury Park, CA: Sage: 136–67.

Dowbiggin, Ian. 2003. *A Merciful End: The Euthanasia Movement in Modern America*. New York: Oxford University Press.

Dumont, Louis. 1985. "A Modified View of Our Origins: The Christian Beginnings of Modern Individualism." In *The Category of the Person: Anthropology, Philosophy, History*. Edited by M. Carrithers, S. Collins, and S. Lukes. Cambridge, MA: Harvard University Press: 46–82.

Durkheim, Emile. 1973. "Individualism and the Intellectuals." In *Emile Durkheim on Morality and Society*. Edited by R.N. Bellah. University of Chicago Press: 43–57.

Dworkin, Ronald. 1993. *Life's Dominion: An Argument About Abortion, Euthanasia, and Individual Freedom*. New York: Alfred A. Knopf.

Dworkin, Gerald, R. G. Frey, and Sissela Bok. 1998. *Euthanasia and Physician-Assisted Suicide: For and Against*. Boston: Cambridge University Press.

Edelman, M. 1988. *Constructing the Political Spectacle*. University of Chicago Press.

Elliott, Carl. (2003). *Better than Well: American Medicine Meets the American Dream*. New York: W.W. Norton & Company.

Emanuel, Ezekiel. 1994. "The History of Euthanasia Debates in the United States and Britain." *Annals of Internal Medicine* 121: 793–803.

_____. 1988. "A Review of the Ethical and Legal Aspects of Terminating Medical Care." *American Journal of Medicine* 84: 291–301.

_____. Apr. 1999. "What is the Great Benefit of Legalizing Euthanasia or Physician-Assisted Suicide?" *Ethics* 109:3: 629.

Emanuel, Ezekiel J., and Linda L. Emanuel. 24 Jul. 1997. "Assisted Suicide? Not in My State." *The New York Times* A15.

Entman, Robert M. 1991. "Framing U.S. Coverage of International News: Contrasts in Narratives of the KAL and Iran Air Incidents." *Journal of Communication* 41: 6–27.

_____. Autumn 1993. "Framing: Toward Clarification of a Fractured Paradigm." *Journal of Communication* 43: 4.

Entman, R. M. and Rojecki, A. 1993. "Freezing Out the Public: Elite and Media Framing of the U.S. Anti-Nuclear Movement." *Political Communication* 10:2: 151–67.

Epstein, Edward J. 1973. *News from Nowhere: Television and the News*. New York: Vintage Books.

Ericson, Richard V., Patricia M. Baranek, and Janet B. L. Chan. (1991). *Representing Order: Crime, Law, and Justice in the News Media*. University of Toronto Press.

Ettema, J. S. Dec. 1990. "Press Rites and Race Relations: A Study of Mass-Mediated Ritual." *Critical Studies in Mass Communication* 7:4: 309–331.

Fairbairn, Gavin J. 1995. *Contemplating Suicide: The Language and Ethics of Self Harm*. New York: Routledge.

Fairclough, Norman. 1992. "Discourse and Text: Linguistic and Intertextual Analysis within Discourse Analysis." *Discourse & Society* 3: 193–217.

_____.1995. *Media Discourse*. New York: Edward Arnold.

Featherstone, M. 1992. "The Heroic Life and Everyday Life." *Theory, Culture and Society* 9: 159–182.

Featherstone, M., and A. Wernick, eds. 1995. *Images of Aging: Cultural Representations of Later Life*. New York: Routledge.

Feifel, H. 1959. *The Meaning of Death*." New York: McGraw-Hill.

_____. 1974. "Religious Conviction and Fear of Death Among the Healthy and the Terminally Ill." *Journal for the Scientific Study of Religion* 13: 353–60.

Ferrell, James J. 1980. *Inventing the American Way of Death, 1830–1920*. Philadelphia: Temple University Press.

Field, Marilyn J., and Christine K. Cassell, Eds. 1997. "Approaching Death: Improving Care at the End of Life." Washington, DC: National Academy Press, downloaded from the WWW on July 15, 2001, URL: http://stills.nap.edu/html/approaching/.

Filene, Peter G. 1999. *In the Arms of Others: A Cultural History of the Right-to-Die in America*. Chicago: Ivan R. Dee.

Fine, Alan. 1995. "Public Narration and Group Culture: Discerning Discourse in Social Movements." In *Social Movements and Culture: Social Movements, Protest, and Contention*, vol. 4. Edited by H. Johnston and B. Klandermans. Minneapolis: University of Minnesota Press: 127–43.

Fiske, John. 1994. *Media Matters: Everyday Culture and Political Change*. Minneapolis: University of Minnesota Press.

_____. 1987. *Television Culture*. London: Methuen.

Fishman, Mark. 1980. *Manufacturing the News*. Austin: University of Texas Press.

Fletcher, Joseph. 1981. "In Defense of Suicide." In *Suicide and Euthanasia: The Rights of Personhood*. Edited by Samuel E. Wallace and Albin Eser. Knoxville: University of Tennessee Press.

Foss, Sonja K. 1989. *Rhetorical Criticism: Exploration & Practice*. Prospect Heights, IL: Waveland Press.

Foucault, Michel. 1973. *The Order of Things: An Archeology of the Human Sciences*. New York: Vintage.

_____. 1954/1976. *Mental Illness and Psychology*. New York: Harper & Row.

_____. 1975/1977. *Discipline and Punish*. New York: Pantheon.

_____. 1984. "The Order of Discourse." In *Language and Politics*. Edited by M. Shapiro. London: Blackwell.

_____. 1980. *Power/Knowledge: Selected Interviews and Other Writings, 1972–1977*." Edited by Colin Gordon. New York: Pantheon.

_____. 1988/1995. "Strategies of Power." In *The Truth about the Truth: De-Confusing and Re-Constructing the Postmodern World*. Edited by Walter T. Anderson. New York: Jeremy P. Tarcher.

Fowler, Roger, Robert Hodge, Gunther Kress, and Tony Trew, eds. 1979. *Language and Control*. London: Routledge & Kegan Paul.

Fox, Renne C. 1977. "The Medicalization and Demedicalization of American Society." *Daedalus*. 106:1: 9–22, reprinted in Kenneth Thompson, ed. 1996. *Key Quotations in Sociology*. New York: Routledge: 61–62.

Freidson, E. 1970. *The Profession of Medicine*. New York: Harper & Row.

Gamson, William A. 1988a. "Political Discourse and Collective Action." In *From Structure to Action: Comparing Social Movements Across Cultures*. Edited by B. Klandermans, H. Criesi, and S. Tarrow, Eds. Greenwich, CT: JAI Press: 219–46.

_____. 1988b. "The 1987 Distinguished Lecture. A Constructionist Approach to Mass Media and Public Opinion." *Symbolic Interaction* 11: 161–74.

_____. 1989. "Media Discourse and Public Opinion on Nuclear Power: A Constructionist Approach." *American Journal of Sociology* 95: 1–37.

_____. 1990. *The Strategy of Social Protest*. 2nd Edition. Belmont, CA: Wadsworth.

_____. 1992a. *Talking Politics*. New York: Cambridge University Press.

_____. 1992b. "The Social Psychology of Collective Action." In *Frontiers in Social Movement Theory*. Edited by A. D. Morris and McClurg Mueller. New Haven: Yale University Press: 53–76.

_____. 1995. "Constructing Social Protest." In *Movements and Culture: Social Movements, Protest, and Contention*: 85–106.

Gamson, William A., Bruce Fireman, and Steven Rytina. 1982. *Encounters with Unjust Authority*. Homewood, IL: Dorsey Press.

Gamson, W. A. and Lasch, K. E. 1983. "The Political Culture of Social Welfare Policy." In *Evaluating the Welfare State*. Edited by S. Spiro and E. Ycchtman-Year. San Diego: Academic Press: 397–415.

Gamson, William A. and Andre Modigliani. Jul. 1989. "Media Discourse and Public Opinion on Nuclear Power: A Constructionist Approach." *American Journal of Sociology* 95:1: 1–37.

_____. 1987. "The Changing Culture of Affirmative Action.: In *Frontiers in Social Movement Theory Research in Political Sociology*. Edited by R. G. Braungart and M. Braungart. New Haven, CT: Yale University Press: 53–76.

Gamson, William A., and G. Wolfsfeld Jul. 1993. "Movements and Media as Interacting Systems." *Annals of the American Academy of Political and Social Science* 528: 114–25.

Gans, Herbert J. 1979. *Deciding What's News: A Study of the CBS Evening News, NBC Nightly News, New York and Time*. New York: Pantheon.

Gavin, William J. 1995. *Cuttin' the Body Loose: Historical, Biological, and Personal Approaches to Death and Dying*. Philadelphia, PA: Temple University Press.

Geertz, Clifford. 1968. *Islam Observed. Religious Development in Morocco and Indonesia*. New Haven, CT: Yale University Press.

_____. 1973. *The Interpretation of Cultures*. New York: Basic Books.

_____. 1984. "'From the Native's Point of View': On the Nature of Anthropological Understanding." In *Culture Theory: Essays on Mind, Self, and Emotion*. Edited by R. A. Shweder and R. A. Levine. New York: Cambridge University Press: 123–36.

Gelman, David, and Daniel Pedersen. 16 Jan. 1984. "The Most Painful Question" *New York Times* 72.

Gerbner, George. 1973. "Cultural Indicators: The Third Voice." In *Communications Technology and Social Policy: Understanding the New "Social Revolution."* Edited by G. Gerbner, L. Gross, and W. Melody. New York: John Wiley: 555–73.

Gerbner, G., L. Gross, M. Jackson-Beeck, S. Jeffries-Fox, and N. Signorielli. 1978. "Cultural Indicators: Violence Profile no. 9." *Journal of Communication* 28: 176–207.

Gergen, Kenneth J. and Gun R. Semin. 1990. "Everyday Understanding in Science and Life." In *Everyday Understanding: Social and Scientific Implications*. Edited by Gun R. Semin and Kenneth Gergen. London: Sage: 1–18.

Gest, Ted, and Sarah Burke. 11 Dec. 1989. "Is There a Right to Die?" *U.S. News & World Report* 17: 23:35.

Gest, Ted, Steven Findlay, Dorian Friedman, and Richard Chesnoff. 9 July 1990. "Changing the Rules on Dying." *U.S. News & World Report* 109:2: 22.

Gianelli, Diane M. 13 Nov. 1995. "New Hampshire Considers Physician-Assisted Suicide." *American Medical News* 38: 42:14.

Gibbs, Nancy. 19 Mar. 1990. "Love and Let Die; In an Era of Untamed Medical Technology, How Are Patients and Families to Decide Whether to Halt Treatment—or Even to Help Death Along?" *Time* 67.

_____. 18 June 1990. "Dr. Death's Suicide Machine: An Ailing Teacher's Last Decision Inflames the Euthanasia Debate." *Time* 69.

_____. 4 Nov. 1991. "Dr. Death Strikes Again; While Lawmakers Agonize Over Euthanasia, Jack Kevorkian Keeps Taking Matters into his Own Hands." *Time* 78.

_____. 28 Dec. 1992. "Mercy's Friend or Foe? As Dr. Kevorkian Takes on the State of Michigan Over Physician-Assisted Suicide, He May be Undermining his Own Crusade." *Time* 36.

_____. 31 May 1993. "Rx for Death." *Time* 34.

Giddens, Anthony. 1990. *The Consequences of Modernity*. Palo Alto, CA: Stanford University Press.

_____. 1991. *Modernity and Self-Identity*. Cambridge, MA: Polity Press.

Giroux, Henry A. 1996. "Is There a Place for Cultural Studies in Colleges of Education?" In *Counternarratives: Cultural Studies and Critical Pedagogies in Postmodern Spaces*. Edited by G. Giroux, C. Lankshear, P. McLaren, and M. Peters. New York: Routledge: 231–47.

Girsh, Faye J. 1992. "Physician Aid in Dying." *Western Journal of Medicine* 157: 188.

Gitlin, Todd. 1977. "Spotlights and Shadows: Television and the Culture of Politics." *College English* 38.

_____. 1979. "News as Ideology and Contested Area: Toward a Theory of Hegemony, Crisis, and Opposition." *Socialist Review* 9: 11–54.

_____. 1980. *The Whole World is Watching: Mass Media in the Making and Unmaking of the New Left*. Berkeley: University of California Press.

Givens, Ron, Susan Agrest, et al. 9 Sept. 1985. "Mercy—or Murder?" *New York Times* 25.

Glasgow University Media Group. 1976. *Bad News*. London: Routledge and Kegan Paul.

Glendon, Mary Ann. 1991. *Rights Talk: The Impoverishment of Political Discourse*. New York: Free Press.

Glick, Henry R. 1992. *The Right to Die: Policy Innovation and its Consequences*. New York: Columbia University Press.

Goffman, Erving. 1974. *Frame Analysis: An Essay on the Organization of Experience*. Cambridge, MA: Harvard University Press.

_____. 1976. *Gender Advertisements*. Cambridge, MA: Harvard University Press.

Goldberg, Carey. 10 June 1997. "Oregon Moves Nearer to Revote On Allowing Assisted Suicide." *The New York Times*, national edition, A18.

Goldman, Daniel. 31 Jan. 1999. Interview, "New Dimensions." National Public Radio.

Gonos, G. 1977. "'Situation' versus 'Frame': The 'Interactionist' and the 'Structuralist' Analyses of Everyday Life." *American Sociological Review* 42:6: 854–67.

Goodman, David. 21 Nov. 1998. "Kevorkian Claims Euthanasia Victim." *The Chattanooga Times* E1.

Goodman, Ellen. 24 Apr. 1997. "Euthanasia as an Option." *The Boston Globe* A27.

Gorer, Geoffrey. 1955/1976. "The Pornography of Death." In *Death: Current Perspectives*. Edited by E. S. Sheneidman. Palo Alto, CA: Mayfield Publishing Company.

Gorman, Christine. 27 June 1994. "A Sick Boy Says 'Enough!'" *Time* 65.

Gorsuch, Neil M. 2000. "The Right to Assisted Suicide and Euthanasia." *Harvard Journal of Law & Public Policy* 23:3: 599.

Graber, Doris. 1988. *Processing the News: How People Tame the Information Tide.* New York: Longman.

Grady, Denise. 15 Feb. 1988. "The Doctor Decided on Death: A Candid Tale of Mercy Killing Inflames the Profession." *Time* 88.

Greenblatt, Stephen. 1992. *Marvelous Possessions: The Wonder of the New World.* University of Chicago Press.

Greenhouse, Linda. 27 June 1997. "No Help for Dying; But Justices Leave Door Open to Future Claim of a Right to Aid." *The New York Times* A1.

Grindstaff, Laura. 1994. "Abortion and the Popular Press: Mapping Media Discourse from Roe to Webster." In *Abortion Politics in the United States and Canada: Studies in Public Opinion.* Edited by T. G. Jelen and M. A. Chandler. Westport, CT: Praeger Publishers: 57–88.

Groneman, Carol. 2000. *Nymphomania: A History.* New York: W. W. Norton & Company.

Gross, Jane. 2 Jan. 1997. "New York Doctor at Center of Supreme Court Case on Assisted Suicide." *The New York Times* 146, A12.

Gurevitch, Michael, and Mark R. Levy, eds. 1985. *Mass Communication Review Yearbook*, vol. 5. Beverly Hills, CA: Sage.

Gusfield, Joseph R. 1970. In *Protest, Reform, and Revolt: a Reader in Social Movements.* New York: John Wiley & Sons.

_____. 1981. *The Culture of Public Problems: Drinking, Driving, and the Symbolic Order.* University of Chicago Press.

Habermas, J. 1989. *The Structural Transformation of the Public Sphere: An Inquiry into a Category of Bourgeois Society.* Cambridge, MA: MIT Press.

Hacking, Ian. 1986. "Making Up People." In *Reconstructing Individualism: Autonomy, Individuality, and the Self in Western Thought.* Edited by T. C. Heller, M. Sosna, and D. E. Wellbery. Stanford University Press.

Hall, E.T. 1976. *Beyond Culture.* New York: Anchor/Doubleday.

Hall, Robert T. Nov. 1994. "Final Act: Sorting out the Ethics of Physician–Assisted Suicide." *The Humanist* 54:6: 10.

Hall, Stuart. 1973. "The Determination of News Photographs." In *The Manufacture of News: A Reader.* Edited by S. Cohen and J. Young. Beverly Hills: Sage: 176–90.

_____. 1977. "Culture, the Media and the 'Ideological Effect.'" In *Mass Communication and Society.* Edited by J. Curran, M. Gurevitch, and J. Woollacott. Beverly Hills, CA: Sage: 315–48.

_____. 1978. "Some Paradigms in Cultural Studies." *Annali* 3: 23.

_____. 1982. "The 'Rediscovery' of Ideology: Return to the Repressed in Media Studies." In *Culture, Society, and the Media.* Edited by M. Gurevitch, T. Bennett, J. Curran, and J. Wollacott. London: Metheun: 86–87.

_____. 1984. "The Narrative Construction of Reality." *Southern Review* 17.

_____. 1986. "Cultural Studies: Two Paradigms." In *Media, Culture and Society: A Critical Reader.* Edited by R. Collins, J. Curran, N. Garnham, P. Scannell, P. Schlesinger, and C. Sparks. Beverly Hills: Sage: 33–48.

_____. 1990. "Cultural Identity and Diaspora." In *Identity: Community, Culture, Difference*. Edited by J. Rutherford. London: Lawrence and Wishart: 235–36.

Hall, Stuart, Charles Critcher, Tony Jefferson, John Clarke, and Brian Roberts. 1978. *Policing the Crisis: Mugging, the State and Law and Order*. New York: Holmes and Meier.

Hallin, Daniel C. 1986. "Cartography, Community, and the Cold War." In *Reading the News*. Edited by R. K. Manoff and M. Schudson. New York: Pantheon.

_____. 1992. "The Media, the War in Vietnam, and Political Support: A Critique of the Thesis of an Oppositional Media." In *Media Voices: An Historical Perspective*. Edited by J. Folkerts. New York: Macmillan Publishing Company: 418–44.

_____. 1994. *We Keep America on Top of the World*. New York: Routledge.

Halloran, J., P. Elliott, and G. Murdock. 1970. *Demonstrations and Communications: A Case Study*. London: Penguin.

Halpern, Ben. 1961. "'Myth' and 'Ideology.'" *Modern Usage, History and Theory*, 1:129: 49.

Hamil-Luker, Jenifer, and Christian Smith. Winter 1998. "Religious Authority and Public Opinion on the Right to Die." *Sociology of Religion* 59:4: 373.

Handler, Joel F. 1978. *Social Movements and the Legal System: A Theory of Law Reform and Social Change*. New York: Academic Press.

Hardt, Hanno, ed. 1992. *Critical Communication Studies: Communication, History, and Theory in America*. New York: Routledge.

Hareven, Tamara K. 1995. "Changing Images of Aging and the Social Construction of the Life Course." In *Images of Aging: Cultural Representations of Later Life*: 119–34.

Harmon, Louise. Nov. 1992. "Fragments on the Deathwatch." *Minnesota Law Review* 77:1: 10.

Harris, Louis. 1987. *Inside America*. New York: Vintage Books.

Hartley, J. 1982. *Understanding News*. London: Methuen.

Hauerwas, Stanley. 1986. *Suffering Presence: Theological Reflections on Medicine, the Mentally Handicapped & the Church*. Indiana: Notre Dame University Press.

Hedberg, Katrina, M.D., and Melvin Kohn, M.D. 6 Mar. 2003. "Fifth Annual Report on Oregon's Death with Dignity Act." Oregon Department of Human Services, Office of Disease Prevention and Epidemiology, Portland, Oregon.

Heffernan, Robert B., and Charles C. Maynard. 1976. "Living and Dying with Dignity: The Rise of Old Age and Dying as Social Problems." In *This Land of Promises: The Rise and Fall of Social Problems in America*. Edited by A. L. Mauss and J. C. Wolfe. Philadelphia: J.B. Lippincott Company.

Hendin, Herbert. 1996. *Seduced by Death: Doctors, Patients, and the Dutch Cure*. New York: W. W. Norton & Company.

_____. 1995. *Suicide in America*. New York: W. W. Norton & Company .

Hernandez, Romel, and Rob Eure. 26 Mar. 1998. "Two Die Using Suicide Law– Reaction." *The Oregonian* A1.

Hilgartner, Stephen, and Charles L. Bosk. Jul. 1988. "The Rise and Fall of Social Problems: A Public Arenas Model." *American Journal of Sociology* 94:1: 53–78.

Hillyard, Daniel, and John Dombrink. 2001. *Dying Right: The Death with Dignity Movement*. New York: Routledge.

Hilts, Philip J. 1 June 1999. "Life at Age 100 Is Surprisingly Healthy: Study Challenges Conventional Wisdom About the Very Old." *The New York Times* D7.

Hodge, R. and G. Kress. 1979. *Language as Ideology*. New York: Routledge.

Hoefler, James M., and Brian E. Kamoie. 1994. *Deathright: Culture, Medicine, Politics and the Right to Die*. Boulder, CO: Westview Press.

Hofstadter, Richard. 1983. *Social Darwinism in American Thought*. Boston: Beacon Press.

Hoover, Stewart M., and Shalini S. Venturelli. 1996. "The Category of the Religious: The Blindspot of Contemporary Media Theory?" *Critical Studies in Mass Communication* 13: 251–65.

Hosenball, Mark. 6 Dec. 1993. "The Real Jack Kevorkian; His Obsession Goes Beyond Mercy to Fascination with the Macabre." *Newsweek* 28.

Hsia, H.J. 1988. Mass *Communication Research Methods: A Step-by-Step Approach*. Hillsdale, NJ: Lawrence Erlbaum Associates.

Hubert, Cynthia. 20 Nov. 1994. "New Assisted Suicide Law Splits Oregon." *Sacramento Bee* A1.

Hufker, Brian, and Gray Cavender. 1990. "From Freedom Flotilla to America's Burden: The Social Construction of the Mariel Immigrants." *The Sociological Quarterly* 31:2: 321–335.

Humphry, Derek, and Ann Wickett. 1986. *The Right to Die: Understanding Euthanasia*. New York: Harper & Row.

Hymes, Dell. 1974. *Studies in the History of Linguistics: Traditions and Paradigms*. Ann Arbor, MI: Books on Demand.

Illich, Ivan. 1975. "The Political Uses of Death." In *Death Inside Out*. Edited by P. Steinfels and R. Veatch. New York: Harper & Row.

_____. 1976. *Medical Nemesis: The Expropriation of Health*. New York: Pantheon.

In re L.W., 482.N.W.2d 60 Wisc. 1992.

Inglis, Fred. 1993. *Cultural Studies*. Oxford, UK: Blackwell.

Ingrassia, Michele. 7 Feb. 1994. "Should We Not Go Gentle?" *New York Times* 54.

Iyengar, Shanto. 1990. "Framing Responsibility for Political Issues: The Case of Poverty." *Political Behavior* 12:1:19–40.

_____. 1991. *Is Anyone Responsible? How Television Frames Political Issues*. The University of Chicago Press.

Iyengar, S. and D. Kinder. 1987. *News That Matters*. University of Chicago Press.

Iyengar, Shanto, and Adam Simon. June 1993. "News Coverage of the Gulf Crisis and Public Opinion: A Study of Agenda-Setting, Priming, and Framing." *Communication Research* 369.

Jacoby, Tamar, and Cheryl H. Miller. 7 Nov. 1988. "'I Helped Her on Her Way.'" *New York Times* 101.

Jalbert, Paul L. 1995. "Critique and Analysis in Media Studies: Media Criticism as Practical Action." *Discourse & Society* 6:1: 7–26.

Jasanoff, Sheila. 1995. *Science at the Bar*. Cambridge, MA: Harvard Univrsity Press.

Johnston, Hank. 1995. "A Methodology for Frame Analysis: From Discourse to Cognitive Schema." In *Social Movements and Culture: Social Movements, Protest, and Contention*: 217–46.

Johnston, Hank and Bert Klandermans, eds. 1995. *Social Movements and Culture*, vol. 4. Minneapolis: University of Minnesota Press.

Kahneman, Daniel, and Amos Tversky. 1984. "Choice, Values, and Frames." *American Psychologist* 39: 341–50.

Kahneman, Daniel, Paul Slovic, and Amos Tversky. 1982. *Judgement Under Uncertainty: Heuristics and Biases*. New York: Cambridge University Press.

Kalwinsky, Robert K. Jan. 1998. "Framing Life and Death: Physician-Assisted Suicide and *The New York Times* from 1991 to 1996." *Journal of Communication Inquiry* 22:1: 93–112.

Kamisar, Yale. 4 Nov. 1998. "Details Doom Assisted-Suicide Measures." *The New York Times* Op-Ed section, A27.

_____. 21 Nov. 1989. "Whose Right Does the Right to Die Protect?" *Manhattan Lawyer* 12.

Kaplan, David A., and Ann McDaniel. 9 July 1990. "The Family vs. the State; Who Decides About Abortion and the Right to Die?" *The New York Times* 22.

Kaplan, David A., and Nina A. Biddle. 15 Apr. 1996. "Is It a Wonderful Life? Two Federal Courts Strike Down Bans on Assisted Suicide and Set Stage for a Supreme Court Battle." *The New York Times* 62.

Kaplan, Stuart Jay. 1990. "Visual Metaphors in the Representation of Communication Technology." *Critical Studies in Mass Communication* 7: 37–47.

Kastenbaum, Robert. 1972. "While the Old Man Dies: Our Conflicting Attitudes." In *Psychosocial Aspects of Terminal Care*. Edited by B. Schoenbert. New York: Columbia University Press.

Katz, Elihu. 1980. "On Conceptualizing Media Effect." In *Studies in Communication*, vol. 1. Edited by T. McCormack. Greenwich, CT: JAI Press: 119–41.

Katz, Michael. 1986. *In the Shadow of the Poorhouse: A Social History of Welfare in America*. New York: Basic Books.

Kearl, Michael C. 1989. *Endings: A Sociology of Death and Dying*. New York: Oxford University Press.

Keenan, James F. 14 Nov. 1998. "The Case for Physician-Assisted Suicide?" *America* 14.

Kenny, Robert W. 2000. "The Rhetoric of Kevorkian's Battle." *The Quarterly Journal of Speech* 86:4: 386–402.

Kevorkian, Jack. Nov. 1994. "A Modern Inquisition." *The Humanist* 54:6: 7.

Kielbowicz, Richard B., and Clifford Scherer. 1986. "The Role of the Press in the Dynamics of Social Movements." *Research in Social Movements, Conflicts, and Change* 9: 71–96.

Kinder, D. R., and L. M. Sanders. 1990. "Mimicking Political Debate with Survey Questions: The Case of White Opinion on Affirmative Action for Blacks." *Social Cognition* 8: 73–103.

Klandermans, Bert. 1988. "The Formation and Mobilization of Consensus." *International Social Movement Research* 1: 173–96.

_____. 1995. "The Politics of Social Protest: Comparative Perspectives on States and Social Movements." In *Social Movements, Protest, and Contention*, vol. 3. Edited by J. Craig Jenkins and Bert Klandermans. Minneapolis: University of Minnesota Press: 3–13.

Klandermans, Bert, and Sjoerd Goslinga. 1996. "Media Discourse, Movement Publicity, and the Generation of Collective Action Frames." In *Comparative Perspectives on Social Movements: Political Opportunities, Mobilizing Structures, and Cultural Framings*. Edited by D. McAdam, J. D. McCarthy, and M. N. Zald. Massachusetts: Cambridge University Press: 312–37.

Klemesrud, Judy. 1 Mar. 1971. "There's a Time, They Say, to Let People Die." *The New York Times* 35.

Kral, Michael J. Fall 1994. "Suicide as Social Logic." *Suicide and Life-Threatening Behavior* 24:3: 245–55.

Kress, G. 1983. "Linguistic and Ideological Transformations in News Reporting." In *Language, Image, Media*. Edited by H. Davis and P. Walton. Oxford: Basil Blackwell: 120–38.

Kübler-Ross, Elizabeth. 1969. *On Death and Dying*. New York: Macmillan.

Kurtz, Paul. 22 Mar. 1994. "The Growth of Antiscience." *Skeptical Inquirer* 18:3: 255–60.

Kurtz, Sheldon. 7 Jan. 1991. "Should Physicians Perform Euthanasia?" *American Medical News* 12: 15.

Lake, Randall A. 1986. "The Metaethical Framework of Anti-Abortion Rhetoric." *Signs* 11: 478–99.

Lakoff, G. and M. Johnson. 1980. *Metaphors We Live By*. University of Chicago Press.

Lakoff, G. 1987. *Women, Fire and Dangerous Things: What Categories Reveal about the Mind*. University of Chicago Press.

Lang, G., and K. Lang. 1983. *The Battle for Public Opinion*. New York: Ballantine.

Larson, Edward J., and Darrel W. Amundsen. 1998. *A Different Death: Euthanasia & the Christian Tradition*. Downers Grove: Intervarsity Press.

Larson, M.S. 1977. *The Rise of Professionalism*. Berkeley: University of California Press.

Larue, Gerald. 1996. *Playing God: 50 Religions' Views of Your Right to Die*. Wakefield, RI: Moyer Bell.

Lazar, Neil, Sam Shemie, George Webster, and Bernard Dickens. 20 Mar. 2001. "Bioethics for Physicians: Brain Death." *Canadian Medical Association Journal*, 164:6: 833–36.

Lemonick, Michael D. 15 Apr. 1996. "Defining the Right to Die." *Time* 147:16: 821.

Levi-Strauss, Claude. 1966. *The Savage Mind*. University of Chicago Press.

Lifton, Robert Jay. 1986. *The Nazi Doctors: Medical Killing and the Psychology of Genocide*. New York: Random House.

_____. 1979. *The Broken Connection: On Death and the Continuity of Life*. New York: Simon and Schuster.

Longino, Charles F., Jr. 1988. "Who Are the Oldest Americans." *Gerontologist* 28: 516.

_____. Aug. 1994. "Myths of an Aging America." *American Demographics* 36.

Lown, Bernard, M.D. 1998. "Physicians Need to Fight the Business Model of Medicine." *Hippocrates* 12:5: 25–28.

Luhmann, Niklas. 1986. "The Individuality of the Individual: Historical Meanings and Contemporary Problems." In *Reconstructing Individualism: Autonomy, Individuality, and the Self in Western Thought*. Edited by T. C. Heller, M. Sosna, and D. E. Wellbery. Palo Alto, CA: Stanford University Press: 313- 25.

Lundberg, George D. 1988. "'It's Over Debbie' and the Euthanasia Debate." *JAMA, Journal of the American Medical Association* 259: 2142.

MacDonald, Michael. 1991. "The Medicalization of Suicide." In *Framing Disease: Studies in Cultural History*. Edited by Charles Rosenberg and Janet Golden. New Brunswick, NJ: Rutgers University Press: 85–103.

Mahony, Roger. 9 May 1994. "Ending Pain Shouldn't Mean Ending Lives." *Los Angeles Times* A11.

Malcolm, Andrew H. 23 Sept. 1984. "Many See Mercy in Ending Empty Lives." *The New York Times*, section 1, page 1.

_____. 12 May 1985. "Family Seeks a Mercy Death Accord." *The New York Times* 20.

_____. 3 Dec. 1989. "The Ultimate Decision." *The New York Times Magazine* 138: 38.

Malcolm, Noel. 19 Oct. 1998. "The Roots of Bosnian Horror Lie Not So Deep." *The New York Times* B6.

Malinowski, Bronislav. 1949. "Death and the Reintegration of the Group." in *Magic, Science and Religion*. New York: Doubleday: 47–53.

_____. 1972. "The Role of Magic and Religion." In *Reader in Comparative Religion*. Edited by W. A. Lessa and E. Z. Volt. New York: Harper & Row: 63–72.

Maloney, Lawrence. 11 July 1983. "A New Understanding About Death." *U.S. News & World Report* 62.

Marker, Rita L. 1992. *Euthanasia: Killing or Caring*. Lewiston, New York: Life Cycle Books.

Markson, Elizabeth. 1995. "To Be or Not to Be: Assisted Suicide Revisited." *Omega* 31:3: 221–35.

Mauss, Armand L., and Julie C. Wolfe, eds. 1975. *This Land of Promises: The Rise and Fall of Social Problems in America*. Philadelphia: J.B. Lippincott Company.

McCombs, Maxwell E., Donald L. Shaw, and Eugene Shaw. 1972. "The News and Public Response: Three Studies of the Agenda-Setting Power of the Press." Paper presented at the annual conference for the Association for Education in Journalism, Carbondale, Illinois.

McCue, Jack. 5 Apr. 1995. "The Naturalness of Dying." *JAMA, Journal of the American Medical Association* 273:13: 1039.

McGee, Michael Calvin. Feb. 1980. "The 'Ideograph': A link Between Rhetoric and Ideology." *The Quarterly Journal of Speech* 66:1: 1–16.

McLuhan, Marshall. 1964. *Understanding Media: The Extensions of Man*. New York: McGraw-Hill.

McNeil, Barbara, Steven Parker, Harold Sox, Jr., and Amos Tversky. 1982. "On the Elicitation of Preferences for Alternative Therapies." *New England Journal of Medicine* 301: 1259–262.

McQuail, Dennis. 1979. "The Influence and Effects of Mass Media." In *Mass Communication and Society*: 70-94.

_____. 1987. *Mass Communication Theory: An Introduction*. 2nd edition. Beverly Hills: Sage.

Mellor, P. 1993. "Death in High Modernity: The Contemporary Presence and Absence of Death." In *The Sociology of Death*. Edited by D. Clark. Oxford, UK: Blackwell.

Meier, Diane E. 24 Apr. 1998. "A Change of Heart on Assisted Suicide." *The New York Times* A23.

Meier, Diane, and Christine Cassel. 1983. "Euthanasia in Old Age: Case Study and Ethical Analysis." *Journal of the American Geriatrics Society* 31: 294.

_____. 1990. "Morals and Moralism in the Debate Over Euthanasia and Assisted Suicide." *New England Journal of Medicine* 232: 750.

Messinger, Thane J. 1993. "A Gentle and Easy Death: From Ancient Greece to Beyond Cruzan: Toward a Reasoned Legal Response to the Societal Dilemma of Euthanasia." *University of Denver Law Review* 71: 175.

Mills, C. Wright. 1956. *The Power Elite*. New York: Oxford University Press.

Minogue, Brendan P. July 1990. "The Exclusion of Theology from Public Policy: the Case of Euthanasia." *Second Opinion* 14: 84.

Minois, G. 2001. *History of Suicide: Voluntary Death in Western Culture* (trans. by Lydia G. Cochrane). Baltimore: Johns Hopkins University Press.

Minsky, M. 1975. "A Framework for Representing Knowledge." In *The Psychology of Computer Vision*. New York: McGraw-Hill: 211–77.

Mitchell, Basil. 1990. "The Value of Human Life." In *Medicine, Medical Ethics and the Value of Life*. Edited by Peter Byme. New Jersey: John Wiley & Sons: 34–46.

Mitford, Jessica. 1963. *The American Way of Death, 1830–1920*. Philadelphia: Temple University Press.

Moller, David W. 1996. *Confronting Death: Values, Institutions, and Human Mortality*. New York: Oxford University Press.

Molotch, Harvey. 1979. "Media and Movements." In *The Dynamics of Social Movements: Resource Mobilization, Social Control, and Tactics.* Edited by M. N. Zald and J. D. McCarthy. Cambridge, MA: Winthrop Publishers: 71–93.

Molotch, Harvey, and Lester, Marilyn. 1974. "News as Purposive Behavior: On the Strategic Uses of Routine Events, Accidents, and Scandals." *American Sociological Review* 39: 101–12.

Mordarski, Daniel R. 1995. "Medical Futility: Has Ending Life Support Become the Next 'Pro-Choice/Right to Life' Debate?" *Cleveland State Law Review* 41: 751.

Moreland, J.P. and Geisler, Norman L. 1990. *The Life and Death Debate: Moral Issues of Our Time.* Westport, CT: Praeger Publishers.

Morley, D. 1980. *The "Nationwide" Audience: Structure and Decoding.* London: British Film Institute.

Morris, M. 1974. "The Public Definition of a Social Movement: Women's Liberation." *Sociology and Social Research* 57: 526–43.

Moscovici, S. 1984. "The Phenomenon of Social Representations." In *Social Representations.* Edited by R. Farr and S. Moscovici. UK: Cambridge University Press: 3–69.

Mullens, Anne. 1996. *Timely Death: Considering Our Last Rights* Toronto, California: Alfred A. Knopf.

Munk, William. 1977. *Euthanasia: Or, Medical Treatment in Aid of an Easy Death.* New York: Arno Press.

Nakagawa, G. 1993. "Deformed Subjects, Docile Bodies." In *Narrative and Social Control: Critical Perspectives,* Sage Series in Communication Research, vol. 21. Edited by Dennis K. Mumby. Thousand Oaks, CA: Sage.

Neergaard, Lauren. 15 Nov. 2000. "Deathly Ill Patients Want Options." Associated Press reprinted on C-Health website, http://www.canoe.ca/Health0011/_life-ap.html.

Nelkin, Dorothy. 1987. *Selling Science: How the Press Covers Science and Technology.* New York: Freeman.

_____. 22 June 1991. "AIDS and the News Media." *The Milbank Quarterly* 69: 2.

_____. 1994. "Promotional Metaphors and their Popular Appeal." *Public Understanding of Science* 3: 25–31.

Neuzil, Mark, and William Kovarik. 1996. *Mass Media & Environmental Conflict: America's Green Crusades.* Thousand Oaks, CA: Sage.

Newcomb, H., and P. Hirsch. 1984. "Television as a Cultural Forum." In *Interpreting Television: Current Research Perspectives.* Edited by W. Rowland and B. Watkins. Beverly Hills: Sage: 58–73.

Newman, Stephen. Fall 1991. "Euthanasia: Orchestrating 'the Last Syllable of Time.'" *University of Pittsburgh Law Review* 53: 153.

Niedelmann, Jacob. 10 Jan. 1999. Interview with Michael Toms, "New Dimensions" National Public Radio.

Noelle-Neuman, E. 1974. "The Spiral of Silence: A Theory of Public Opinion." *Journal of Communication* 24: 43–51.

Nuland, Sherwin B. 13 Jan. 1997. "How We Die is Our Business." *The New York Times* A15.

Ochs, Donovan J. 1993. *Consolatory Rhetoric: Grief, Symbol, and Ritual in the Greco-Roman Era.* Columbia: University of South Carolina Press.

O'Keefe, Mark. 12 Nov. 1994. "Outsiders Ignored in Oregon Suicide Vote." *The Oregonian* A1.

Olien, C. N., P. T. Tichenor, and G. A. Donahue. 1989. "Media Coverage and Social Movements." In *Information Campaigns: Balancing Social Values and Social Change.* Edited by C. T. Salmon. Beverly Hills: Sage: 139–63.

Olien, C. N., G. A. Donohue, and P. T. Tichenor. Nov. 1984. "Media and Stages of Social Conflict." *Journalism Monographs* No. 90.

Omicinski, John. 6 Jan. 1999. "Aging Population Gives All Gray Hairs." *USA Today* A12.

O'Neill, Anne-Marie.12 June 1995. "Kinder, Gentler Death?" *Time* 28.

Osgood, Nancy J. 22 Mar. 1995. "Assisted Suicide and Older People: A Deadly Combination." *Issues in Law & Medicine* 10:4: 415.

Oski, Frank A. 24 Jan. 1994. "Opting Out; Jack Kevorkian and Euthanasia." *The Nation* 258:3: 77.

O'Sullivan, T., J. Hartley, D. Saunders, M. Montgomery, and J. Fiske. 1994. *Key Concepts in Communication and Cultural Studies*. New York: Routledge.

Ostling, Richard N. 23 Feb 1987. "Is It Wrong to Cut Off Feeding? Experts Debate the Denial of Nourishment for Comatose Patients." *Time* 71.

Paletz, D., and R. M. Entman. 1981. *Media Power Politics*. New York: Free Press.

Palmer, Larry I. 2000. *Endings and Beginnings; Law, Medicine, and Society in Assisted Life and Death*. Westport, CT: Greenwood Press.

Pan, Zhongdangpan, and Gerald M. Kosicki. 1993. "Framing Analysis: An Approach to News Discourse." *Political Communication* 10: 55–75.

Parenti, Michael. 1996. *Dirty Truths*. San Francisco: City Lights Bookstore.

Park, Robert. 1941. "News and the Power of the Press." *American Journal of Sociology* 47:1: 1–11.

Parsons, T., and V. Lidz. 1967. "Death in American Society." In *Essays in Self Destruction*. Edited by E. Shneidman. New York: Science House.

Patterson, Maggie J., and Megan W. Hall. June 1998. "Abortion, Moral Maturity and Civic Journalism." *Critical Studies in Mass Communication* 15:2: 91.

Pearson, David E. July 1993. "Post-Mass Culture." *Society* 30:5: 17.

Peck, M. Scott. 10 Mar. 1997. "Living Is the Mystery; I Believe We Should Enlarge the Debate on Euthanasia and Not Rush to Resolve It." *Newsweek* 18.

Phillips, Pat. 24 Sept. 1997. "Views of Assisted Suicide from Several Nations." *JAMA Journal of the American Medical Association* 278:12: 969.

Polan, Dana. 1986. *Power and Paranoia: History, Narrative, and the American Cinema, 1940–1950*. New York: Columbia University Press.

Postman, Neil, and Steve Powers. 1992. *How to Watch TV News*. New York: Viking Penguin.

Potter, J. and M. Wetherell. 1987. *Discourse and Social Psychology: Beyond Attitudes and Behaviour*. London: Sage.

Press, Aric, and Nancy Cooper. 28 Nov. 1983. "The Case of Baby Jane Doe." *The New York Times* 45.

Press, Aric, David T. Friendly, et al. 7 Jan. 1985. "Arguing the Right to Die." *The New York Times* 18.

Price, Joyce. 10 Nov. 1994. "Euthanasia Measure Leading in Oregon: Law Would Allow Doctors to Aid Death." *The Washington Times* A17.

Price, Vincent, David Tewksbury, and Elizabeth Powers. Oct. 1997. "Switching Trains of Thought: The Impact of News Frames on Readers' Cognitive Responses." *Communication Research* 24:5: 481–506.

Pride, Richard A. 1995. "How Activists and Media Frame Social Problems: Critical Events Versus Performance Trends for Schools." *Political Communication* 12: 5–26.

Pugliese, J. Aug. 1993. "Don't Ask—Don't Tell: The Secret Practice of Physician-Assisted Suicide." *Hastings Law Journal* 44: 1291–1330.

"Question: Who Will Play God?" 9 Aug. 1984. *Time* 68.

Quill, Timothy E. 1991. "Death and Dignity: A Case of Individualized Decision Making." *New England Journal of Medicine* 324:10: 691–94.

Rachels, James, ed. 1979. *Moral Problems.* 3rd edition. New York: Harper & Row.

_____. 1986. *The End of Life: Euthanasia and Morality.* New York: Oxford University Press.

_____. 1989. "Passive and Active Euthanasia Are Equally Acceptable." In *Euthanasia: Opposing Viewpoints.* Edited by Neal Bernards. New York: Oxford University Press.

Radway, J.C. 1984. *Reading the Romance.* Chapel Hill: University of North Carolina Press.

Redlich, Fredrick C. 1978. "Medical Ethics Under National Socialism." In *Encyclopedia of Bioethics.* Edited by Walter Reich. 3: 1016–17.

Reinhold, Robert. 21 Jul. 1974. "Attitudes to Death Grow More Realistic." *The New York Times* A1.

Reitman, James S. 22 Dec. 1995. "The Debate on Assisted Suicide—Redefining Morally Appropriate Care for People with Intractable Suffering." *Issues in Law & Medicine.* 11:3: 299.

Report of the Ad Hoc Committee. 1968. "A Definition of Irreversible Coma: Report of the Ad Hoc Committee of the Harvard Medical School to Examine the Definition of Brain Death." *Journal of American Medical Association* 205: 337.

Roberts, Carolyn S., and Martha Gorman. 1996. *Euthanasia: A Reference Handbook.* Santa Barbara: ABC-CLIO, Inc.

Roberts, D., and N. Maccoby. 1985. "Effects of Mass Communication." In *Handbook of Social Psychology,* vol 2. Edited by G. Lindzey and E. Aronson. New York: Random House.

Robin, Eugene D., and Robert F. McCauley. 3 June 1995. "Cultural Lag and the Hippocratic Oath." *The Lancet* 345:8962: 1422.

Roeh, Itzhak and Raphael Nir. 1993. "Reporting the Intifada in the Israeli Press: How Mainstream Ideology Overrides 'Quality' and 'Melodrama,'" In *Framing the Intifada.* Edited by A. A. Cohan and G. Wolfsfeld. Norwood, NJ: Ablex Pub. Co.

Rollins, Betty. 1985. *Last Wish.* New York: Simon and Schuster.

Roper Poll. 1991. *Hemlock Quarterly* 44:9.

Rorty, Richard. June 1996. "What's Wrong with 'Rights.'" *Harper's* 292:1753: 15–18.

Rosenberg, Charles E. 24 Nov. 1996. "Slippery Slope: A Psychiatrist Looks at Physician-Assisted Suicide and Shudders." *The New York Times Book Review* 22.

Rosellini, Lynn. 7 Nov. 1994. "The Final Struggle of Jamie Butcher." *U.S. News & World Report* 67-70.

Rubenstein, Ruth P. 1995. *Dress Codes: Meanings and Messages in American Culture.* Boulder, CO: Westview Press.

Rucht, D. and T. Ohlemacher. 1992. "Protest Event Data: Collection, Uses and Perspectives." In *Studying Collective Action.* Newbury Park, CA: Sage.

Russell, O. Ruth. 14 Feb. 1972. "The Right to Choose Death." *The New York Times* 29.

_____. 1977. *Freedom to Die: Moral and Legal Aspects of Euthanasia.* New York: Human Sciences Press.

Ryan, Charlotte. 1991. *Prime Time Activism: Media Strategies for Grassroots Organizations.* Boston: South End Press.

Sahlins, Marshall. 1985. *Islands of History.* University of Chicago Press.

Sanders, Alain L. 11 Dec. 1989. "Whose Right to Die?" *Time* 80.

Saner, Robert J. Feb. 2000. "A New Focus on Pain Care, Pain Medicine Network." *American Academy of Pain Medicine* 15:1. http://www.painmed.org/productpub/newsletter/feb00/fromthehill.htm.

Schaffner, Christina. 1995. "The 'Balance' Metaphor in Relation to Peace." In *Language and Peace*.

Schanker, David R. Summer 1993. "Of Suicide Machines, Euthanasia Legislation, and the Health Care Crisis." *Indiana Law Journal* 68: 977.

Scheingold, Stuart A. 1989. "Constitutional Rights and Social Change: Civil Rights in Perspective." In *Judging the Constitution*. Edited by M. McCann and G. Houseman. Boston: Little, Brown.

Scheufele, Dietram A. Winter 1999. "Framing as a Theory of Media Effects." *Journal of Communication* 49:1: 103–22.

Schneider, Carl E. 2000. *Law at the End of Life: The Supreme Court and Assisted Suicide*. Ann Arbor: University of Michigan Press.

Schudson, Michael. 1978. *Discovering the News: A Social History of American Newspapers*. New York: Basic Books.

_____. 1982. "The Politics of Narrative Form: The Emergence of News Conventions in Print and Television." *Daedalus* 3: 4.

_____. 1989. "The Sociology of News Production." Media, *Culture and Society* 11: 263–82.

_____. 1989. "How Culture Works: Perspectives from Media Studies on the Efficacy of Symbols." *Theory and Society* 18: 153–80.

_____. 1995. *The Power of News*. Cambridge, MA: Harvard University Press.

Schuller, Diane E. 1996. "The 'Business' of Medicine: Hippocratic or Hypocritical?" Presidential Address, *Annals of Allergy, Asthma & Immunology* 77: 28–32.

Schumach, Murray. 22 Mar. 1963. "Kildare Commits a Mercy Killing: Use of Euthanasia Episode a new Step in TV." *The New York Times* 7.

Seale, Clive. Nov. 1995. "Heroic Death." *Sociology* 29:4: 597–613.

Seravalli, E. and J. Fashing. 1992. "Medical Art and Immortality." *Society* 29: 37–38.

Shapiro, Joseph 30 Sept. 1991. "A Vote on Legal Euthanasia: The Right-to-Die Movement Makes its Mark in Washington." *U.S. News & World Report* 111:14: 322.

Sheed, Wilfrid. 3 June 1996. "Dr. Death, a '90s Celebrity: By Passing into the Eye of Hoopla, Jack Kevorkian Jeopardizes the Cause He Champions." *Time* 80.

Sheils, Merrill, and Susan Agrest. 29 Sept. 1975. "Cruel Questions." *The New York Times* 76.

Siebold, Cathy. 1992. *The Hospice Movement: Easing Death's Pains*. New York: Twayne Publishers.

Siegler, Mark, and Carlos F. Gomez. 9 May 1992. "U.S. Consensus on Euthanasia?" *The Lancet* 339:8802: 1164.

Sigal, Leon V. 1973. *Reporters and Officials*. Lexington, MA: D.C. Heath and Company.

Sigman, S., and D. Fry. 1985. "Differential Ideology and Language Use: Readers' Reconstructions and Descriptions of News Events." *Critical Studies in Mass Communication* 2: 307–22.

Silverstein, Helena. 1992. "Unleashing Rights: Law and the Politics of the Animal Rights Movement." Ph.D diss., University of Washington.

Simon, Rita J., and Jennifer M. Scherer. 1999. *Euthanasia and the Right to Die: A Comparative View*. New York: Rowman and Littlefield Publishers.

Smith, Barbara Hernstein. 1984. "Contingencies of Value." In *Canons*. Edited by Robert von Hallberg. University of Chicago Press.

Smith, A. 1989. "All's Well that Ends Well: Toward a Policy of Assisted Rational Suicide or Merely Enlightened Self-Determination?" *U.C. Davis Law Review* 22: 286–87.

Smith, Dinitia. 13 May 2000. "The Opposites of Sex: The Normal and the Not." *The New York Times* A13.

Smith, Tom. 1987. "That Which We Call Welfare by any Other Name Would Smell Sweeter: An Analysis of the Impact of Question Wording on Response Patterns." *Public Opinion Quarterly* 51: 75–83.

Smith, Wesley. Summer 1998. "The Serial Killer as Folk Hero." *The Human Life Review.* 24:3: 107–9.

Snow, David A., E. Burke Rochford, Jr., Steven K. Worden, and Robert Benford. 1986. "Frame Alignment Processes, Micromobilization, and Movement Participation." *American Sociological Review* 51: 464–81.

Snow, David, and Robert Benford. 1988. "Ideology, Frame Resonance, and Participant Mobilization." in *International Social Movement Research* 1: 197–217.

_____. 1992. "Master Frames and Cycles of Protest." In *Frontiers in Social Movement Theory.* Edited by A. Morris and C. Mueller. New Haven, CT: Yale University Press.

Solomon, William S. 1992. "News Frames and Media Packages: Covering El Salvador." *Critical Studies in Mass Communication* 9: 56–74.

Somerville, Margaret A. Spring 1993. "The Song of Death." *Journal of Contemporary Health Law & Policy* 9:1: 1–15.

Stannard, David. E. 1977. *The Puritan Way of Death: A Study of Religion, Culture, and Social Change.* New York: Praeger Publishers.

Stern, Andrew. 25 June 1996. "U.S. Doctor's Group Opposes Assisted Suicide Again." Reuters North American Wire, 1.

Stolberg, Sheryl G. 11 June 1997. "Assisted Suicide." *The New York Times* A22.

_____. 3 Oct. 1999. "Buying Time for Women on the Biological Clock." *The New York Times,* Week in Review, Section 4, 3.

Stone, Alan, M.D. 1988. "The Right to Die: New Problems For Law and Medicine and Psychiatry." *Emory Law Journal* 37: 627.

Storey, John. 1993. *An Introductory Guide to Cultural Theory and Popular Culture.* Athens, GA: University of Georgia Press.

Strong, P.M. 1979. "Sociological Imperialism and the Profession of Medicine: A Critical Examination of the Thesis of Medical Imperialism." *Social Science Medicine* 13A: 199–215.

Strouse, Jean. 10 June 2001. "Where They Got Their Ideas." *The New York Times Book Review* 10.

Sullivan, John L., James Piereson, and George L. Marcus. 1982. *Political Tolerance and American Democracy.* University of Chicago Press.

Sullivan, Joseph F. 25 June 1987. "Right of Patients who Wish to Die Widened in Jersey." *The New York Times* A1.

Sulmasy, Daniel P. 23 Sept. 1998. "Physician Resource Use and Willingness to Participate in Assisted Suicide." *JAMA, Journal of the American Medical Association* 280:12: 1034.

Swidler, Ann. 1995. "Cultural Power and Social Movements." In *Social Movements and Culture: Social Movements, Protest, and Contention*: 25–40.

_____. Apr. 1986. "Culture in Action: Symbols and Strategies." *American Sociological Review.* 51: 273–86.

Tannen, Deborah. 1998. *The Argument Culture: Moving from Debate to Dialogue.* New York: Random House.

_____. 1993. "What's In a Frame? Surface Evidence for Underlying Expectations." In *Framing in Discourse.* Edited by Deborah Tannen. New York: Oxford University Press.

_____. 1998. "Agreeing to Disagree: The Culture of Argument in America." Interview with Michael Toms, New Dimensions Radio: www/newdimensions.org.

Tarrow, Sidney. 1994. Power *in Movement: Social Movements, Collective Action and Politics*. New York: Cambridge University Press.

Taylor, Humphrey. 9 Jan. 2002. "2-to-1 Majorities Continue to Support Rights to Both Euthanasia and Doctor-Assisted Suicide." Harris Interactive, downloaded from the Internet on 4 June 2002, http://www.harrisinteractive.com/harris_poll/index.asp? PID=278.

Taylor, Verta, and Whittier, Nancy. 1995. "Analytical Approaches to Social Movement Culture: The Culture of the Women's Movement." In *Social Movements and Culture: Social Movements, Protest, and Contention*: 163–87.

Terkildsen, Nayda, and Frauke Schnell. Dec. 1997. "How Media Frames Move Public Opinion: An Analysis of the Women's Movement." *Political Research Quarterly* 50:4: 879–900.

"The Right to Die." 3 July 1973. *The New York Times* A22.

"The Right to Die: Who Can Play Fate and How?" 11 Feb. 1980. *Time* 95.

Thompson, John B. 1990. *Ideology and Modern Culture: Critical Social Theory in the Era of Mass Communication*. Cambridge, UK: Polity Press.

Tifft, Susan. 11 Apr. 1983. "Debate on the Boundary of Life; Medical Miracles and the Patient's Right to Die." *Time* 68.

Tiryakin, Edward A. 1988. "From Durkheim to Managua: Revolutions as Religious Revivals." In *Durkheimian Sociology: Cultural Studies*. Edited by Jeffrey C. Alexander. Cambridge, UK: Cambridge University Press.

Tocqueville, Alexis de. 1835/1966. *Democracy in America*. Edited by J.P. Mayer and M. Lerner. New York: Harper & Row.

Toulmin, Stephen Edelston. 1958. *The Uses of Argument*. Cambridge, UK: Cambridge University Press.

Treichler, Paula A. 1989. "What Definitions Do: Childbirth, Cultural Crisis, and the Challenge to Medical Discourse." In *Rethinking Communication*, vol. 2. Edited by Brenda Dervin. Newbury Park, CA: Sage: 424–53.

Trew, Tony. 1979. "What the Papers Say: Linguistic Variation and Ideological Difference." In *Language and Control*: 117–56.

Tuchman, Gaye. 1972. "Objectivity as Strategic Ritual: An Examination of Newsmen's Notions of Objectivity." *American Journal of Sociology* 77: 670–73.

_____. 1973. "Making News by Doing Work; Routinizing the Unexpected." *American Journal of Sociology* 79: 110–131.

_____. Autumn 1976. "Telling Stories." *Journal of Communication* 26:4: 93–97.

_____. 1978. *Making News: A Study in the Construction of Reality*. New York: Free Press.

_____. 1981. "Myth and the Consciousness Industry: A New Look at the Effects of the Mass Media." In *Mass Media and Social Change*. Edited by E. Katz and T. Szecsko. Beverly Hills: Sage: 83–100.

Turner, Victor. 1969. *The Ritual Process: Structure and Anti-Structure*. Chicago: Aldine.

Turow, Joseph. 1989. "Television and Institutional Power: The Case of Medicine." In *Rethinking Communication* 2: 454-73.

Tversky, Amos, and Daniel Kahneman. 1977. "Judgement under Uncertainty: Heuristics and Biases." In *Statistics and Public Policy*. Edited by W. B. Fairly and F. Mosteller. Reading, MA: Addison-Wesley: 309–27.

_____.1990. "Rational Choice and the Framing of Decisions" In *The Limits of Rationality*. Edited by K. Cook and M. Levi. University of Chicago Press.

Urofsky, Melvin I. 2000. *Lethal Judgments: Assisted Suicide & American Law*. Lawrence, KS: University Press of Kansas.

U.S. Census Bureau. 15 May 2001. "Table DP-1Profile of General Demographic Characteristics for the United States." downloaded June 2002 from http://www.census.gov/Press-Release/www/2002/cb01cn67html.

Van Biema, David. 31 May 1993. "Sisters of Mercy; A Few Months After Sue Weaver went to Kevorkian to End Her Life, Her Sisters Talked to Time about How They Came to Respect that Decision." *Time* 42.

_____. 11 Oct. 1993. "An Education in Death" *Time* 60.

_____. 13 Jan. 1997. "Is There a Right to Die?" *Time* 60.

_____. 7 July 1997. "Death's Door Left Ajar." *Time* 30.

Van Dijk, Teun A. 1988. *News as Discourse*. Hillsdale, NJ: Lawrence Erlbaum.

_____. 1992. *Racism and the Press*. London: Routledge.

_____. 1995. "Discourse Analysis as Ideology Analysis." In *Language and Peace*.

Veatch, Robert M. 1976. "Death, Dying and the Biological Revolution: Our Last Quest for Responsibility." New Haven, CT: Yale University Press.

Verhovek, Sam H. 18 Feb. 1999. "Oregon Reporting 15 Deaths in year Under Suicide Law." *The New York Times* A1.

Wallis, Claudia. 31 Mar. 1986. "To Feed or Not to Feed? An AMA Panel Rules on the Ethics of Treating the Comatose." *Time* 60.

Walter, Tony, Jane Littlewood, Michael Pickering. Nov. 1995. "Death in the News: the Public Invigilation of Private Emotion." *Sociology* 29:4: 579–96.

Walter, Tony. 1994. *The Revival of Death*. New York: Routledge.

Wanzer, Sidney H. et al. 1989. "The Physician's Responsibility Toward Hopelessly Ill Patients: A Second Look." *New England Journal of Medicine* 320: 844.

Warrick, Pamela. 12 Sept. 1991. "Lethal Advice: Fast-Selling 'Final Exit' Has Made Suicide a Hot Topic." *Los Angeles Times* E1.

Weaver, D. H., and G. C. Wilhoit. 1986. *The American Journalist: A Portrait of U.S. News People and their Work*. Bloomington: Indiana University Press.

Weber, Max. 1968. *Economy and Society*. New York: Bedminster.

Weisman, A. 1972. *On Dying and Denying*. New York: Behavioral Publications.

Weiss, Gregory L., and Lonnquist, Lynne E. 1994. *The Sociology of Health, Healing, and Illness*. Englewood Cliffs, NJ: Prentice Hall.

Wells, Robert V. 2000. *Facing the "King of Terrors": Death and Society in an American Community, 1750–1990*. New York: Simon & Schuster.

Wennberg, Robert N. 1990. *Terminal Choices: Euthanasia, Suicide, and the Right to Die*. Grand Rapids, Mich.: William B. Eerdmans Publishing Company.

Wernick, Andrew. 1995. "Selling Funerals, Imaging Death." In *Images of Aging: Cultural Representations of Later Life*. Edited by M. Featherstone and A. Wernick. New York: Routledge: 280–93.

Wetherell, M. and J. Potter. 1992. *Mappi g the Language of Racism: Discourse and the Legitmation of Exploitation*. New York: Harvester Wheatsheaf.

White, David M. 1964. "The Gatekeeper: A Case Study in the Selection of News." In *Society and Mass Communication*. Edited by L. A. Dexter and D. M. White. New York: Free Press.

White, David. M. 1950. "The Gatekeeper: A Case Study in the Selection of News." *Journalism Quarterly* 27: 383–90.

Wiley, Lindsay F. 24 May 2002. "Ashcroft Appeals Assisted Suicide Decision, *Pain & the Law*, accessed June 04, 2002 from http:painandthelaw.org/palliative/Ashcroft_053002.php.

Wilkerson, Isabel. 7 June 1990. "Physician Fulfills a Goal: Aiding a Person in Suicide." *The New York Times* A16.

_____. 25 Oct. 1991. "Rage and Support for Doctor's Role in Suicide." *The New York Times* A1.

Wilkes, Paul. 21 July 1996. "The Next Pro-Lifers." *The New York Times Magazine* 22–51.

Will, George F. 9 Jan. 1978. "A Good Death." *Newsweek* 72.

_____. 14 Apr. 1980. "The Case of Phillip Becker." *Newsweek* 112.

Williams, Glanville. 1959. "Mercy-Killing Legislation: A Rejoinder." *Minnesota Law Review* 43:1: 9–11.

Williams, Raymond. 1976. *Television: Technology and Cultural Form*. New York: Schocken.

Wolf, Susan M. 1996. "Gender, Feminism, and Death: Physician-Assisted Suicide and Euthanasia." In *Feminism & Bioethics: Beyond Reproduction*. Edited by S. Wolf. New York: Oxford University Press: 282–317.

Wolfsfeld, G. 1993. "Introduction: Framing Political Conflict." In *Framing the Intifada: People and Media*. Edited by A. A. Cohen and G. Wolfsfeld, Norwood, NJ: Ablex Publishing.

Woodman, Sue. 1998. Last *Rights: The Struggle Over the Right to Die*. New York: Plenum Trade.

Wyden, Ron. 23 Oct. 1999. "Tying the Healing Hands." *The New York Times* A26.

Yuen, Amy. 22 June 1996. "Kevorkian Death Toll Up by 3 in 10 Days." *Austin American-Statesman* A15.

Yuen, Michele. Feb. 1992. "Letting Daddy Die: Adopting New Standards for Surrogate Decisionmaking." *UCLA Law Review* 39: 581.

Zarefsky, David. 1986. *President Johnson's War on Poverty: Rhetoric and History*. Birmingham: University of Alabama Press.

Zola, Irving. 1972. "Medicine as an Institution of Social Control." *Sociological Review* 20: 487–504.

Zucker, H.G. 1978. "The Variable Nature of News Media Influence." In *Communication Yearbook*, 2. Edited by B. D. Ruben. New Brunswick, NJ: Transaction.

Zucker, Marjorie B., ed. 1999. *The Right to Die Debate: A Documentary History*. Westport, CT: Greenwood Press.

INDEX

About the Author

ELIZABETH ATWOOD GAILEY is Assistant Professor of Communication at the University of Tennessee, Chatanooga. Her research focuses on media cultural studies and the mass media's role in social change.